Chicago Transformed

CHICAGO TRANSFORMED

World War I and the Windy City

Joseph Gustaitis

Southern Illinois University Press
Carbondale

Southern Illinois University Press
www.siupress.com

19 18 17 16   4 3 2 1

Cover illustration: postcard of the Merchant Marines marching in
Chicago during World War I. Author's collection

Library of Congress Cataloging-in-Publication Data
Names: Gustaitis, Joseph Alan, [date] author.
Title: Chicago transformed : World War I and the Windy City /
    Joseph Gustaitis.
Description: Carbondale : Southern Illinois University Press, 2016.
    | Includes bibliographical references and index.
Identifiers: LCCN 2015042807| ISBN 9780809334988 (pbk. : alk.
    paper) | ISBN 9780809334995 (e-book)
Subjects: LCSH: Chicago (Ill.)—History—1875– | World War,
    1914–1918—Illinois—Chicago. | Chicago (Ill.)—Social
    conditions—20th century. | Chicago (Ill.)—Ethnic relations—
    History—20th century.
Classification: LCC F548.5 .G949 2016 | DDC
    305.8009773/110904—dc23 LC record available at
    http://lccn.loc.gov/2015042807

Printed on recycled paper. ♻

This paper meets the requirements of ANSI/NISO Z39.48-1992
(Permanence of Paper) ∞

*To Charles and Cecilia—may they never know war but
always treasure Chicago, their hometown*

Historic events are often said to have "changed everything." In the case of the Great War this is, for once, true. The war really did change everything: not just borders, not just governments and the fate of nations, but the way people have seen the world and themselves ever since. It became a kind of hole in time, leaving the postwar world permanently disconnected from everything that had come before.

—G. J. Meyer, *A World Undone: The Story of the Great War, 1914–1918*

Contents

Illustrations

Chicago Transformed

Introduction:
Chicago, Microcosm of America

Without World War I, there would have been no Soviet Union, no Nazi Germany, no Holocaust, no Communist China. Without the First World War, there would not have been the Second, with all its death and destruction, and the spillover from World War II, the conflicts in Korea and Vietnam, most likely would not have happened. Even some of the struggles of the twenty-first century—the conflicts in the Middle East—might not have occurred, because these nations were artificially stitched together by the victors of the Great War with little regard for religious and ethnic differences.

This is a book about Chicago, but it is also a book about the United States. The First World War had many of the same effects on the city as on the nation as a whole. Chicago can be seen as a microcosm of the United States in which these effects can be studied up close. Trends that shaped the entire country often were more intense in Chicago.

The sexual revolution that began in the second decade of the twentieth century and was accelerated by the war was nationwide, but Chicago is the ideal laboratory in which to study it. The types of job opportunities that the city offered drew thousands of young women, who came not only for employment but also for the social and sexual freedom unavailable in the small towns they left behind. For them, another enticement was music, and Chicago became the capital of jazz, the music that accompanied the nation's first sexual revolution.

All across the country, German-Americans were subject to suspicion, hostility, and violence during the war, but Chicago was the most German of American cities, and it was there that the intimidation and antagonism were most profuse and the results most dramatic, as people changed their surnames, institutions were renamed, monuments were vandalized, and a once vibrant ethnic culture went underground.

Even before the United States entered the war, fear arose about the menace purportedly presented by Imperial Germany and the spies and saboteurs that its cunning officials were supposedly planning to send to the New World. But after America joined the Allies, the mood of suspicion morphed into paranoia. This attitude prevailed nationwide, but it was in Chicago that one patriotic citizen created a national entity to confront the danger—the American Protective League, an idealistic establishment that turned out to be one of the greatest violators of civil liberties in American history. And it was in Chicago that another loyal citizen created the speakers' bureau known as the Four Minute Men, which sent thousands of orators into theaters, churches, union halls, and other venues nationwide to spread the government's message.

Pacifism and isolationism, both strong elements in American thought before the war—and both suppressed during it—also existed throughout the country, but Chicago held a special place in those movements. The city was not only the leading metropolis in a region that tended toward isolationism but also the home of many eloquent antiwar voices, most notably the world-famous reformer Jane Addams of Hull-House, who strove against near-impossible odds to persuade world leaders to come to the negotiating table. Chicago was also the home of the Industrial Workers of the World (IWW), also known as the "Wobblies," a radical antiwar labor organization that for many Americans was nearly as terrifying as German saboteurs. It was in Chicago that the fury of the government came down on this idealistic band of trade unionists, socialists, and anarchists.

The famed "Rosie the Riveter" of World War II actually had thousands of predecessors during the First World War, when women worked in many jobs formerly held only by men. After making these gains, women never turned back and continued to press for workplace equality. As the industrial heart of the United States, Chicago was again the focal point of a national trend, and its working women were vocal and determined. At the same time, the rising wages and shortage of workers that characterized the war years gave new hope to the labor movement, whose leaders grew more confident, aggressive, and willing to strike. Chicago again, with its large industrial working class—employed especially in steel and the stockyards—was one of the central areas of this development and the site of some of the great labor strikes of the era.

The anti-German mindset gave the forces of prohibition the final ammunition they needed to impose their agenda, amend the Constitution, and ban alcoholic beverages. As is well known, their success created a flamboyant age of speakeasies and bathtub gin and stirred a new brand of organized crime. No metropolis is more associated with that development than Chicago, home of Al Capone and Eliot Ness.

On New Year's Day 1919 Chicagoans were in a buoyant mood. The terrible war was over, their country had won, and the men (and a few women) were coming home. Chicago's ethnic population was pleased that impediments to immigration would soon be gone, and many of the city's immigrants were delighted that their European homelands were now independent. The labor movement hoped to build on the gains it had made during the war, and Chicago's manufacturers saw no reason why the prosperity they had enjoyed during the Great War should not continue.

Chicago was a much different place than it had been in 1913. When the war was over, there was a new Chicago.

But 1919 did not turn out that way. Unemployment mounted and labor strife was rampant. Labor leaders, once so optimistic, saw their efforts crushed, and they were subjugated, not to rise again until the Great Depression. Indeed, Chicago was a much different place than it had been in 1913. When the war was over, there was a new Chicago. It was no longer a city with a strong German character; African Americans and Mexicans were now becoming a dominant presence. When black people left the South to settle in northern cities, the single metropolis that many dreamed about and sang about was Chicago and nowhere else. A black-owned newspaper called the *Chicago Defender* promoted the Great Migration, a huge population shift that brought millions of black southerners to the North. Pullman porters carried the *Defender* throughout the South, and its editorials lured migrants by condemning southern ways and extolling northern freedom. Chicago was also the home base of the Illinois Central Railroad, whose lines penetrated deep into Dixie and ferried thousands of African Americans to new homes. This influx led to a race riot, and battles among incoming African Americans and Mexicans and the old-line ethnics for neighborhood turf became a feature of Chicago life that would last for decades.

Readers might be surprised to find that this book mentions aspects of Chicago that occurred well after World War I. For example, it discusses the Maxwell Street blues scene in the 1950s and 1960s and the establishment of the National Museum of Mexican Art in 1982. One of the major points of the book is that events that transpired during the Great War still affect Chicago today. Thus guidebooks to Chicago invariably advise tourists to go to one of Chicago's blues clubs; this book tries to explain why the blues has become so identified with the city. And the museum, one of the most vivid examples of the large Mexican presence in Chicago, would not be where it is if not for the historical changes wrought by World War I.

Because of the Great War, Chicago was a city transformed.

PART ONE

Before the War

1

"Throw the Dictionary at It": Chicago in 1913

As 1913 began, revelers crammed into Chicago's Loop in a display of merriment not seen in years. Sidewalk vendors did a lively business selling feather "ticklers," which rowdies used to tease pretty women. Confetti filled the air, and the cafés and cabarets were packed. The crowd on State Street grew to a hundred thousand, and then "pandemonium broke loose at midnight. Thirty thousand horns were blown together. Thousands of men and women cheered. Everyone did all in his or her power to make all the racket possible. Automobilists turned loose the siren horns, street car motormen pumped the gongs until their legs ached, maudlin shouts and song floated out of the smoky atmosphere of crowded saloons, strangers slapped each other on the back. For ten minutes half the pedestrians were in a semi-delirium."[1]

Mayor Carter Harrison II declared that Chicago looked forward to 1913 "with several definite hopes and ambitions, and with good prospect to have them realized."[2] Among the items

Automobiles were not yet common on Chicago's busy State Street in 1913, but pedestrians jammed the sidewalks. Author's collection

7

on his agenda were subway construction, a consolidation and rationalization of the streetcar lines, and the city's eventual ownership of the transit system. He also looked forward to a new harbor bill that would enable the city to complete an ambitious pier project. He announced that Chicago had been making progress toward cleaner air through a smoke abatement effort, thousands of electric streetlights would be added in 1913, and a new sewer system was in the works for downtown.

In April, Edwin Romberg, chairman of the real estate committee of the Association of Commerce, delivered a buoyant paper on Chicago real estate. He marveled that a piece of land purchased in 1836 for $410 was now worth $12 million. "What other city," he asked, "can point to a specific instance in which land values have multiplied more than twenty-five thousand fold in the span of a lifetime?" The last three years had seen "phenomenal development," and "men familiar with real estate conditions in all the great cities of the country, or the world, are practically unanimous in the opinion that Chicago central business property offers in a greater measure all the elements which make for thoroughly high class land investments than are to be found in any other city."[3]

Chicago's "Big Things"

A guide to Chicago published in 1905 began by saying, "The stranger entering Chicago . . . should be prepared for big things. . . . To one unaccustomed to large cities the noise, incident to the enormous traffic on the down-town streets, supplemented by the roar of the elevated trains, will be confusing and bewildering."[4] Chicago on the eve of World War I was described by visitors as marvelous, cosmopolitan, sordid, busy, strong, dominating, congested, sprawling, disorderly, and stupefying. Chicago-born author Julian Street wrote in 1913, "Call Chicago mighty, monstrous, multifarious, vital, lusty, stupendous, indomitable, intense, unnatural, aspiring, puissant, preposterous, transcendent—call it what you like—throw the dictionary at it! It is all that you can do, except to shoot it with statistics. And even the statistics of Chicago are not deadly, as most statistics are."[5]

Chicago in 1913 was only eighty years old—extremely young for a major world city. People still cherished the "old settlers" who survived from Chicago's pioneer days. On August 4, 1913,

Just three years old in 1913, the ornate Blackstone Hotel anchored the southern end of downtown Michigan Avenue. In 1920 the hotel would be the site of the "smoke-filled room" in which Republican Party leaders agreed to nominate Warren G. Harding for president. Author's collection

the old settlers met for their annual picnic, which they had been holding since 1874. Two of them, John J. O'Neil and Catherine Clark, had come to Chicago in 1838. According to the *Chicago Tribune*, the old settlers "took their children's children upon their laps and told them how the Indians roamed the nearby prairies, and how there were bears, and wolves, and things, 'right in this very spot.'"[6]

Most travelers to Chicago arrived by train from the East.[7] They rode past the steel mills in Gary and South Chicago, as well as rows and rows of simple workers' houses. Their coaches crossed over dozens of other railroad lines and passed by long freight trains, a sign of Chicago's preeminence in the nation's railroad system. Some fourteen hundred trains entered the city every day, and every one of them ended its run in Chicago. Lake Michigan looked like a blue haven of tranquillity next to the restless urban conglomeration. But just as a storm can quickly stir the lake into a seething mass of waves, so would the approaching world war transform the city by the lake.

A guide to the city published in 1909 reports 300 public schools, 19 high schools, 1,077 churches, almost 100 banks, over 50 hospitals, and 8,159 manufacturing plants churning out goods with a combined annual value of about a billion dollars. The busiest street crossing was at State and Madison: "The streams of pedestrians and vehicles pass this corner in constant and almost solid masses." However, "thirteen hundred and fifty

Every single day, some fourteen hundred railroad trains entered Chicago, the undisputed railroad capital of the nation. Library of Congress

miles of surface and elevated railway traverse the city upon which ride daily an average of 1,354,000 passengers." A visitor did not need to get on a tour bus—the guide describes five "sight seeing" trolley car rides totaling seventy-five miles that would show the tourist all sections of Chicago.[8]

To visitors, Chicago seemed a city of paradoxes. Culture in the form of museums, auditoriums, theaters, and universities clashed with political corruption and ravenous capitalism. The city's hotels, skyscrapers, and department stores were staggering; so were its slums. The stockyards—the city's biggest tourist attraction—were a marvel of efficiency and a house of horrors, but the extensive parks, connected by a necklace of broad boulevards, sparked envy. Visitors noted that this Midwestern metropolis was American through and through, a place of back-slapping familiarity, pragmatism, and eagerness to get things done. As a visitor named Edward Hungerford expressed it in 1913, "So you see that Chicago is only America, not boastful, not arrogant, but strong in her convictions, strong in her sincerity, strong in her poise between right and power together, and not merely power without right."[9]

But although it was American, Chicago was also cosmopolitan. When Julian Street visited the stockyards, he saw "signs printed in English, Russian, Slovak, Polish, Bohemian, Hungarian, Lithuanian, German, Norwegian, Swedish, Croatian, Italian, and Greek." According to the 1909 guide, "During recent years Constantinople, with its mature reputation as the most cosmopolitan city of the world, has been compelled by

linguistic statisticians to yield the palm to Chicago, the world's newest large city." There were "fourteen languages besides English spoken here by permanent colonies of more than 10,000 persons each, and in all some forty different tongues. . . . Chicago is the second largest Bohemian city in the world, the third Swedish, the third Norwegian, the fourth Polish, the fifth German."[10] The Germans were by far the largest ethnic group, with a population of half a million, followed by the Irish (180,000), Polish (125,000), Swedish (100,000), and Bohemians (90,000). In the summer of 1913, *Tribune* columnist Henry M. Hyde reported that every month some four thousand immigrants were arriving at the Dearborn Street Station alone—and this was just one of six major railroad terminals in the city. In his view, Chicago's citizens disdained these industrious newcomers as "wops," "dagoes," and "sheenies" and left them at the mercy of swindlers and charlatans—bankers who cheated them of their savings and labor agents who took payment for jobs that never materialized. However, he said, this situation would change when these people got the vote.[11] Businessmen saw these immigrants as a source of cheap labor; others wondered how all these nationalities could ever be assimilated.

The census of 1910 reported Chicago's population as 2,185,283. Ten years later, the number had climbed to 2,701,705, which puts the population of the city at the time of the First World War at about 2.5 million. Given that the estimated population in 2013 was about 2.7 million, the city isn't much bigger today, although this statistic can be misleading, because with the growth of the suburbs after World War II, the entire Chicago metropolitan area now has a population over 10 million.

Chicago at Work

The heart of Chicago's economy was downtown, where the department stores, banks, commercial firms, and railroad stations were located. The leading financial institutions were on LaSalle Street, where stood the Board of Trade, the nation's mightiest commodities exchange. As a banking center, Chicago was second only to New York. George E. Hooker, secretary of the City Club, described downtown Chicago in 1910: "Within an area of less than a square mile there are found the railway terminals and business offices, the big retail stores, the wholesale and jobbing business, the financial center, the main offices of the chief firms of the city, a considerable portion of the medical and dental professions, the legal profession, the city and country government, the post office, the courts, the leading social and political clubs, the hotels, theatres, Art Institute, principal libraries, the labor headquarters, and a great number of lesser factors of city life."[12]

Outside the hectic downtown, Chicago was very much a working man's city. The largest single employer in the city was the meatpacking industry. In 1900 there were sixty-eight thousand packinghouse employees in the entire United States, and twenty-five thousand of them worked in Chicago.[13] At the end of the Great War, the yards processed almost nineteen million head of livestock every year.[14] The South Works of U.S. Steel in Chicago employed some eleven thousand people in 1910; four years earlier, U.S. Steel, the world's largest corporation, had also built a massive steel mill in nearby Gary, Indiana. Acme Steel, Republic Steel, Union Steel, Wisconsin Steel, Inland Steel, and Youngstown Sheet & Tube also operated steel mills in the Chicago area. Another major factory was the McCormick Reaper Plant, which made farm equipment; in 1902 McCormick merged with International Harvester. The Pullman Sleeping Car Company had ten thousand employees in 1910 and peaked at twenty thousand in the 1920s. Other important trades in Chicago were printing and clothing manufacture. Printing

Outside the hectic downtown, Chicago was very much a working man's city.

and publishing businesses employed twenty thousand people at the beginning of the twentieth century, and by 1914 Chicago was responsible for 18 percent of the men's clothing produced in the United States.[15]

Chicago at Play

Chicago's two major league baseball teams, the Cubs and the White Sox, both were usually competitive in this era. The White Sox won the World Series in 1917, and the Cubs finished first the following year, losing the World Series to Babe Ruth's Boston Red Sox. African Americans had their own Chicago team, Rube Foster's American Giants, founded in 1911. It became the most popular black team in the country, and the Negro Leagues All-Star game was annually held in Chicago. In 1913 John T. Powers formed the Federal League, which he hoped would be a third major league. The Chicago entry was the Chicago Whales, which newspapers called the "Chifeds" in the team's early days. It played in a new stadium named Weeghman Park after the team's owner, Charles Weeghman, and finished second in 1914 and first in 1915. The league then went out of business, and Weeghman arranged to purchase the Cubs. One of his partners was the chewing gum mogul William Wrigley, who eventually became sole owner of the team. Weeghman Park then became Wrigley Field.

Football was popular in Chicago, but it was considered mostly a college game or one played by athletic clubs or amateur neighborhood groups that played in the parks.[16] The city's most celebrated football personality was coach Amos Alonzo Stagg, who turned the University of Chicago into a national powerhouse. His players, who won the national championship in 1913, were the original "Monsters of the Midway." The Chicago Cardinals professional football team began as early as 1898 as an amateur squad. The team purchased some surplus jerseys from the University of Chicago and acquired its nickname because the shirts were cardinal red. In 1917 the Cardinals won the championship of the Chicago Football League, which had sixteen clubs.

Chicago was an early adopter of basketball. The game was invented in Springfield, Massachusetts, in 1891 by Dr. James Naismith, and one of the players in the first public basketball game was Amos Alonzo Stagg, who brought the game to Chicago in 1893. The University of Chicago had one of the best teams in the United States. In the 1890s soccer was most popular among immigrants from the United Kingdom, but by 1913 it had spread to other ethnic groups. Chicago was also the headquarters of the Western Golf Association, and in 1919 *American Golfer* magazine counted fifty-two courses in and around the city. Chicago was known for being especially strong in women's golf.[17] The parks department provided free tennis courts, and Chicago high school students dominated the state championships. Other leisure activities listed in the 1909 guide to Chicago included bowling, billiards, yachting, swimming, cricket, fencing, and handball.[18]

But the most prevalent outdoor activity may have been simply going to the beach. In fact, Chicago advertised itself as an "ideal summer resort." Not only did it have beaches and boats, but it also had amusement parks, summer gardens, outdoor concerts, and boulevards that were ideal for automobiles and bicycles, while educational institutes offered summer courses "for serious study of the arts, sciences and literature." At the time of the Great War, Chicago had three public beaches and five pools with an annual attendance of 1.2 million.[19] In August 1913 twenty thousand beachgoers were treated to the strange sight of a motorboat towing a "raftlike contraption called a skimmer," on which was standing an adventurer named Walter Walker. He explained that the new sport (the forerunner of waterskiing) was common in South America and was "the greatest ever."[20]

A whimsical advertisement by Chicago cartoonist Quin Hall shows how the city promoted itself as the "ideal summer resort." Author's collection

In 1911 around eighty-six thousand patrons poured into Chicago's 275 dance halls every night.[21] Chicago was second only to New York as a theater town. The theater district, bordered by Randolph, Clark, Washington, and LaSalle Streets, was known as the Rialto. The city was also noted for its "little theater" scene, with amateur theater groups operating in community auditoriums and settlement houses. Maurice Browne's Little Theatre of Chicago, founded in 1912, may be considered the forerunner of the city's many contemporary theater companies. The conductor of the Chicago Symphony Orchestra was the German-born Frederick Stock, who led the orchestra for a remarkable thirty-seven years (1905–42). Opera lovers went to the four-thousand-seat Auditorium Theater, the home of the Chicago Grand Opera Company since its founding in 1910. The company's music director, Cleofante Campanini, had turned Chicago into an internationally recognized opera center. At the beginning of February 1914, the *Tribune*'s opera critic reported, "During the last ten weeks thirty-seven operas have been presented in seventy-two performances," an amount of music unthinkable for any opera company today. Among the operas were ones that are still popular, such as *Madama Butterfly*, *Carmen*, and *Die Walküre*, as well as now-forgotten works like Wilhelm Kienzl's *Der Kuhreigen*.[22] Many amateur groups, such as the Irish Choral Society, the Wanda Polish Ladies Singing Society, and the Germania Männerchor, also served Chicago's immigrant communities.

In 2014 Chicago had about 70 movie theaters, but in 1914 it had 620.[23] The city's first "movie palace" was the opulent, eighteen-hundred-seat Central Park on Roosevelt Road, which opened in 1917. It was owned by the team of Barney Balaban and Sam Katz, who went on to develop a chain of prestigious Chicago movie theaters. Movies were becoming an integral part of American culture, and Chicago played an important role in this development before filmmakers discovered Hollywood. At first entrepreneurs who wanted to show movies had to buy them, but the film exchange, allowing theater owners to rent and screen many more movies, was created in Chicago. By 1907 the city had more than fifteen film exchanges, controlling 80 percent of the market for film distribution.[24]

Chicago was also home to some of the early film studios. The two most famous were the Selig Polyscope Company, founded by William Selig as early as 1896, and Essanay, dating to 1907. On Essanay's roster were such soon-to-be-famous players as Gloria Swanson, Wallace Beery, Harold Lloyd, Tom Mix, Francis X. Bushman, and Edward Arnold. The studio's biggest acquisition was the hugely popular Charlie Chaplin, who signed an unprecedentedly large contract and arrived in Chicago in late December 1914. However, the great comedian stayed in the city for all of twenty-three days and made just one film, *His New Job*. Having arrived in the middle of winter, Chaplin hated the climate, and he disliked even more what he viewed as Essanay's unambitious artistic standards. He left Chicago for Essanay's western studio in Niles, California, which he didn't like much either, and in February 1916 he signed with the Mutual Film Corporation. Also in 1913 William Foster opened a film production company in Chicago called the Foster Photoplay Company, the first to be owned and operated by African Americans.[25] Foster saw the movie business as "the Negro business man's only international chance to make money and put his race right with the world."[26] He was followed by Peter P. Jones, who opened a second black film studio on the South Side in 1914. Jones made both documentaries and features; his second film, *The Troubles of Sambo and Dinah*, was an "uplift comedy" that was intended to counter the demeaning stereotypes of African Americans in white-made films.

The Selig Polyscope Company was, along with Essanay, one of the two major film studios that made Chicago the film capital of the United States before World War I. *An Embarrassing Predicament* (1914) was one of its typically zany comedies.

Library of Congress

The major cinematic excitement in Chicago in 1913–14 was Selig's *The Adventures of Kathlyn*, the first serial in movie history, which preceded the better-known *Perils of Pauline* by a year. Each of thirteen biweekly episodes concluded with the heroine, played by the blond and beautiful Kathlyn Williams, confronting calamity, often in the form of wild beasts. The production was sponsored by the *Chicago Tribune*, whose editor viewed it as a terrific publicity stunt and published advertisements targeted at young women: "Young Ladies! Watch your Sweethearts! Kathlyn is coming!" The *Tribune* published the plot of each installment as it was released and reported that its circulation increased 10 percent during the run of the serial. There were Kathlyn postcards, a Kathlyn dance, a Kathlyn cocktail, and eventually a spin-off book also titled *The Adventures of Kathlyn*. A feature-length movie based on the serial was released in 1916.

When all this activity is taken into account, it is clear that Chicago played a major role in filmmaking around the turn of the century. According to Michael Glover Smith and Adam Selzer in their book on Chicago's film industry, "The astonishing reality is that Chicago filmmakers produced literally thousands of movies between 1896 and 1918, perhaps more than any other single city in the country during this time. It has been estimated that the Chicago film industry at its most prolific, at the end of the first decade of the twentieth century, was responsible for producing the majority of the American movies on the market."[27] However, it is estimated that at least 90 percent of the films made by the early Chicago studios did not survive. Once sound films appeared, studios deemed silent movies worthless and deliberately destroyed them, usually because they took up valuable storage space.

Progressivism

The mayor of Chicago in 1913 was Carter Harrison II, a Democrat, who was serving the last of his five terms (his father had also served five terms).[28] Harrison was something of a reformer, though perhaps a half-hearted one. Although he did not believe in legislating morality, he established the Chicago Vice Commission and in 1911 shut down Chicago's most infamous brothel, the Everleigh Club. He also battled the transportation mogul Charles Yerkes and prevented him from acquiring monopoly control of Chicago's streetcar lines. Like his father, Harrison II was successful in attracting the votes of immigrants and workingmen, and he rewarded his constituents with extended city services and public playgrounds.

It was the age of Progressive politics. Former president Theodore Roosevelt (1901–09), the Progressives' champion, had backed many of the reforms championed by the journalists known as the "muckrakers," several of whom were Chicagoans. He advocated trust busting, the breaking up of monopolistic corporations; established the U.S. Department of Commerce and Labor; supported the Pure Food and Drug Act; and turned millions of acres of land into national parks. In 1913 the president was Woodrow Wilson, a Democrat; he furthered the Progressive legacy with a series of reforms of his own, which he called the New Freedom. He continued Roosevelt's policy of fighting the trusts by setting up the Federal Trade Commission and signing the Clayton Antitrust Act. In 1913, in an attempt to control the all-too-frequent Wall Street panics, he established the Federal Reserve System, which aimed at stabilizing prices, maximizing employment, and setting beneficial interest rates. Wilson was also a strong friend of labor.

Chicago had its own local Progressive movement. Ever since the gambling boss Michael C. McDonald organized the "saloon Democrats" in the 1870s–80s and built the city's "machine," Chicago had acquired a reputation for corruption.[29] But at the same time, concerned citizens were countering with "good government" associations, which gave rise to the term "goo-goos" to describe these reformers. The first was the Citizens Association of 1874. In 1893 the Civic Federation was established; it was followed three years later by the Municipal Voters League (MVL) and then by the City Club (1903) and the Bureau of Public Efficiency (1910). In the 1896 election the MVL targeted twenty-six aldermen for removal, and to nearly everyone's surprise, twenty were defeated. This success was repeated, and by the 1920s the reformer Charles E. Merriam was able to write, "As a result of the League's Herculean labors, Chicago for a twenty-year period had the best legislative body of any American city."[30] By the 1920s, however, the antireform forces, led by Republican mayor William Hale ("Big Bill") Thompson, were back in control. Nevertheless, by 1913 the Progressive forces had left their mark on Chicago. As historian Dominic A. Pacyga has written, "Chicagoans played a lead role in the development of city planning, housing, working conditions, construction of playgrounds and parks, reform of the court system, advanced education, and the role of the university in the modern city. The Progressive community acted as the conscience of the city and helped to formulate policies that made Chicago a better place to live."[31]

Women and the Vote

Ratification of the Nineteenth Amendment, which gave women the right to vote nationally, occurred in 1920, but women obtained this right much earlier in some places. Wyoming women had the right to vote as early as 1869, and suffragists were successful in many other western states before World War I. The first state east of the Mississippi in which women won the right to vote for president was Illinois, and a group of women from Chicago led the campaign. Foremost among them was Grace Wilbur Trout, known as "the woman who never fails."[32] She pioneered campaigning by automobile and

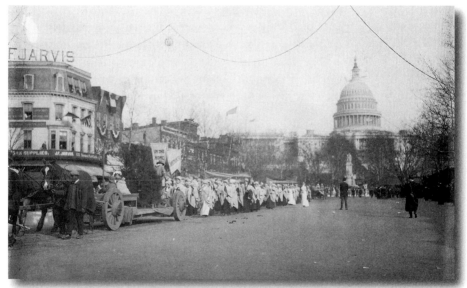

Illinois women made up a prominent contingent in the massive national suffrage parade held in Washington, D.C., on March 8, 1913. Illinois was the first state east of the Mississippi in which women won the right to vote. Library of Congress

led the Illinois delegation to the great national suffrage parade held in Washington, D.C., on March 8, 1913. Standing in a red automobile, she gave a two-hour oration in which she berated the local police for not protecting the marchers from jeering onlookers. According to a *Tribune* reporter, "Many of the men lingered as the motor drove away, loudly cheering and applauding."[33] After the parade, Trout spent much time in Springfield to lobby Illinois legislators, and Governor Edward F. Dunne signed the suffrage bill on June 26, giving the vote to a million and a half Illinois women. The next spring more than 150,000 women registered to vote in Chicago.

Known as "the woman who never fails," Grace Wilbur Trout spearheaded the drive that won the vote for women in Illinois in 1913.
Library of Congress

The victory of women's suffrage in Illinois had a national impact. As historian Suellen Hoy has explained, "What Illinois did in 1913 was significant to women in the state and nation. Suffragist leader Carrie Chapman Catt remembered it in her history of the national campaign as a 'turning point' since 'suffrage sentiment doubled over night' as a result."[34]

Modern Art

In mid-February 1913 Chicagoans began hearing of some peculiar goings-on in New York City, where a large exhibition of strange artwork was being staged at the Sixty-Eighth Regiment Armory. The artists were little known at the time—among them Vincent van Gogh, Claude Monet, Edgar Degas, Auguste Rodin, Paul Gauguin, Paul Cezanne, Pablo Picasso, Marcel Duchamp, Henri Matisse, and Americans George Bellows and Edward Hopper—and many viewers considered their creations insults or jokes. The most famous jibe was the description of Duchamp's *Nude Descending a Staircase, No. 2* as "an explosion in a shingle factory," a comment by the same

Julian Street who described Chicago as "mighty, monstrous, and multifarious." Harriet Monroe, however, who covered the show for the *Tribune*, considered the exhibition "exuberant" and wrote, "We cannot always tell what they mean, but at least they are having a good time." She considered Cezanne "an original master" and described Van Gogh's paintings as "masterpieces."[35]

After the New York armory show closed, Chicagoans got a chance to see what all the fuss was about when 634 works, about half of the original contents, were shipped to the Art Institute. The Chicago organizers wanted the most radical artists and omitted most of the older ones, many of whom were already represented in the Art Institute anyway, and most of the sculptures were too expensive to transport. The exhibition opened on March 24 and ran for about three weeks. The show was greeted with wisecracks, and *cubism* became a vogue word in Chicago. The Edgewater Catholic Women's Club hosted a "cubist" food exposition, and an article in the *Tribune* titled "The Cubist Costume: Milady in Crazyquilt" imagined celebrity women sporting costumes based on this artwork: "step right in line and get a cubist or a futurist, an impressionist or a secessionist to build you a nice little dress of blocks, or a costume of circles."[36] One might have expected the students of the Art Institute to have been receptive, but they staged a mock trial of an artist named "Henri Hairmattress" and burned imitations of two Matisse paintings. However, the *Evening Post* beseeched Chicagoans to give the show "a fair hearing and serious consideration," and Monroe asked, "Why should we not acquaint ourselves with the facts, learn what is going on?"[37] Attendance surpassed the organizers' hopes: the Chicago exhibition had 188,650 visitors, more than in New York, although it did not make money and not many pictures were sold. The New York armory show was a breakthrough in American cultural history. Modernism had planted its flag in America, and it would never retreat. In 2013, the Art Institute of Chicago commemorated the centennial of the show by mounting the exhibition "Picasso and Chicago," noting that in 1913 the Art Institute became the first museum in the United States to show Picasso's works (the Sixty-Eighth Regiment Armory, of course, was not a museum).

"The Baseless Fear of War"

The literary historian I. F. Clarke once observed that in every year between 1871 and 1914, at least one book or short story prophesying a devastating war appeared in Europe.[38] For many Europeans, the next great conflict was just a matter of time, and since the 1890s the European powers had been constructing an elaborate system of alliances. Their militaries were conducting vast armament programs, and Britain and Germany were engaged in an expensive naval arms race. Just ten weeks into 1913 a London-based *Tribune* correspondent named T. P. O'Connor reported that war scares were enflaming Europe. Conflict in the Balkans, he said, threatened to trigger war between Austria and Russia, which would inevitably draw in France, Britain, Germany, and Italy, and politicians feared that "the mighty war cloud so long hanging in the European sky would at last burst."[39]

But the Balkans were a long way from Chicago, and the idea that their boys might be thrown into a gigantic European war was the farthest thing from the minds of Chicagoans in 1913. In an article published in the *Independent* in February 1913, titled "The Baseless Fear of War," the steel magnate Andrew Carnegie assured everyone there would never be a war between Germany and "ourselves, members of the same Teutonic race." "All nations are our friends," he said, "and we are the friends of all."[40]

As 1913 ended, Chicagoans found one more reason to celebrate: on Christmas Eve the city erected its first municipal Christmas tree. Grant Park was turned into a "winter wonderland," and twenty-five thousand children from all over the city were given free tickets. Music was provided by members of the Chicago Grand Opera Company, as well as the Swedish and Paulist choruses, and movies "intended especially for children" were projected onto a mammoth screen. Mayor Harrison, accompanied by mounted police and trumpeters, touched the switch that illuminated the lights. He cheerfully declared, "Nowhere in the world does the spirit of Christmas Tide find more hearty welcome and meet with more ready response than in the hearts of the people of Chicago."[41]

2

Preparedness and Public Opinion:
Why Chicago Went to War

When Chicagoans picked up their newspapers in late June 1914, they read about an assassination in some faraway place called Sarajevo, which, it's safe to say, few of them had ever heard of. The victims were the Archduke Franz Ferdinand, heir to the throne of Austria-Hungary, and his wife, Sophie. The *Chicago Daily News* printed a dispatch on the funeral, and the *Chicago Tribune* interviewed a historian at the University of Chicago who speculated that the incident might stir a rebellion among the Slavs in the Austro-Hungarian Empire. No one talked of war, and the matter was then largely forgotten.[1]

However, the European powers had constructed a system of alliances that made it nearly inevitable that if two countries went to war, their allies would do the same. The archduke had been murdered by a Yugoslavian nationalist who hoped that his action would result in the liberation of the south Slavs from Austro-Hungarian rule. Austria-Hungary demanded satisfaction from Serbia, didn't get it, and declared war on July 18. Then the dominoes began to topple. Russia, Serbia's ally, mobilized against Austria-Hungary, and Germany declared war on Russia and on Russia's ally, France. Germany then invaded Belgium, and Great Britain declared war on Germany. Eventually, Italy and Japan joined with France and Britain, while the Ottoman Empire and Bulgaria sided with Austria-Hungary and Germany. The two warring coalitions became known as the Triple Entente, an alliance between Britain, France, and Russia, and the Central Powers, consisting of Germany, Austria-Hungary, Bulgaria, and the Ottoman Empire.

A month after the assassination, Europe was in crisis, and Henry M. Hyde of the *Tribune* wrote that "the greatest war in history is in progress and western civilization has relapsed into a bloody chaos." The assassination, he astutely analyzed, "would have resulted in nothing more than added sorrow for the house of Hapsburg if there had not been just under the surface a seething furnace of racial hatred, dynastic jealousy, and commercial envy."[2] Two shots fired into an open car had started a world war.

At Chicago's Board of Trade on July 28, what the *Tribune* characterized as a "panic" caused wheat prices to skyrocket by about 10 cents a bushel.[3] But once the traders calmed down, they realized that American wheat was bound to become a coveted commodity when agricultural production in Europe plummeted. By October Chicago's famed attorney Clarence Darrow was predicting a boom even greater than the one following the Civil War. "The European war," he said in a speech, "is bringing to the United States the greatest prosperity it has ever experienced."[4]

War and Business

Some historians have argued that the economic links between the United States and the Triple Entente were a main reason for the U.S. entry into the war. As Francis G. Walett has written, by April 1917, "the American economy was linked to the allied cause: huge shipments of supplies were being sent to England and France; private loans to the Allies amounted to 2.5 billion dollars, those to Germany only 35 million dollars."[5] New York banks made most of the loans, but Chicago banks also got in on the action. In 1916, for example, the Merchant's Loan and Trust Company and the First National Bank "helped underwrite credits for the French government's machinery and supply orders from Chicago manufacturers."[6] Chicago commerce would do very well during the war; not only was wheat greatly needed in Europe, but so were steel and meat, two commodities Chicago produced in abundance.

Chicagoan James Lewis Kraft is one example of how some U.S. businessmen benefited from the war. He started out in the cheese business in Chicago in 1903 with a rented cart and a horse named Paddy. In 1916 he received a patent for a processed cheese product that could be packaged in tins and shipped long distances. When the war came, the U.S. government ordered more than six million pounds of Kraft's new canned cheese, ensuring the company's success. Today Kraft Foods is a giant; in 2015 it merged with the H. J. Heinz Company to form the fifth-largest food and beverage company in the world. It then moved its headquarters to the Aon Center in downtown Chicago.

Chicago's bankers and industrialists not only profited from selling goods and equipment to the Allies and the U.S. government but also saw opportunities south of the border. For years Chicago businessmen had watched European powers profit from trade with Latin America and South America, regions they believed should be trading primarily with the United States. Especially annoying to them was the transport of American products to these regions in

Many Chicago businesses profited from the war, none more so than the Kraft Cheese Company. During the war the U.S. government ordered more than six million pounds of its newly invented processed cheese. Author's collection

foreign ships. The interests of Chicagoans were represented by the Illinois Manufacturers Association, which lobbied for federal legislation that opened up free trade with the rest of the Western Hemisphere. Chicagoans were instrumental in the creation of the Mississippi Valley Foreign Trade Bank, with Harry H. Merrick of Chicago as president. This bank was designed to boost trade between the Midwest and Latin America and to establish bank branches throughout the hemisphere. The *Chicago Banker* called the new bank "the biggest development of American resources since the Louisiana Purchase," and the *Tribune* hailed the bank's creators as "empire builders without cannon, or menace, or armies, or ships of war, but even so, militant builders and joyously out to subdue the earth!"[7] According to historian James A. Martin, "By 1919 the I.M.A. and Chicago's bankers . . . had united to build the essential foreign trade apparatus capable of assuring American predominance over Latin America in the post war years," and the result was a commercial network that would "allow American business interests to topple and replace German and British economic control of Latin America and the world."[8] U.S. exports to Latin America had increased by at least 20 percent by the mid-1920s and exceeded those of Britain and Germany by the end of the decade.[9]

The total exports of the United States soared from $2.8 billion in 1913 to $7.3 billion in 1918. U.S. wheat exports were $142 million in 1913 and $505 million in 1918.[10] In just two years, from 1915 to 1917, exports of steel and iron went from $251 million to $1.1 billion.[11] In November 1914 the *New York Times* reported "great activity in the iron and steel industry in the Chicago district." "Big orders are coming in," the story said. "Several thousand men were put back to work in the great industrial plants with the probability that their number will be increased nearly 10,000 a week hence."[12] Profits surged as well. "As early as 1915 net industrial profits were some 20 per cent above the pre-war level, and in 1918 as much as 120 per cent"—and these estimates were conservative.[13] In 1919 the *New York Times* reported that during the war, the profits of the "Big Five" Chicago packinghouses "were from two and a quarter to three times as great as during pre-war years."[14]

The War and Chicago's Ethnic Communities

World War I lasted about fifty months. The United States was in it for about twenty months and in combat for only about twelve. In other words, most of the time America was on the sidelines.

One of the first effects of the war on daily life in Chicago was shortages of imported goods, such as Scotch whiskey, French champagne and fashions, and German toys. In 1914 aspirin and quinine were produced only in Germany, and Chicagoans, like other Americans, would have to do without. Even opera singers were in short supply. The Chicago Grand Opera Company announced it was suspending its season because "the war made it impossible to bring over the necessary continental singers," and in September 1914 the *Tribune* reported that three opera company members, all French, had been killed in action.[15] Chicagoans stranded in Europe were among those who found it difficult to cross the ocean. The newspapers related the adventures of many, although most of them reached home after enduring what were merely inconveniences.

At first there was little enthusiasm in Chicago for U.S. participation in the war. It was a standard refrain that greedy monarchs and oppressive aristocracies had caused the war. As one historian has put it, "Neither the British nor the Continental monarchies came off blameless in newspaper accounts of the period from 1910 to 1914. . . . That America would involve itself in a war to defend any of the monarchies governing Europe seemed unthinkable."[16] When stories of atrocities committed by German soldiers in Belgium were first reported, the *Chicago Tribune* printed skeptical views, such as a February 1915 article by reporter Robert J. Thompson in which he asserted that most stories of atrocities by German soldiers were fabricated. He even argued that British sea rule was worse than German militarism and that the German Army was built "primarily for defensive purposes."[17]

> *Feelings were different in Chicago's ethnic communities, where people began to choose sides.*

Feelings were different in Chicago's ethnic communities, where people began to choose sides. The *Chicago Daily News* reported that in the Serbian cafés, "war talk ran high and war speeches were fiery." One speaker, a former member of the Serbian Army, shouted, "There won't be a single man of us left in America if Servia calls us to its aid. I'm going tomorrow."[18] On July 29 a large meeting of Chicago Serbians was held at Best Hall, where cries of "To hell with Austria!" rang out.

On the same night, the city's Bohemians pledged their solidarity with the Serbs at an outdoor rally. Like other Eastern European ethnic groups, the Czechs and Slovaks were under the rule of the Austro-Hungarian Empire, and many of them saw the war as an opportunity to press for that empire's dissolution and independence for their peoples. The Austrian Consulate in Chicago actually had the temerity to tell Chicago's young Czechs to get ready to be drafted into the Austrian Army, an announcement met with ridicule; instead, Chicago's Czechs began calling for independence.[19] In Europe many young Bohemians deserted the Austrian Army and formed the Czechoslovak Legion to fight on the side of the Allies. The largest contingent fought in Russia; others saw action in France and Italy.

Czechs and Slovaks in Chicago also joined the legion; one of the first was Josef Novak, an editor of the Czech-language newspaper *Spravedlnost*. One of the most active Czech leaders in Chicago was future mayor Anton J. Cermak. According to his biographer, Cermak "had perhaps the greatest number of war-organizational responsibilities among all Czechs."[20] He spoke tirelessly at rallies, helped drive the Liberty Loan campaigns, and served as chairman of all of Czech war activities in the United States. A vigorous supporter of Czech-Slovak solidarity, his anti-German rhetoric was so fierce that even some of his supporters thought it excessive. So high was Cermak's prestige that after the war he was invited to Prague to act as an adviser to the new democratic government. Much of the activity of the Czechs and Slovaks in Chicago centered on agitating for independence; the movement received a major boost with the visit to Chicago of the Czech leader Tomas Masaryk in the spring of 1918. At a massive rally in Pilsen Park, Masaryk told the crowd, "You in America know what liberty means. We want to build the independent Czechoslovak state upon the same principles."[21] When the United States recognized Czechoslovak independence in September 1918, a massive parade was staged in Chicago. According to historian Dominic A. Pacyga, "The cry for Czechoslovak independence rose up first from Chicago's South Lawndale neighborhood."[22] As one historian has said, "The magnitude of Chicago's contribution to the founding of a free Czechoslovakia is yet to be fully appreciated."[23]

Chicago's Hungarians generally remained loyal to the Austrian emperor. Most of the city's Russians were Jews who had little love for the czar, but when a group of fifty loyal Russians staged a rally on July 30, a party of Austrians set out to confront them, and only the intervention of the police prevented a violent clash. Chicago's Poles were in a unique situation. Their country did not exist as an independent state; what was once Poland was now divided among Russia, Germany, and Austria-Hungary, and all three countries conscripted Poles into their armies (about seven hundred thousand in Russia and seven hundred thousand in Germany and Austria).[24] Poles had long thought that a major European conflict might restore their lost nation, and many saw the Great War as an opportunity. Some, usually those who tended toward socialism in politics, viewed Russia as the enemy. They were organized into a fighting force under the politician and paramilitary leader Joseph Pilsudski. Others, of more conservative inclinations, were anti-German; their representative in the United States was the illustrious Polish pianist and statesman Ignace Paderewski.

In Chicago, as in the rest of the country, most Poles favored the anti-German faction, which made life much easier for them after the United States entered the war and anti-German hysteria began. Two major Polish figures in Chicago—the politician and banker John Smulski and Bishop Paul Rhode—served on the board of the committee backing Paderewski. January 24, 1915, was proclaimed Polish Relief Day in Chicago, and $25,000 was collected through the sale of tags. When the Poles raised an army of twenty-five thousand to fight under the French on the western front, three thousand of the volunteers came from Chicago.[25] After the U.S. declaration of war, young Poles eagerly volunteered for the U.S. military; in three weeks, seventeen hundred men enlisted at a draft board located in the Polish Roman Catholic Union building.[26] The Poles' faith was rewarded when President Woodrow Wilson announced his support for Polish independence, and in the presidential election of 1916, Chicago's Poles voted overwhelmingly for the president's reelection. Another sign of Polish backing of the war effort was in the purchase of Liberty Bonds; it was reported that the Poles bought more than any other immigrant group.[27]

Meanwhile, it seemed as if German flags were fluttering from every building on North Avenue, and bands were playing "Die Wacht am Rhein" on every corner. On August 3, 1914, nearly seven hundred men, many of them former German soldiers, crowded into the German consulate office to register for service in the German Army. The *Tribune* reported that "mechanics, artisans, clerks, and bookkeepers were in the crowd" and noted a group of officers who "wore the proverbial upward curling mustaches."[28] Two days later more than ten thousand Germans attended a rally at the Auditorium Theater and began collecting funds for the German and Austrian Red Cross. As late as March 1916 a grand affair was held at the Coliseum to raise funds for "German war sufferers." It was reported that Archbishop George Mundelein purchased a soldier doll for $10.[29] As one historian has expressed it, "No nationality group in Chicago's history had ever unleashed such a spectacular display of patriotism as had Chicago's *Deutschtum*."[30] However, Chicago Germans' enthusiasm for the kaiser's regime quickly went underground after the U.S. declaration of war.

Shortly after the outbreak of war in Europe, Chicago Germans crowd into the German consulate office on South Michigan Avenue to register for service in the German Army. Chicago History Museum, DN-0063292, cropped; *Chicago Daily News* photograph

A Shift in Public Opinion

Although many of Chicago's ethnic groups had made their choice of whom to support, most Americans were unsure. Public opinion, however, slowly shifted. The British operated an extremely successful secret propaganda bureau known as Wellington House. One of their earliest and most effective efforts was a document known as the Bryce Report, after its principal author, James Bryce, a former ambassador to the United States. It was created by a commission established to investigate stories of German atrocities during the invasion of Belgium in 1914, and its conclusions were sensational—babies speared on bayonets, boys with their hands cut off, women raped by the hundreds, hospitals shelled. Historians have concluded that although the Germans did shoot civilians suspected of being snipers, most of the evidence was dubious, if not bogus. Chicagoan Clarence Darrow offered a $1,000 reward for anyone who could produce a Belgian boy without hands; he never had to pay. Chicagoans were able to read the Bryce Report's sickening details in a *Tribune* piece published on May 13, 1915, but two months later the newspaper published an even longer article containing the German government's rebuttal.

Such evenhanded reporting by the *Tribune* also characterized the sinking of the ocean liner *Lusitania* by a German submarine on May 7, 1915. This disaster, which took the lives of 1,198 passengers, 128 of them U.S. civilians, has sometimes been cited as the event that drew the United States into World War I, but the declaration of war didn't come for nearly two more years. The *Tribune* printed samples of editorials from around the country, and although many expressed outrage, quite a few counseled patience, and none called for war. The *Tribune* also reported that the German embassy had warned that "travelers intending to embark on British ships did so at risk of the ships being destroyed in accordance with the German zone decree" and that the owners of the *Lusitania* had assured the public that the ship was "too fast for torpedoing."[31]

Before the war, one of the most intensely debated topics in the United States was preparedness, a movement backed largely by Republicans such as former president Theodore Roosevelt and Senator Henry Cabot Lodge. They

Lurid posters depicting alleged German atrocities in Belgium were instrumental in convincing Americans of the need to enter the war. Library of Congress

thought that U.S. entrance into the war was inescapable and that it was vital to build up the military immediately. Many Americans believed that the United States was vulnerable to occupation by German forces, who would perpetrate the same horrors they had in Belgium. A whole genre of fiction known as "conquest novels" fanned the hysteria. These books had such titles as *Defenseless America* and *America Fallen!* and some were made into movies. One was *The Fall of a Nation*, by Thomas Dixon, author of *The Clansman*, the novel that D. W. Griffith turned into the film *The Birth of a Nation*. Chicagoans knew *The Fall of a Nation* well because the *Tribune* serialized the book between September 1915 and March 1916, which must have provided both a boost to the preparedness crusade and a jolt of terror. The *Tribune* lent credulity to the scare with an article

Many Americans genuinely believed that their homeland was vulnerable to a German conquest, a fear quickened by various "invasion" novels and films, such as *The Fall of a Nation* (1916), a frightening depiction of a German invasion.
Wikimedia Commons

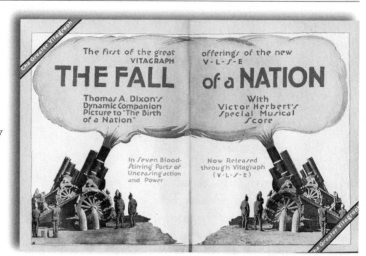

by reporter Burton Rascoe, who described a "mimic invasion" exercise conducted by the U.S. Navy in June 1915. "The inadequacy of our defense is terrifying," he wrote, adding that the huge German Army could easily capture Washington, D.C., "inaugurate the crown prince as sovereign of the dominion of German-America," and then conquer the "industrial center of the United States," by which he obviously meant Chicago.[32] *Tribune* editor Robert R. McCormick cowrote his own invasion novel, titled *1917*.

Chicago mayor Big Bill Thompson urged the United States to stay out of the war, and many of his constituents agreed. The Chicago Federation of Labor, for example, opposed the preparedness movement, arguing that "democracy and militarism cannot be combined," and many on the left viewed preparedness as a Wall Street plot to drag the nation into war.[33] But Thompson succumbed to political pressure and agreed to host a "preparedness parade" on June 3, 1916. A contingent of police officers, followed by a group of judges and government employees, led the massive procession. The rest of the marchers included nurses and physicians, department store owners and employees, insurance men, messenger boys, railroad clerks, architects, art students, "girls of the great mail order houses," bankers, and electricians. Ethnic contingents also were in line, even Germans. The number of marchers was reckoned at 130,214, and the *Tribune* called the parade the "largest in the history of America."[34]

In June 1916 Chicago staged a "preparedness parade," described as the largest parade in the history of America. Preparedness was one of the most contested topics of the day, with many intellectuals and politicians urging the need to make ready for war. Library of Congress

A month after the preparedness parade, on the Fourth of July, fifty thousand Chicagoans flocked onto the new Municipal Pier. It jutted thirty-three hundred feet into Lake Michigan and had freight and passenger buildings, a roof garden, loggias, terraces, and a concert hall with a hundred-foot-high dome. "No city in the world," crowed the *Tribune*, "has any structure on a water front that compares with the new Municipal pier."[35] When city planner Daniel Burnham set out his *Plan of Chicago* in 1909, he envisioned two long "public recreation piers." The Harbor Commission proposed no fewer than five piers, to be used mostly for commercial shipping, but it was pointed out that 95 percent of Chicago's freight traffic was carried by rail and that the cost would be astronomical. So just one pier was constructed, but by combining recreation with commerce, it satisfied both backers of Burnham's plan and the Harbor Commission.[36] During the war, it served as a recruiting center and a training ground for the army, navy, and Red Cross. When a stadium named Soldier Field opened in the 1920s, the sentiment arose that the navy deserved equal recognition. So on December 28, 1927, the city council approved renaming the Municipal Pier as the Navy Pier, today the most visited attraction in Illinois.

Although neither the rape of Belgium nor the sinking of the *Lusitania* was enough to persuade Americans to go to war, two events of early 1917 did push many in that direction: Germany's resumption of unrestricted submarine warfare and Britain's interception of the Zimmermann telegram. After a German submarine torpedoed the *Sussex*, a ship carrying two Americans, on March 24, 1916, Wilson threatened to break off diplomatic relations with Germany. The Germans backed down and issued the Sussex Pledge, promising no further attacks on merchant and passenger vessels. By January 1917, however, the kaiser was persuaded that abandoning the pledge would secure victory over the exhausted Allies, and once again the U-boats went into action. Many U.S. newspapers considered this the last straw, but in mid-March, when three American vessels were sunk, Wilson still resisted pressure to declare war.[37]

On March 1, 1917, the *Tribune* trumpeted the news of the Zimmermann telegram with a headline reading "U.S. Bares War Plot." A message sent by the German foreign minister, Arthur Zimmermann, to Germany's ambassador to Mexico had been intercepted and deciphered by British cryptographers. It proposed that if Mexico formed an alliance with Germany, it might regain Arizona, New Mexico, and Texas. At the same time, Mexico would join with Japan to wage war on the United States. The notion that Mexico might serve as the staging area for a German invasion had already been raised in the conquest novels, and now it seemed as if fiction might become reality.

THE TEMPTATION

A primary cause of the American decision to go to war was the discovery that the German foreign minister had proposed to Mexico that an alliance with Germany might enable Mexico to regain Arizona, New Mexico, and Texas. Wikimedia Commons

Declaration of War

When news of the Zimmermann telegram became public, as historian Thomas Fleming has put it, "outrage simmered from sea to shining sea."[38] To a man, Wilson's cabinet favored taking up arms. And thus the president who had won reelection in 1916 with the campaign slogan "He kept us out of war" found himself before Congress on April 2, 1917, calling for a declaration of war. The vote in the Senate was 82–6; both Illinois senators, Lawrence J. Sherman and J. Hamilton Lewis, voted yea. The vote in the House was 373–50, with six Illinois congressmen voting no. The two from Chicago were Frederick (Fred) A. Britten, who represented the heavily German Ninth District, and William E. Mason, a congressman at large. Britten "stirred a furor when he estimated that 75 percent of the representatives secretly opposed the war but were afraid to say so." Mason said, "I am against this war because I know the people in my state are not for it."[39]

Chicago had a strong pacifist, progressive, and socialist tradition that made many of its leading intellectuals antiwar; by the late nineteenth century, Chicago had become known as "the center of leftist publishing in the English-speaking world."[40] Like most progressives, the Chicago reformer Jane Addams viewed war as "a kind of lunatic vestige from the feudal past that had incredibly intruded its way into the modern world."[41] Isolationism tended to be strong in the Midwest, where many suspected that war fever was being stirred up by eastern capitalists eager to profit from war. As publisher of the *International Socialist Review*, Charles H. Kerr of Chicago was one of the most nationally prominent opponents of the war. "Wars are fought today to hold or to gain some economic advantage for the capitalist classes of the various nations," one of his editorials declared.[42] Robert Herrick, writing in the *Tribune*, quoted a "friend from the prairies," who told him, "You can't get the folks out this way to interest themselves in preparedness until the guns are going off in the next county."[43] Although patriotic songs remained popular, "the vast majority of tunes clearly favored non-participation prior to America's involvement."[44] One of the most popular songs in 1915 was "I Didn't Raise My Boy to Be a Soldier." That same year also saw the publication of a tune by Chicago songwriter Jack Frost called "Neutrality Rag," which said the monarchs of Europe "don't know what they are fighting for" and urged Americans to stay out of the conflict. When Congress instituted the draft, two-thirds of the three hundred thousand Chicagoans who registered sought exemptions, another sign of a lack of war enthusiasm.[45] A record-breaking number of men rushed to get married; some did so as a pledge to their sweethearts before going to war, and so that their wives might get government aid if something should happen to them, but most, it seems, got married so they could claim exemption from the draft.

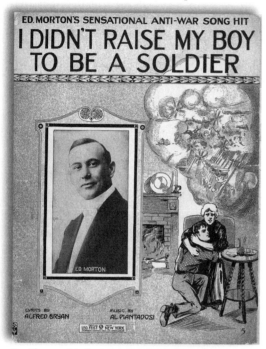

Pacifism and isolationism were widespread in Chicago and the Midwest in 1915, when one of the most popular songs was "I Didn't Raise My Boy to Be a Soldier." Wikimedia Commons

Nevertheless, once the war was declared, most citizens supported it. Even many pacifists swallowed hard and accepted its reality. As author Louisa Thomas put it, "Most of the peace advocates in Europe and, eventually, the United States joined the fight, not because they were rejecting their own beliefs but because they were told repeatedly that it would be a war to end war."[46] "The war to end all wars"—that phrase would be recited over and over. Another popular expression, one created by President Wilson, was "the war that would make the world safe for democracy." With such idealistic justifications, nearly all Americans could cheer the crusade. This was not a war for territory or treasure; this was a war to make the world safe and decent. *Tribune* columnist Caroline Kirkland, who wrote under the pseudonym "Mme X," told her readers, "It is safe to prophesy that when the war ends this little, round globe of ours will be girdled with democracies."[47] A *Tribune* editorial said the war meant "the Twilight of the Kings." It was "killing medievalism and crowning modernity."[48]

"Within an hour" after the proclamation of war, two Chicago lads, Harry Glen Velle and Edward Bamrick, had been accepted for aviation training, an act that the *Tribune* called "a record for speedy enlistment." The Chicago Yacht Club began conducting courses in navigation, signaling, and radio transmission, while members of a military club began drilling in Washington Park and the Illinois National Guard commenced a recruiting campaign at the University of Chicago.[49] On the evening of April 8 the first volunteer contingent left Chicago—450 naval militiamen bound for the East Coast.[50] By the end of the month the *Tribune* was describing the city as "war mad." Recruiting stations were "swamped," university and high school students were practicing military drill, physicians were lining up to volunteer, restaurant bands were playing patriotic songs, and on the South Side a meeting was held to organize "a new volunteer negro regiment of 1,300 men."[51]

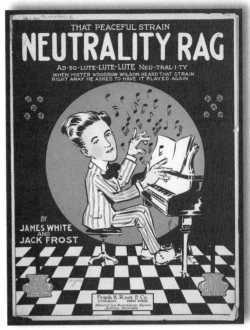

Jack Frost, a Chicago songwriter, composed the antiwar song "Neutrality Rag," which said that the monarchs of Europe "don't know what they are fighting for." Library of Congress

As the soldiers and sailors reported for duty, as men reported for the draft, and as women prepared to take up war work, hopeful Chicagoans anticipated that they were seeing the start of a new era, one in which liberty would enlighten the globe and democracy would elevate the world's nations. There is scant evidence that they thought much about how the war would change their own city. But it would.

One Chicagoan's War

Jane Addams. Library of Congress

Jane Addams
The "Impertinent Old Maid"

When World War I began, Jane Addams of Chicago had been a public figure for a long time. In September 1889, at age twenty-nine, she and a friend had converted an old mansion in a seedy West Side neighborhood into Hull-House, which became the best-known settlement house in the United States and an inspiration to crusaders for social reform. Among her causes were child welfare, political ethics, urban sanitation, protections for working women, improved public education, and labor legislation. As historian Alan Valentine has put it, "Many who never read a word she wrote knew what Jane Addams stood for, and her example set new goals for an awakening sense of social responsibility."[1] By age fifty, Jane Addams was not just famous; she was world famous.

Another cause Addams embraced was the peace movement. Inspired by Leo Tolstoy's writing on nonviolence, as early as 1892 she had joined the Chicago Peace Society. Although her doubts about the wisdom of the Spanish-American War and the U.S. occupation of the Philippines brought her some disapproval, her pacifism was largely uncontroversial—until the Great War.

Six months after the war began in Europe, Addams was elected head of a new national organization called the Women's Peace Party. The members, many of whom were suffragists, insisted that, just as women deserved the vote, they deserved to have their voices heard on foreign affairs: "We demand that women be given a share in deciding between war and peace in all the courts of high debate."[2]

Meanwhile, women in Europe were also organizing a peace movement. Dr. Aletta Jacobs of Amsterdam, a woman Addams had "long warmly admired," created the Women's International League for Peace and Freedom (WILPF).[3] The first meeting was scheduled to be held in The Hague; it would assemble women from many countries, and Addams was asked to preside. While sailing to Europe, Addams read in the British newspapers that the delegates were being mocked as "Peacettes" and her endeavors were "being loaded with ridicule of the sort with which we later became only too familiar."[4] British women were barred from attending, although three managed to get there, and no delegates came from France, Russia, or Serbia. But Belgian and German women were there, as well as many from neutral countries and forty-three from the United States, bringing the total to eleven hundred.

Addams did her job expertly. "To see her handle difficult situations, difficult personalities, conflicts," an observer said, "was as exhilarating as watching skillful rapier play." No one, least of all Addams, expected the gathering to end the war; her best hope, she said, was to "state a new point of view."[5] The conference adopted twenty resolutions, one of which called for a conference of neutral nations to offer "continuous mediation." The delegates also agreed to form a permanent peace organization and to dispatch delegates to the capitals of the warring nations. Addams, accompanied by three others, visited London, Berlin, Vienna, Rome, Paris, and elsewhere and "conferred with eight prime ministers or presidents, and nine foreign ministers; also with the Pope."[6] These statesmen encouraged the formation of a conference of neutrals to attempt arbitration. Attitudes had not yet hardened. As Addams later put it, "it still seems marvelous to me that the people we met were so outspoken against war, with a freedom of expression which was not allowed later in any of the belligerent nations."[7]

Unfortunately, while Addams was on her tour, a German submarine sank the *Lusitania*, which encouraged American militarists to demand preparation for war. Addams's efforts were widely derided. The *Louisville Courier-Journal* labeled her a "foolish, garrulous old woman," and *New York Topics* said she was a "silly, vain, impertinent old maid."[8] A French poet named Jane Catulle Mendès wrote an "open letter" saying that Addams was "making a great deal of noise for nothing" and charging her with "pretentious egotism," while a women's club newspaper asserted, "Jane Addams is losing her grip. She is becoming a bore."[9]

Addams hoped to persuade President Woodrow Wilson to convene a meeting of neutral countries, but he resisted. Late in 1915, however, Henry Ford, the automobile tycoon, decided to finance an unofficial meeting of neutrals in Stockholm and chartered a "peace ship" to transport U.S. representatives. Addams would have gone, but she caught pneumonia and missed the trip. She recovered but was sporadically ill over the next three years, which curtailed her activity.

Despite the dreadful losses, as the war progressed the European combatants became less, not more, responsive to peace talks. And when the United States entered the war, many of Addams's colleagues supported it. She refrained from censuring the government but continued to decry war in general. After a propacifist speech to the Chicago Woman's Club was coldly received, she said, "I do not suppose that I shall ever be applauded in Chicago again."[10] She supported conscientious objectors and delivered speeches on behalf of the Department of Food Administration's efforts to alleviate starvation in Europe.

Although the war years were probably the most difficult of Addams's life, her woes continued after the armistice. The WILPF met again in Zurich in 1919 (Addams served as president until 1929), but many still viewed the organization as unpatriotic, if not downright Communist. As time went on, however, the prospect of another war made efforts to establish international mechanisms for peace and disarmament seem more important, and Addams's reputation rose. When Addams received the Nobel Peace Prize in 1931, the presenter noted that "sometimes her views were at odds with public opinion both at home and abroad. But she never gave in, and in the end she regained the place of honor she had had before in the hearts of her people."

Big Bill Thompson. Library of Congress

William Hale Thompson
"Kaiser Bill"

For most Americans during World War I, the most hated person in the world was the man they nicknamed "Kaiser Bill"—Wilhelm II, Friedrich Victor Albert von Preussen Hohenzollern, the bellicose German tyrant whose hunger for conquest, as Americans saw it, had single-handedly caused the worst conflict in history. But Chicagoans had their own "Kaiser Bill" to detest—Mayor William Hale ("Big Bill") Thompson, who was also branded "Wilhelm der Grosse," "Burgomaster Bill," and "Herr von Thompson."[1]

The reason for Thompson's vilification was his lukewarm support of the war. In September 1918 the *Chicago Tribune* published an article on "Thompsonism," a catalog of his unpatriotic misdeeds that ran to twenty-two paragraphs and included the following:

- He "coddled the pro-German vote."
- "He denounced conscription."
- "He refrained from encouraging recruiting," "sneered at enlistments," and was "languid over the draft enrollment."
- "He did not attend the farewell ceremonies when Chicago's quota began to move to Camp Grant."
- He "encouraged war objectors" and "launched an anti-war propaganda that brought it under the eye of the department of justice."[2]

Big Bill Thompson was not always so detested. When Republican leaders asked him to run for alderman of the Second Ward in 1901, he was an ideal candidate. Although he had been born in Boston in 1867, there was nothing of New England about him. His father was a wealthy real estate developer who had brought his family to Chicago when Bill was just a year old. Like other boys of his era, Bill became infatuated with tales of the Wild West, but unlike most of them, his family had the means to fulfill his wish to be a cowboy. His father bought him a ranch in western Nebraska, and Bill became an authentic buckaroo. He could build a campfire and rope a steer, and he once laid out three hostile cowpokes in a saloon with a cue stick. Later, as mayor, he warned his foes that he was "an ex-cowboy" who knew "how to be quick on the trigger."[3]

When Thompson returned to Chicago in 1891 to take over the family business after his father died, he kept up the strenuous life by joining the Chicago Athletic Club and becoming a nationally re-nowned athlete, especially in water polo and football, while also racing his yacht on Lake Michigan. Tall, handsome, and a model sportsman, he was a golden boy when the Republicans came calling. In politics, Thompson's secret weapon was his crafty campaign manager, Fred Lundin, a.k.a. the "Poor Swede," who was key to winning the mayor-alty for Big Bill in 1915, just as the debate over the war was beginning.

Lundin had vast ambitions for his protégé; even the presidency was not considered out of the question. Hoping to gain national at-tention for Thompson, Lundin positioned him as a man of restraint who might become the voice for those who opposed American involvement in the European conflict. Isolationism and pacifism had substantial appeal among certain segments of the American popula-tion, but when the United States entered the war, such sentiments were largely buried under an avalanche of patriotism, and Thompson was censured for pointing out that Chicago was the fifth-largest German city. It was true, however, and there was a civic constituency for his antiwar views. Chicago's Germans were sympathetic to Thompson's blaming the British for the conflict, and the Scandinavians were skeptical about America's need to fight. In addition, Chicago's large Irish population had little motivation to back Britain. Finally, little enthusiasm for the war existed, at least initially, among Chicago's black population, who tended to ask why second-class citizens should rally around the flag. (And Thompson was already popular with black voters for having boldly put African Americans on the city payroll.) Thus there was an antiwar coalition to be forged. Even when American jingoism reached its height, Thompson and Lundin kept up their hopes that Big Bill might still have national appeal when, as Lundin explained, "the people realize what's happened to them and they start to think about things."[4]

Still, Thompson managed to hedge his bets. Before the war, he was willing to march in Chicago's "preparedness parade," a rally designed to get the city ready just in case. And after the declaration of war, he agreed that, although the people did not support sending soldiers to Europe, raising an army might be necessary to defend the country from invasion. He said that a draft should not be instituted unless the very existence of the nation was in jeopardy. One incident that damaged his reputation concerned the visit to Chicago of Marshal Joseph Joffre, the French victor of the Marne, and René Viviani, the French minister of justice. His reluctance to issue them a formal invitation brought cries of "traitor." Eventually, the city council delivered the invitation, and Thompson greeted the Frenchmen at the railroad station, but the damage was done.

Lundin and Thompson had their own newspaper, the *Republican*, which continued to decry the war with editorials labeling it a "moneybags' war" and saying that "our entrance into the great war . . . was unnecessary, unwise, unwarranted, and contrary to the self-interest of this country and its people."[5] Few of Thompson's actions were more provocative than his allowing an antiwar group to meet in Chicago. This pacifist organization, the People's Council of America for Democracy and Terms of Peace, had sought in vain to find a Midwestern city in which to gather, but Thompson welcomed them in September 1917, five months after the U.S. declaration of war. Many comments were made that Big Bill deserved a noose or a firing squad, and the VFW hanged the mayor in effigy on the lakefront.

The Democratic Cook County state attorney made Thompson a special target and used the new technology of telephone wiretapping to spy on the mayor and his police chief.

Thompson's antiwar gestures softened in 1918, and Lundin, continuing to believe that higher office was still possible, put Big Bill forth as a candidate for the U.S. Senate. In downstate Illinois, however, Thompson was viewed as little short of a Hun, and the opposition rallies were fierce. He lost the Republican Senate primary to Medill McCormick, who went on to win the general election.

But Thompson was hardly washed up in Chicago. By the time of the mayoral election of 1919, the war was over and the "Kaiser Bill" epithet had lost its sting. Thompson put himself forward as "Big Bill the Builder" who was doing great things for the city and would do more, and he easily won reelection by piling up votes in the minority wards, those inhabited by his coalition of German, Irish, and black voters.

Thompson had barely begun his second term when he had to deal with a colossal race riot. After that, the ills spawned by prohibition sickened the city, and Thompson saw fit to ally himself with Al Capone and other Chicago gangsters. His reputation grew so dim that he didn't run for reelection in 1923, when he was replaced by a reform candidate. Reform, however, meant the unpopular closing of hundreds of speakeasies, and by 1927 Chicagoans were ready to welcome Big Bill back. His final term marked the apex of bootlegging and organized crime in the city, and he was defeated by Democrat Anton Cermak in 1931. William Hale Thompson was the last Republican mayor of Chicago.

PART TWO

Chicago's Soldiers

3

"Kia-Kiak":
The Black Hawk Division

It has been claimed—and it just might be true—that the very first private drafted into the U.S. Army in World War I was one J. Bradley Smollen of 5063 Winthrop Avenue in Chicago. Smollen, a screenwriter for Essanay Studios, reported for duty at Camp Grant on September 2, 1917. The problem was that he wasn't due to report until September 5. At headquarters Smollen was told that he couldn't be housed until he "was sent in the regular way," but he decided to stick around anyhow. Asked where he would sleep, he replied, "A nice soft spot on the riverbank is good enough for me."[1] Shortly after his arrival, Smollen was joined by another early bird, a sportswriter named Tom A. Martin, and "for days this pair of eager patriots walked about the camp, misfits in the midst of a sea of officers."[2]

The Draft

When the United States declared war on Germany, many believed that American troops would not need to get into the fight. An aide to the secretary of war went before the Senate Finance Committee to report the military's requirements and said, "We may have to have an army in France." Whereupon an astonished senator, Thomas S. Martin, burst out, "Good Lord! You're not going to send soldiers over there, are you?"[3] The United States eventually sent two million.

Assembling that many men took a lot of effort; the U.S. Army was minuscule, with 127,588 men, plus 80,446 in the National Guard. In February President Woodrow Wilson stated that he favored voluntary enlistment, but even before war was declared he had come to realize that a draft would be needed. One of the things that changed his mind was former president Theodore Roosevelt's public gesture of volunteering to raise a regiment and take it into combat. Wilson cringed at the idea of his bumptious rival let loose in France and quickly scrapped any idea of a volunteer force. The example of Great Britain, which had successfully introduced conscription in 1916, also swayed his decision.

Quite a few influential congressmen, however, opposed conscription, especially those from the West and South. For example, House Speaker Champ Clark of Missouri said, "There is precious little difference between a conscript and a convict," and Missouri Senator Jim Reed asserted that the streets would "run red with blood" if Congress passed a conscription bill.[4] Nevertheless, conscription passed in the Senate, 81–8, and in the House, 397–24. The blow was softened by a plan to have 4,557 local draft boards composed of civilians, and not the military, oversee the procedure, thus giving the draft the appearance of decentralization and not something forced on people by high-handed generals and politicians in Washington. As one historian has put it, "Most Americans . . . typically experienced federal power not through the physical coercion of 'heavily browed officers' but through the efforts of 'trim little school teachers' and 'mild-mannered citizens' who staffed Selective Service draft boards. Every one of them was a volunteer."[5] The agency that oversaw the draft was known as the Selective Service System. This was truly mass conscription. In the Civil War, draftees made up about 8 percent of the army; in World War I, the figure was 72 percent.[6]

Despite the ominous predictions, the national draft went off calmly. On June 26, 1917, Wilson released the names of the members of local draft boards, also known as exemption boards, in twenty-four states, including Illinois. Chicago was divided into eighty-six exemption districts. The *Chicago Tribune* noted with satisfaction that few politicians had been placed on the boards and that Mayor Big Bill Thompson "was without influence in the selection," although some of the members had close ties to City Hall. Other members included a University of Chicago professor, the president of the tuberculosis sanitarium, a bank president, and Michael H. Rogers, "the west side coal man."[7]

The first thing eligible young men needed to do was to determine their serial numbers. This would tell them where they stood in the upcoming draft lottery, in which inductees would be selected by chance. Men were issued draft cards, but the numbers were not on them. To find out their numbers, men had to go to their local exemption offices, the addresses of which were printed in the newspapers. Some offices were understaffed and swamped. Many men tried to obtain their numbers by phone, but not enough people were available to answer, and in some places the phones were taken off the hooks. One of the buildings used as a draft board office was a Lincoln Park clubhouse that was unfinished and had no lights. The lighting of hundreds of matches was required when two hundred men showed up after dark demanding their serial numbers. Some in the overburdened offices decided it would be easier just to mail out postcards containing registration numbers, an effort that required overtime work.

Chicago's draft boards eventually compiled a list of 313,510 eligible prospective soldiers between ages twenty-one and thirty. How many would actually be called depended on the quota that would be determined in Washington. On national draft day, June 20, for sixteen hours blindfolded officials in the nation's capital pulled numbers from a glass jar. The first number drawn was 258, which applied to each man holding that number in each district. In this first round of the lottery, nearly 1.4 million were designated in order to obtain the 687,000 that the military had requested. The task then became one of choosing those who would actually serve.

On national draft day, June 20, 1917, for sixteen hours blindfolded officials pulled draft lottery numbers from a glass jar. Library of Congress

During the war the Selective Service registered many more men than were conscripted; about 23.9 million were registered and 2.8 million were drafted. Chicago's quota was set at 24,982. In order to reach this figure, twice that number, 49,964 men, were called for physical examination. Men who had volunteered before the draft began were deducted from the gross quota of each district. At the beginning of August an official of the provost marshal's office in Washington addressed a large gathering of Chicago draft board members and explained the guidelines, addressing especially the issue of women who were dependent on their husbands' incomes. The army was very reluctant to draft married men who had children, and 43 percent of all the exemptions went to married men with dependents.[8] Once the examinations began, it was found that only about one out of three men were eligible; about 30 percent were rejected for disability, and 40 percent claimed exemption (it was estimated that only 3 to 4 percent would have their exemption denied). Officials then realized it would be necessary to examine men totaling three times the quota instead of two times. On August 18, 1917, the *Tribune* reported that 66,726 men had been examined; of these, 15,720 had been rejected, 31,732 had claimed exemption, and 19,274 had been accepted. This left the city 5,708 short of its quota, but the gap was closed within a week, and the quota was fulfilled.

Statistics compiled by the draft boards give a fascinating picture of the average recruit of 1917. For one thing, obesity was not a problem in early twentieth-century Chicago. One physician reported that he was "struck by the number of men under size and under weight." The average recruit stood five feet, six inches; weighed about 150 pounds; and measured a slender thirty-four inches around the chest. Social class was found to be a determinant of health: the young men of the Gold Coast and Hyde Park were much fitter than their counterparts in poorer neighborhoods. The most common cause of rejection was hernia, which was attributed to "flabby abdominal muscles, due to lack of exercise." About 25 percent had bad teeth and the same number had eye trouble, but both conditions were considered correctable. Tuberculosis was uncommon, as were deafness and venereal disease, but a surprising number of recruits were found to have "heart affection." Despite these troubles, a doctor

Officers from Fort Sheridan and soldiers of the National Guard march up Michigan Avenue on August 4, 1917. The parade, initiated by the *Chicago Tribune,* included seven thousand Chicagoans who had been summoned in the first quota of the draft and would soon be called up for service. Author's collection

reported, "On the whole I feel proud of Chicago's young men. They are a husky lot with plenty of vitality and stamina."[9]

Camp Grant

Chicago's "husky" young men were sent for training to Camp Grant. In June Chicago architect Edward H. Bennett had driven around the designated site, a three-thousand-acre tract on the banks of the Rock River about five miles south of Rockford, Illinois. Even before the day was over, he had submitted a preliminary sketch to the authorities in Washington. Soon a throng of workers frantically erected the facilities, which covered six square miles and came to include at least fourteen hundred buildings and twelve miles of paved roads.[10] The first load of lumber was delivered on June 25, and exactly two months later the camp was ready to welcome its commander, Major General Thomas H. Barry. He had been in charge of the Central Department, which was headquartered in Chicago. As he boarded the train to Rockford, Barry said, "I and all the officers assigned

Most of the Chicagoans who went into the army trained at Camp Grant, a three-thousand-acre tract about five miles south of Rockford, Illinois. Camp Grant Museum

to my command will be not only the instructors of the men, but their friends in every sense of the word."[11] As his comradely statement might suggest, Barry became highly popular with his soldiers. The unit he was commanding was now known as the Eighty-Sixth Division.

Most of the officers were new to the army and had received three months of training at Fort Sheridan, north of Chicago. They arrived about the same time as Barry, long before the enlisted men. Many who envisioned themselves as gallant cavalry officers were disappointed to learn they would be commanding machine gun units. As it turned out, Smollen's premature appearance worked out well for him. The officers were so glad to

have an enlisted man available for chores, and he did them so willingly, that he kept being promoted, eventually becoming a lieutenant.[12]

On September 5, 1917, the train bearing the first contingent of 350 enlisted men pulled into the camp station. The men disembarked singing, "Hail, hail, the gang's all here; What the hell do we care now!" and were treated to an ample supper of beef short ribs, browned potatoes, stewed corn, pickles, bread, syrup, prunes, and coffee. The men stuffed their bed sacks with straw, took to their iron cots, and spent their first night beneath a driving thunderstorm, which only worsened their homesickness.

The outfit to which a man was assigned depended on which neighborhood he came from—that is, the different units were drawn from specific draft districts. For example, the men from Districts 1, 3, 4, and 29 were put into the divisional supply train, men from the Lake Shore Drive district formed an infantry regiment, and soldiers from Oak Park went into the trench mortar battery. These assignments were not inflexible, and provision was made for moving men to different outfits depending on their talents and experience. A former football star named Lawrence H. Whiting was made personnel officer and put in charge of assigning men to posts that suited them.

By September 9 the number of trainees in camp had grown to two thousand, and training was set to begin. (By 1918 the camp would house fifty thousand men and cover 5,460 acres.) When a publicity agent from Chicago named Spearman Lewis arrived, Barry had him organize a press headquarters to keep the soldiers and their families informed of events and to provide copy to reporters. On September 10 Barry gathered his soldiers

The men of the Eighty-Sixth Division, also known as the Black Hawk Division, pose for an impressive group portrait at Camp Grant. Library of Congress

53

into a tree-shaded semicircle and addressed them from a small knoll. It was reported that the assembly was characterized by "puzzled frowns, anxious looks, and other signs of bewilderment." Barry said, "As we live together, work together, fight together, and—some of us—die together, why shouldn't we be friends and comrades . . . ? Most of you are making greater sacrifices than your officers, are entitled to the best there is in us, and you'll get it. We shall play no favorites in this camp. So let us all get together, stay together, and pull together for the cause we have joined hands to defend." The soldiers were won over, and a sergeant called out, "We're Barry's boys now!" Another cried that their motto would be "Barry's boys to Berlin or bust."[13]

The Eighty-Sixth Division began training in September 1917; orders to proceed to Hoboken, New Jersey, their port of embarkation, arrived on August 8, 1918. It might seem that such a long duration meant that the division was superbly trained, but that was not necessarily the case. At that point in the war, the U.S. military was still adhering to the old-school doctrine of open warfare, a charge-the-enemy style of combat that relied heavily on bayonets but that had been rendered practically obsolete by advances in technology such as machine guns, rapid-fire artillery, poison gas, airplanes, and tanks. Bitter combat experiences would eventually change strategy, but that would be late in the war.[14] Also, the U.S. Army was lacking in weapons and equipment. As historian Edward Lengel has described it, "Most of the men landed in Europe without having touched a machine gun or grenade, fired a cannon, operated signals or engineering equipment, or learned how to apply basic infantry tactics in either attack or defense. The Doughboys were as unprepared as the country that sent them."[15]

Major General Thomas H. Barry, seen here with his wife, was the first commander of the Black Hawk Division. He was very popular with his men, who called themselves "Barry's boys." Library of Congress

For the Eighty-Sixth Division, the long months of training were interspersed with boredom, dulling education, training, and a few memorable moments. The first week was composed of days that began with reveille at 5:45 A.M. and ended with taps at 11 P.M., with the intervening hours filled with such activities as assembly, mess, guard duty, inoculations, issuing of uniforms and equipment, drill, and lessons in various soldierly necessities, such as hygiene and military courtesy. At least some of the new soldiers found the going at Camp Grant rough. Interviewed late in the war, some described their feelings of humiliation at being sworn at by harsh noncommissioned officers and their frustration with being punished for unexplained misdeeds.[16] The officer in charge of the division's MPs had been the founder and head of Chicago's mounted police, a coach from Northwestern University became the athletic director, and a former contender for the lightweight championship became the boxing instructor. Boxing was a common activity in the army's training camps, and the Eighty-Sixth Division appears to have become known for its boxing prowess—in June 1918 four of its finest fighters staged an exhibition at a Chamber of Commerce luncheon in Chicago.

One of the most vivid episodes in the history of Camp Grant was a visit by none other than Teddy Roosevelt, who gave a speech there on September 17, 1917, at which time the camp housed eighteen thousand troops. He used the opportunity to lament how the nation's unpreparedness had left it with an inadequate military and to criticize the War Department for inefficiency, and his dour assessment evoked criticism from some of the men. The next day Secretary of War Newton Baker's secretary visited and pronounced Camp Grant to be the best military cantonment he had seen. A really invigorating moment came in late June 1918, when the men were visited by Dr. A. J. ("Old Doc") Woodcock of Bryon, Illinois, who was described as an "old Indian fighter and scout." Wearing "hip boots, a cowman's vest, flowing red tie, and a campaign hat," Old Doc was taken to the shooting range, where he was handed an Enfield rifle and drilled a bull's-eye at six hundred yards. Even better, he taught the boys the old Black Hawk war cry, "Kia-Kiak," a shortened form of Chief Black Hawk's Indian name, Ma-ka-tai-me-she-kia-kiak. Woodcock, who was born in 1857, was not a veteran of the Black Hawk War of 1832, but he apparently had known more than a few who were and was something of an expert on Indians. Soon the cry "Kia-Kiak" was sounding throughout the camp, and the Eighty-Sixth became known as the "Black Hawk Division."[17]

After instruction in military protocols and other matters, the men were trained in the use of Enfield rifles, mortars, fortifications, camouflage, observation, and sniping, as well as how to survive gas warfare. Officers oversaw the construction of replica trenches complete with barbed wire, while engineers constructed a bridge over the Rock River in case they might have to do a similar job in France. British and French veterans of the western front conducted part of the training. The soldiers' high morale was evident in their readiness to take part in the Liberty Loan drive. They contributed more than $2 million, which was described as the highest of any training camp in the country. One soldier, Harry Horwitz, earned a headline in the *Tribune* by donating the royal sum of $15,000 to the Red Cross. It was explained that Horwitz had been born in Russia and that Germans had not only killed his two brothers, who had been fighting with the Russian Army, but also had slaughtered his father, mother, and sister in their home.[18]

The Black Hawk Division parade into Rockford on July 4, 1917. When the head of the column reached the bridge, the end was still at Camp Grant, five miles away. Camp Grant Museum

The warriors of the Black Hawk Division had expected to fight together in Europe, but the army began poaching trained units and assigning them to other divisions. In the first such action fifty-six hundred men were ordered to Camp Logan in Texas. In February and March 1918 four thousand Black Hawks were assigned to the Fourth Division, which was then sent to the western front; another eight thousand left for Camp Logan at about the same time. The army had an especially annoying habit of stealing trained men with special skills, such as carpenters, mechanics, and telegraphers, and shipping them off to France to serve in other divisions. To add to the gloom, the winter of 1917–18 was severe, with blizzards, temperatures as low as –27 degrees Fahrenheit, and snowdrifts that reached the barracks' roofs. Perhaps most demoralizing was the departure of General Barry, who in March 1918 was reassigned to his old job as head of the Central Department. Barry's immediate successor was Brigadier General Lyman W. V. Kennon, who was then followed by Brigadier General Charles Henry Martin.

The transfer of soldiers from the Black Hawk Division to other army units accelerated; between November 1917 and June 1918 eighty-seven thousand men were taken out of the Eighty-Sixth and sent elsewhere.[19] Transfers from other units and new recruits made up the division's losses. The Black Hawk Division now had many soldiers who were not only not from Chicago, but not even from Illinois—a situation not unusual in the later stages of the war. Other divisions suffered from the same practice, as the army was "constantly pilfering skilled men from already formed divisions." In October 1918, when seven newly created combat divisions arrived in France, the army immediately broke them up and sent their members into already existing divisions.[20]

Over There

Finally, after many months, General Martin received orders on August 8, 1918, to send the division to Hoboken, New Jersey, one of the U.S. Army's two main ports of embarkation. The Eighty-Sixth traveled first to Liverpool and then caught trains to Southampton, where the men boarded ships to cross the channel. The great influenza epidemic of 1918 was building, and many stricken soldiers never left England. Those who did were sent to the Bordeaux region of France, where the weather was delightful and the wine harvest was in progress. Many soldiers remained there until nearly the end of the war—except for those who once again were subjected to the War Department's practice of filching soldiers from the division and sending them elsewhere. In October 1918 an urgent call went out to General Martin requesting twenty-five thousand replacements; he sent twenty-eight thousand. Black Hawks were now being sent into battle, where many were wounded, gassed, or killed, but as members of other units. As correspondent Charles V. Julian of the *Tribune* put it, "The Camp Grant men have been scattered to all parts of France and wherever one goes, from the North Sea to Switzerland, he is bound to meet a soldier from the Blackhawk outfit."[21] It has been estimated that a soldier originally from the Eighty-Sixth could be found in almost every American regiment and that no other division contributed more soldiers to the army in France.[22]

Many of the Black Hawks, as well as others in the U.S. military, were doubtless carrying an absorbing publication produced in Chicago, *The Chicago Daily News War Book for American Soldiers, Sailors and Marines*, a pocket-size 192-page

"It's your turn!" The French and British were ecstatic when the United States entered the war, as shown in this cartoon, which makes the grim western front look like fun and games. Americans were called "Sammies" after Uncle Sam. Author's collection

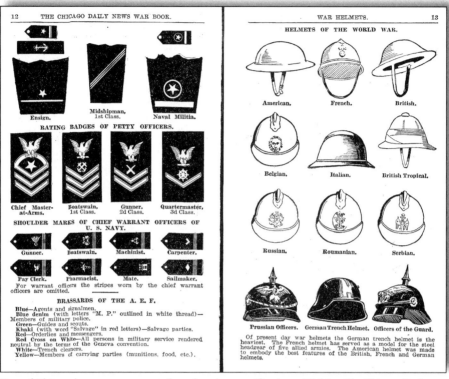

12   THE CHICAGO DAILY NEWS WAR BOOK.

WAR HELMETS.   13

HELMETS OF THE WORLD WAR.

American.   French.   British.

Belgian.   Italian.   British Tropical.

Russian.   Roumanian.   Serbian.

Prussian Officers.   German Trench Helmet.   Officers of the Guard.

Of present day war helmets the German trench helmet is the heaviest. The French helmet has served as a model for the steel headgear of five allied armies. The American helmet was made to embody the best features of the British, French and German helmets.

Ensign.   Midshipman, 1st Class.   Naval Militia.

RATING BADGES OF PETTY OFFICERS.

Chief Master-at-Arms.   Boatswain, 1st Class.   Gunner, 2d Class.   Quartermaster, 3d Class.

SHOULDER MARKS OF CHIEF WARRANT OFFICERS OF U. S. NAVY.

Gunner.   Boatswain.   Machinist.   Carpenter.

Pay Clerk.   Pharmacist.   Mate.   Sailmaker.

For warrant officers the stripes worn by the chief warrant officers are omitted.

BRASSARDS OF THE A. E. F.

Blue—Agents and signalmen.
Blue denim (with letters "M. P." outlined in white thread)—Members of military police.
Green—Guides and scouts.
Khaki (with word "Salvage" in red letters)—Salvage parties.
Red—Orderlies and messengers.
Red Cross on White—All persons in military service rendered neutral by the terms of the Geneva convention.
White—Trench cleaners.
Yellow—Members of carrying parties (munitions, food, etc.).

One of Chicago's newspapers contributed to the war effort by publishing *The Chicago Daily News War Book,* a remarkably detailed manual for soldiers at the front. Author's collection

hardcover book distributed free to any soldier who requested it. A valuable resource for historians, it contained densely packed information about weapons, insignia, airplanes, travel, German and French phrases, knot tying, map reading, and even a handy map of Paris.

In early November the Eighty-Sixth finally got the order to leave Bordeaux, and on November 8, 1918, the division departed for Le Mans. The plan was that it would travel to the front in Lorraine and on November 14 take part in the assault on Metz, but the armistice was signed on November 11, and as the author of the division's official history expressed it, "For them the curtain had been rung down just as they were about to enter the big show. And it may be said, they had paid scalper prices for their tickets."[23] A *Tribune* reporter said that the armistice had "ruined all hopes they entertained of trying on the Germans the combined effect of their Blackhawk yell and high explosive shells."[24]

Chicago's War Heroes and the Thirty-Third Division

Ten men from Chicago received the Medal of Honor for their deeds in World War I. Six were in the army, one was a pilot in the army air corps, two were in the marines, and one was in the navy. The naval hero was a member of the Dental Corps, an unlikely source for a war hero. Lieutenant Weedon Osborne, a 1915 graduate of Northwestern Dental School, was attached to the Sixth Regiment of the U.S. Marines when it made its assault on the French town of Bouresche in June 1918. His medal citation explains that he "threw himself zealously into the work of rescuing the wounded" and was killed when carrying a suffering officer from the battlefield.

None of the ten medal winners were Black Hawks. Five, however, were soldiers in the Thirty-Third Division, the "Prairie Division," which was also a unit from Illinois. Unlike the Eighty-Sixth, the Thirty-Third remained intact, and it saw a great deal of frontline warfare. Between mid-June 1918 and the armistice, the unit was almost constantly in battle. According to the division's official history, "There were only eighteen days when some part, at least, of the division was not holding a portion of the allied line."[25]

Many Chicagoans who took part in the war were not members of the Eighty-Sixth Division. Besides the numerous Black Hawks who ended up in other divisions, Chicagoans served as sailors, fliers, and marines. Even before the war began, some eager souls took off to Canada and joined the British Army. A few flew with the Lafayette Escadrille, a French volunteer aviation unit, in France; some Italian-Americans returned to Italy to fight; and quite a few women went abroad as nurses, Red Cross workers, and other participants. The Chicago Red Cross operated four complete base hospital units in France. A handful of Chicago Germans went to fight for the Fatherland. A group of railroad men recruited from Chicago formed an outfit called the Thirteenth Engineers, which helped run French railroads in the war zone. A hundred thousand men passed through the Great Lakes Naval Training Station, and many pilots trained at Chanute Flying Field in Rantoul, about 120 miles southwest of Chicago. Then there were separate units for Chicago's black soldiers, who are the subject of the next chapter. Finally, when

German soldiers flee in terror when confronted by the "cold steel" of an assault from U.S. Marines. The postcard was one of about thirty published by the *Chicago Daily News.* Author's collection

the war began, some men from Chicago and elsewhere in Illinois were already serving in the National Guard.

The Thirty-Third Division was formed from these National Guard units. It was commanded by Major General George Bell Jr. and trained at Camp Logan just outside Houston. In late October and early November 1917 the ranks of the division were augmented by the arrival of fifty-six hundred draftees from the Eighty-Sixth Division. Another twenty-seven hundred Black Hawks arrived in Camp Logan in April 1918.[26] These transfers explain how men from Chicago won military honors fighting in the Prairie Division.

In May 1918 the Prairie Division shipped out. The Thirty-Third saw action in four major campaigns: Hamel, Saint-Mihiel, Chipilly, and Meuse-Argonne. At Hamel the soldiers were introduced to combat by fighting alongside Australians, and one of the most often repeated legends of the unit tells how one of Australians remarked, "You'll do me, Yank, but you chaps *are* a bit rough!"[27] That their accomplishments at Hamel were out of the ordinary is attested by the visit on August 12 of King George V of Great Britain to the division's headquarters, where he decorated twelve soldiers—the only such instance of royal recognition for anyone in the U.S. Army during the war.

Of all history's wars, World War I was likely the most hideous in which to have fought. The stench and squalor of trench warfare, the muck and mud, the insane infantry charges into blizzards of machine gun fire, the unending artillery barrages that led to shell shock, the mangled corpses, the reeking clouds of poison gas that slowly asphyxiated their victims, the folly of the generals, the staggeringly high casualty rates, and the literal obliteration of hundreds of thousands of young men made the Great War one of the most successful of humanity's many efforts to re-create hell on earth. The U.S. Army—or the Allied Expeditionary Force (AEF), as it was properly known—did not suffer these horrors to the extent that its British and French allies did, because by the time the Yanks arrived in France, the trench system had begun breaking down on the western front and a campaign of mobility was beginning.

For most of the duration of their involvement, the Thirty-Third Division did not remain wedged in trenches but marched across northeastern France from battle to battle.[28] By November 10 the soldiers had broken through the Kriemhilde Stellung, one of a system of potent German defenses, and the next day they were advancing through the fog toward Metz when word of the armistice arrived. The records show that 989 men of the Thirty-Third Division were killed or died of wounds and 6,266 were wounded, for a total of 7,255 casualties.[29] And although they were not in the frontlines nearly as long as the French and British, U.S. soldiers did not escape shell shock, a condition of extreme mental duress characterized by disorientation, panic, trembling, and loss of motor control. After the war 60 percent of the beds in U.S. government hospitals were filled by veterans suffering from shell shock.[30]

Three of the Medal of Honor winners from Chicago were born outside the United States. Berger Loman was from Norway, Johannes Siegfried Anderson was from Finland, and Jake Allex (Mandusich) was a Serbian, born in the city of Prizren, now in Kosovo. Just skimming through the roster of the Black Hawk Division finds such surnames as Milaszius, Uebel, Vytiska, Drosopoulos, Gnacinski, Noonan, Pristoupimsky, Mulcahy, Solomon, Vanderhulst, Bodzioch, Libakken, Pedersen, Stamelos, and Damato. A large percentage of the names are clearly German. This wide variety is not surprising, given the many immigrants in Chicago, and the polyglot nature of the army was a national phenomenon. After all, one-third of the population of the United States either was born in a foreign country or had a parent born overseas. It's been estimated that one out of five U.S. soldiers in the Great War was born overseas and that a hundred thousand of the soldiers in the U.S. Army couldn't speak English.[31] According to the *Stars and Stripes*, the soldiers' newspaper, "Our army is probably the most 'international' in history. . . . The censor's staff handles mail couched in twenty-five European languages, many tongues and dialects of the Balkan States and a scattering few in Yiddish, Chinese, Japanese, Hindu, Tahitian, Hawaiian, Persian and Greek, to say nothing of a number of Philippine dialects."[32] Officers at Camp Upton on Long Island, New York, reported that the recruits spoke forty-three different languages, and one enlistee at Fort Gordon in Georgia said that three-fourths of his comrades didn't speak English.

Jake Allex's medal citation is an astonishing illustration of the audacity that some of these World War I heroes demonstrated: "At a critical point in the action, when all the officers with his platoon had become casualties, Corporal Allex took command of the platoon and led it forward until the advance was stopped by fire from a machine-gun nest. He then advanced alone for about 30 yards in the face of intense fire and attacked the nest. With his bayonet he killed 5 of the enemy, and when it was broken, used the butt of his rifle, capturing 15 prisoners."[33] One of the most poignant stories from the war is about Frank Lynn Bourne, a member of the Black Hawk Division. He killed a German soldier with a bayonet, and when the fallen enemy's helmet rolled off, Bourne saw attached to the inside a picture of

Frank Lynn Bourne of the Black Hawk Division became so remorseful after killing a German soldier that he vowed he would never bring children into such a heartless world. Camp Grant Museum the man's wife and children. Bourne was so remorseful that he vowed he would never bring children into a world that would permit such things. He kept his promise, and he and his wife never had any children.[34]

The Black Hawks' Legacy

The first Black Hawks to come home—sixty of them—returned to Chicago on January 10, 1919, and trains carrying men of the Eighty-Sixth continued to arrive in the succeeding days and weeks. Prominent citizens formed committees to make sure that each group of veterans would be greeted, and "each of the Black Hawk units received a rousing welcome home."[35] Private R. R. Burch of Oak Park brought with him a fourteen-year-old French orphan boy. As he explained, "We were giving a band concert at base hospital No. 22 when I first saw Noel. He climbed up in the truck when we left and the boys got to talking to him. I am married and have no children and decided to bring him home with me."[36] In June a group of former division members created the 86th Blackhawk Division Association, which was to provide financial assistance to members who were sick or needy, help veterans find employment, and aid those

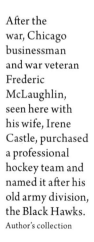

After the war, Chicago businessman and war veteran Frederic McLaughlin, seen here with his wife, Irene Castle, purchased a professional hockey team and named it after his old army division, the Black Hawks.
Author's collection

who had claims against the War Department. In addition, the secretary explained, "Entertainments and social gatherings will be given, enabling members, their relatives and friends to get together and talk over old times."[37]

One more member of the Black Hawk Division deserves mention: Major Frederic McLaughlin, commander of the 333rd Machine Gun Battalion. After the war he went back to running the successful Chicago coffee business he had inherited from his father. He became interested in hockey and decided that his hometown needed a professional team. In 1926 he paid the $12,000 entry fee to join the National Hockey League, which had been founded nine years before, and in order to acquire players he bought the Portland Rosebuds of the Western Hockey League for $200,000. The sissified name Rosebuds didn't seem proper for a team from big-shouldered Chicago, so he had to come up with another one. What could be better than the name of his old outfit? Given the team's logo, many fans might think that the Chicago Blackhawks hockey club is named after the Illinois Indian tribe.[38] It is, but only indirectly. In reality it is named after McLaughlin's old Eighty-Sixth Division. Perhaps the fans should be shouting, "Kia-Kiak."

4

Black Devils and Partridges:
The 370th Infantry Regiment

By 1917 Franklin A. Denison had risen about as high as was possible for a black man in the United States. In 1890 he had been valedictorian of the Union College of Law (today Northwestern University School of Law), and even before his graduation he had become only the twelfth African American to pass the Illinois bar. Because of his "brilliant academic record," Chicago mayor Hempstead Washburne appointed him assistant city prosecutor, and Denison was later promoted to chief assistant prosecuting attorney.[1] He formed a legal partnership with another black attorney, Samuel Asbury Thompson Watkins, and in June 1916 Denison, at age fifty-four, was a member of the Illinois delegation to the Republican National Convention, which met in Chicago's Coliseum.

But Franklin A. Denison of Chicago was destined for an even greater achievement, eventually becoming the highest-ranking black American officer in World War I. For he was also a soldier in the Eighth Regiment of the Illinois National Guard, which was originally formed in 1890 as an all-black militia unit designated as the Ninth Infantry Battalion. In 1895 the battalion, consisting of 18 officers and 407 enlisted men, became part of the National Guard. When the Spanish-American War broke out three years later, Illinois governor John R. Tanner did not call up the battalion, provoking protests from the black community. Consequently, Tanner asked one of the unit's commanders to raise a regiment of black soldiers to be called the Eighth Regiment of the Illinois National Guard. The outfit was sent to Cuba in August 1898, and Denison, a major, was appointed judge of claims in Santiago. When the unit returned to Chicago, it was rewarded with a victory parade down Michigan Avenue. In 1914 Denison, now a colonel, took over the command of the regiment, and the outfit moved into a new armory especially built for it at 3533 South Giles Avenue—the first armory in the country built for black soldiers.[2] The armory was "constructed of fire brick with stone trimmings and ha[d] a drill floor one hundred and sixty feet by ninety, besides corridors, executive offices and company rooms, thirty-eight by twenty-eight feet."[3] In September 1915 a distinguished-looking Denison, in full military regalia, was featured on the cover of the *Crisis*, the magazine of the National Association for the Advancement of Colored People (NAACP). He returned to active duty in 1917, when the Eighth Illinois was sent to the Mexican border as part of the effort to suppress Pancho Villa's raids on U.S. territory. When the United States entered World War I, Denison, along with his regiment, answered the call.[4]

As an indication of the prestige of the regiment, even before the war the pioneering black filmmaker Peter P. Jones of Chicago had made two documentary films about the Eighth Illinois: *For the Honor of the 8th Illinois Regiment* (1914) and *Colored Soldiers Fighting in Mexico* (1916). An advertisement in the February 22, 1919, *Chicago Defender* promoted a film by the black producer Oscar Micheaux of the Eighth Illinois upon its victorious return to its armory. These films apparently no longer exist, but they and similar movies helped counter unfavorable images questioning the competence and loyalty of black soldiers.[5]

Colonel Frederick A. Denison, commander of the Eighth Illinois Regiment, was the highest-ranking black officer in the U.S. Army. In 1915 he was featured on the cover of the *Crisis*, the magazine of the NAACP. Author's collection

Black Soldiers in the Great War

In April 1917 the regular army contained four all-black regiments: the Ninth and Tenth Cavalry and the Twenty-Fourth and Twenty-Fifth Infantry. Even before the draft began, thousands of black volunteers joined the army. On April 16, 1917, for example, the *Day Book*, a Chicago newspaper, reported that the

Eighth Illinois had paraded through the "black belt," "blaring forth jaz [*sic*] music," and "many enlistments resulted." Then, under the first call of the Selective Service System, over a million black men responded to the draft. Not all were certified for service: about 36 percent of those who registered became soldiers (compared with about 25 percent for white men). The forms used by the Selective Service carried a note in the lower left corner that read, "If person is of African descent, tear off this corner." About 2.3 million corners were removed by the time the war was over.[6] Black citizens constituted about 10 percent of the U.S. population, but black men made up about 15 percent of the men who entered the military through the draft. In Illinois, however, African Americans made up only about 4 percent of the draftees.

Many men, black and white, claimed exemptions—mostly because their occupations were essential to the war effort—but although white claimants were more likely to work in factories, they also seemed to be more convincing. Many southern white landholders attempted to have their black employees declared exempt but met with little success. In one Georgia county, the draft board exempted 526 of 815 white men but only 6 out of 202 African Americans, which was considered so egregious (even in Georgia) that the board was replaced.[7]

Young black men from Chicago enlist at the Eighth Illinois Regiment's new armory—the first armory in the country built for black soldiers.
Wikimedia Commons

Eventually, about 370,000 black soldiers entered the U.S. Army. They were a diverse group: rich and poor, urban and rural, northern and southern.[8] Not everyone in the country was eager to arm young black men. The black civil rights leader W. E. B. Du Bois commented that "the white South" was "preoccupied" with the risks of giving arms training to black soldiers. Some whites feared that the black soldiers would return from combat with "revolutionary" tendencies. This was a major reason that most black soldiers were given noncombat roles in stevedore units, salvage companies, labor battalions, and the like.

Although the admission of black men into the army was accepted, there was much debate about who would lead them.[9] During the Civil War the 170,000 black soldiers in the Union army were led by white officers, but as Denison had demonstrated, by the 1890s black men in the National Guard could rise to at least the rank of major. Yet in 1917 the U.S. Army was reluctant to train black officers, the entrenched belief being that black men were incapable of leadership positions. However, under pressure from various quarters, especially the NAACP, in May 1917 the military did establish a segregated training camp for black officers at Fort Des Moines, Iowa. About 1,250 men were posted to the camp; 250 were noncommissioned officers, and the remainder were civilians. The training was poor, and after the war the camp's commander, Charles C. Ballou, no admirer of the black man's martial aptitude, admitted that the white instructors did not take their jobs very seriously. Nevertheless, in October 1917, 639 black men graduated and were commissioned. The camp was then closed, and the training of future black officers was conducted in various scattered locations, some as distant as Puerto Rico and the Philippines.

In this era of Jim Crow, when black Americans were second-class citizens, why did they support the war? Some did not, like the social activist A. Philip Randolph, who in 1918 was sent to jail for his opposition, and others said they'd prefer life under the kaiser than under some of the city governments in the South. A black man in Harlem was quoted as saying, "The Germans ain't done nothin' to me, and if they have, I forgive 'em."[10] But W. E. B. Du Bois said it was time to "forget our special grievances and close our ranks shoulder to shoulder with our own white fellow citizens," although he also said, "absolute loyalty in arms and civil duties need not for a moment lead us to abate our just complaints and just demands."[11] The *Chicago Defender* argued that black participation in the war "will be the biggest possible step toward our equality as citizens."[12] As the historian Christopher Robert Reed has written, "There was no greater claim to the rights and privileges of citizenship than that linked to military service."[13] The hope was widespread that participation in the conflict would advance civil rights. As the black academic M. V. Lynk wrote:

> Standing alone like a man in No Man's Land . . . the Negro fought to make a Man's Name and a place to stand in Every Man's Land—the United States of America. Protecting the women of France from the invading foe . . . the Negro fought for protection of his own women in Dixie. The American Negro fought for a kind word from the American white man whom he has never failed, and to whom he is the only friend not bought with gold. . . . The Negro fought to hold the American ballot without a sigh and mark it without a single fear. Any hand good enough to pull a trigger in defense of the American ballot is good enough to put a cross mark on that ballot and have it counted.[14]

In addition, many black-owned newspapers favored the French, whom they admired for their use of colonial African soldiers in the war as combat troops. In early 1918 the *Chicago Defender* quoted an item from the *Vicksburg Evening Post*: "Fighting in the French army are thousands and thousands of variously tinted men, from all of the so-called races upon earth—yellow Tonkinese and Anmanese, jet black Senegalese, brown Kanakas, swarthy Moroccans, mullatoes from Martinique—fighting for France, giving their blood and life for France. . . . In the French system there are no 'inferior peoples.' All the people of all lands where the French flag waves are free, equal and brothers. They are citizens of the French republic, exactly like all other citizens."[15]

Nevertheless, many young black men were apparently not convinced by the arguments of prowar black leaders. Draft evasion was widespread, especially in the South. According to Chad L. Williams, "African Americans constituted 22 percent—105,831— of the 474,861 reported draft deserters. These numbers reflected a particularly high level of draft evasion among southern African Americans." Williams has argued that a disinclination to enter the military was a factor in the Great Migration of black southerners to northern cities like Chicago.[16]

The Eighth Illinois reported for duty on July 25, 1917. It consisted of 42 officers and 1,405 men, Colonel Franklin A. Denison commanding. *Half-Century Magazine*, a black-owned periodical, called it "the only regiment in America that is colored from the Colonel down to the last buck private."[17] The Headquarters Company, Machine Gun Company, Supply Company, Detachment Medical Department, and Companies A, B, C, D, E, F, G, and H were all mustered in at Chicago; four other companies, I, K, L, and M, reported at downstate locations. The men of the Eighth Illinois did not train at Camp Grant but were sent to Camp Logan in Houston. Although this was the regular training ground for troops of the Illinois National Guard, it was an awkward location. Shortly after the arrival of an advance contingent of the Eighth Regiment, a race riot broke out when two black military policemen were beaten and arrested for objecting to the rough handling of a black woman by white police officers. Over 150 armed

> *The men of the Eighth Illinois did not train at Camp Grant but were sent to Camp Logan in Houston.*

black soldiers of the Third Battalion of the Twenty-Fourth Infantry marched on Houston, and before order was restored twenty people were killed. The advance troops of the Eighth Illinois were commended for taking no part in the unrest, but one of its sergeants later recalled, "The unfortunate incident . . . caused many days of anxiety to our boys, and incidentally a test of discipline on our part. Uneasiness akin to despair swept our ranks."[18]

The First Battalion of the Eighth Illinois arrived at Camp Logan in mid-October, and the rest of the regiment followed a few days later. The *Chicago Tribune* noted, "The Regiment was sent into the South by an order that was not particularly noted for its wisdom."[19] Emmett J. Scott, the author of a history of black soldiers in World War I, described some of what the regiment experienced: "Week by week during the course of the training Col. Denison and his men won the confidence of the best white and colored citizenship of the town. He asked for a 'square deal' for his men, and he resolved that they should not suffer because of the former riot, with which they had nothing to do, although at several places en route to Houston from Illinois they were jeered at along the way, stoned in one or two places, and a riot was barely averted at a way station in Texas."[20] According to William S. Braddan, who wrote a memoir of his service as a chaplain with the regiment, as the soldiers headed south on the train, "we were the center of curiosity, for in every village, city and town through which we passed, we were greeted with the query, 'Where are the White Officers?' 'There's not a one in the regiment,' was our proud reply."[21] At one station the troops tore down signs designating segregated facilities, and when the men of Company F were denied service in a local store, they looted the place.

Inevitably, the Eighth Illinois encountered hostility in Houston. A police officer shot a black soldier for interfering with an arrest, some soldiers were sent to the guardhouse for getting into a fight with local whites, and after refusing to accept segregated seating, the troops were barred from riding Houston's streetcars. However, the training generally went well, and most of the men retained pleasant memories of their stay in Texas. They marched in a parade along with white units, and their smart appearance apparently calmed the tensions of some of Houston's residents. Colonel Denison, his staff, and the regimental band were entertained at a dinner by the leading citizens of Galveston. A highlight of their stay was a baseball game between the Eighth Illinois and white ballplayers of the 124th Field Artillery. The Chicagoans won, 7–5 (one of their players was something of a ringer, having played professionally for the Chicago American Giants). According to Chaplain Braddan, "The Negro population tried to outdo each other in making us welcome and many were the men of the regiment who fell pierced by the arrow of that Little Cherub, Cupid."[22] And at least one of the soldiers met and married a local girl. On January 8, 1918, Corporal Ray Barbee married Savannah Mae Day, "one of Houston's society belles."[23] One asset that black soldiers had was that they were unquestionably American, unlike the dubious soldiers of foreign extraction, those dreaded "hyphenated Americans" (see chapter 13). As the *Baltimore Sun*, a white newspaper, put it, "The Afro-American is the only hyphenate, we believe, who has not been suspected of a divided allegiance."[24]

The officers of the 370th Regiment pose for a group portrait at Camp Logan in Texas. *Left to right*: Major Charles L. Hunt, Captain John H. Patton, Major Otis B. Duncan, Colonel Franklin A. Denison, Major Rufus M. Stokes, Lieutenant Colonel James H. Johnson. Chicago History Museum, DN-0069826, cropped; *Chicago Daily News* photograph

In December the designation of the outfit was changed from the Eighth Illinois to the 370th Infantry Regiment. The military created two black combat divisions for African Americans. The Ninety-Second Division was composed of draftees and officers, and the Ninety-Third Division was made up of mostly National Guard units from New York, Cleveland, Massachusetts, Washington, D.C., and Chicago (the 370th). The 370th was sent to Camp Stuart at Newport News, Virginia, in April 1918. There was still uncertainty in the army about whether these black soldiers should be sent to France under the command of black officers, but apparently Denison's performance and abilities allayed the doubts, and the regiment shipped out in June.

Although among the entire body of the AEF about two out of three soldiers saw combat, the percentage among black soldiers was much lower. About two hundred thousand black soldiers were sent to France, and just over forty thousand of them were combat troops. Besides the worries in the South about giving guns to black men, military leaders had a dim view of their abilities. Although many in the government realized that black soldiers were needed, if for no other reason than to achieve the desired numbers of men, this by no means implied equality, and black soldiers were regularly reminded of their subordinate status. It was no great infraction for a white enlisted man to fail to salute a black officer, and black officers were given second-class quarters on troop ships. The facilities in which black soldiers trained were segregated, the troops were forbidden to leave their bases for recreation, and their training was substandard. The Ninety-Second and Ninety-Third Divisions, for example, never trained together in the United States. A general staff report claimed that "the mass of the colored drafted men cannot be used for combatant troops" and went on to advise that "these colored drafted men be organized in reserve labor battalions."[25] Many of them were therefore employed in that way; there were many cases of black college graduates working as stevedores and ditch diggers.

Ironically, rumors began to circulate in the black community that black soldiers were being deliberately placed in the most dangerous combat situations and that when wounded they were left to die. General John J. Pershing, commander of the AEF, felt compelled to dispel such speculation, even acknowledging that black soldiers regretted "that they are not given [more] dangerous work to do."[26] Even when whites could not deny the obvious success of black soldiers in combat, racist stereotypes often emerged. For example, an editorial in the *Milwaukee Sentinel* opined, "Those two American colored regiments fought well, and it calls for special recognition. Is there no way of getting a cargo of watermelons over there?"[27]

Denison's outfit was one of the few sent into the hell of the frontlines. The 370th Regiment sailed on the USS *President Grant*. The ship passed through a heavy storm and on April 22, 1918, arrived in Brest, where the troops spent two days in the Napoleonic-era Pontanezen Barracks. The unit then arrived for training at Grandvillars in the region of Franche-Comté, where the locals reportedly found the black soldiers to have much better manners than their white counterparts. Although the French were not free from racial prejudice, on the whole their relationships with the black American soldiers were cordial. One reason seems to have been that the white American soldiers tended to be condescending and rude and

Portraits of soldiers of the 370th Regiment taken in the French village of Grandvillars by pharmacist and photographer Lucien Edmond capture the dignity and bearing that the French so admired. Wikimedia Commons

entirely uninterested in French culture, whereas the black soldiers were respectful. One black officer asserted that "the general contrast between our attitude and the typical attitude of the white officers was so great that the townspeople took our side."[28] Members of French military intelligence noted that "many of the inhabitants of villages in which they [black soldiers] are stationed declare that they like them better than whites."[29] Many black soldiers were in no hurry to return to the United States after the armistice, and a few even remained in France, especially in Paris's Montmartre neighborhood.[30]

In mid-June Floyd Gibbons of the *Tribune* reported on some black soldiers in France. Censorship prevented him from identifying the unit, but his account of their singing the song "By the Rivers Gently Flowing, Illinois," revealed who they were. Gibbons assessed the officers and men, writing, "In the village square of a small hamlet serving as headquarters I saw them mingling on the easiest terms with the most cultivated French officers. And as officers they carry out their bearing in their personal appearance. Among no American officers in France now, even the nattiest, whose habitat is at G.H.Q., far from the dust and mud of the camps, have I seen more highly polished shoes and leathers or better pressed uniforms. Pride in the wearing of clothes is something which these negro officers did not have to learn from orders."[31]

Gibbons also described how the regimental band introduced jazz to cheery French onlookers, including an elderly woman in a rocking chair who happily swayed to a swinging version of "I Don't Love Nobody."[32] Other accounts of black American soldiers in France also commented on their music. Another *Tribune* reporter, Charles Wheeler, filed a story titled "Colored Yanks Jazz Their Way through France," and Gibbons related that "it is not an uncommon sight to see a crowd of white doughboys around a piano in some 'Y' or Red Cross hut, singing to beat the band, with a colored jazz band expert pounding the stuffing out of the piano."[33] A black woman who worked in the "colored" YMCA noted, "The average life of a piano was but of short duration. . . . Whatever else he might play, a fellow would finally finish with a touching rendition of some one of the many 'Blues.'"[34] As music historian William Howland Kenney has explained, many Chicago jazz musicians joined the 370th Regiment band "to improve their skills, or, as reedman

Unidentified black bandsmen, probably from the 370th Regiment, perform in a French town near the front. Many Chicago jazz musicians joined the Black Devils Band, and the popularity of jazz in postwar France was largely due to the sensation made by U.S. military bands. Wikimedia Commons

Albert 'Happy' Caldwell put it, 'to get some good, you know, learning, playing all that type of music.'"[35]

The popularity of jazz in postwar France was in great measure due to the sensation made by the military bands. A few of the black soldiers who settled in Paris after the armistice were musicians and contributed greatly to the spread of the new sound. A 1919 article in the *Music Review*, "The Doughboy Carries His Music with Him," described how American soldiers would invariably find a dilapidated piano somewhere and begin to pound out jazz melodies. "Soon," the author went on to say, "no French 'revue' was complete minus a jazz band to play between acts, and no French piano up to date without a sprinkling of jazz songs on the top."[36] The musicians of the 370th Regiment, however, could play a lot more than jazz. The regimental band was considered an expert ensemble; before departing for France, it had given a concert in Hampton, Virginia, at which it played marches, an overture, and an opera selection.

Although the Ninety-Second Division fought under the American flag, the Ninety-Third, including the 370th Regiment, served with the French. Pershing had promised to supply the French with four infantry regiments, and the Ninety-Third Division became the source: "The regiments were apparently not lent but transferred to the French army, and forgotten until after the Armistice. They were the only American regiments completely integrated into the French army."[37] The 370th Regiment was attached to the Seventy-Third Division of the French Army for training, and the men "were given French rifles, pistols, helmets, machine guns, horses, wagons, and even French rations, which consisted of food sufficient for about two meals per day, while the American ration had provided for three meals per day."[38] At first the men grumbled: "This man's army certainly doesn't want us, was heard on all sides." Eventually, however, they adjusted to being part of the French Army and genuinely enjoyed the continuing hospitality of the French. When the unit left Grandvillars for the front, Chaplain Braddan saluted it as a "garden spot where lived God's noblest and best people."[39]

The 370th Regiment in War

The 370th Regiment first went into battle on June 21, 1918, when it was sent into the Saint-Mihiel sector. The Germans assailed the regiment with artillery and machine gun fire, but the 370th took no casualties. In early July the regiment was shipped to the Argonne Forest. Although that sector was relatively tranquil at the time, it was there that the 370th took its first casualty—a private from Chicago with the surprising name of Robert E. Lee. The French general in charge of the division attended Lee's funeral. About this time, Colonel Denison came down with what was described as rheumatism, and on July 12 he was relieved of his command. Historians Arthur E. Barbeau and Florette Henri have expressed skepticism that illness was the main reason for Denison's removal; a member of the division flatly stated that Denison was removed "simply on prejudicial grounds."[40] A white officer named George Marvin had written a biased, unflattering report about the 370th shortly before, and it was evident that a move was being made to replace at least some of the regiment's black officers with white ones. In November two more white officers were attached to the regiment.[41] According to Braddan, the talk among the soldiers was "What's coming off; is it the purpose of this hard boiled egg to slip a bunch of white majors over on us?"[42] Denison was sent to the hospital at Camp Dodge in Des Moines for "recuperation." While he was passing through La Salle Street Station in Chicago, a man came up to him and said that he had four sons "over there." Colonel Denison replied, "I have 3,500."[43]

For the first time, the battalion was put under the charge of a white officer, Colonel Thomas A. Roberts. Not surprisingly, the new commander proved to be unpopular. Braddan called him the "arch enemy, vilifier, and traducer of the Negro soldier" and labeled him a "Modern Judas" who had conspired to have Denison removed.[44] Roberts probably took his assignment with misgivings that were evident to his soldiers, but if so, he learned to appreciate them—after a fashion. He wrote to headquarters, "Please don't think that after a month I am convinced that I have a world beater of a regiment—it hasn't gone that far with me yet; but there is a lot of excellent material that is not doing as much for the cause as it is capable of doing; the men are willing and as apt in most ways as most troops that I have seen; the officers are generally good as far as I have been able to observe them."[45]

The highest-ranking black officer in the unit was now Lieutenant Colonel Otis B. Duncan. Duncan was from Springfield,

Illinois, where his family had lived for generations. His mother's father, a Haitian named William de Fleurville (or Florville) had been Abraham Lincoln's barber and friend for over twenty years and watched his house when Lincoln went to Washington. Duncan, who was born in 1873, held a position with the Office of the Superintendent of Education and joined the Illinois National Guard in 1902, rising to the rank of major. In the Springfield Race Riot of 1908 his house was vandalized. The rioters destroyed a piano, smashed furniture, and used Duncan's military saber to rip the eyes from a portrait of Duncan's mother. Fortunately, Duncan and his family were not home. During the war, he won the Purple Heart and the French Croix de Guerre.

The 370th spent much of the summer being shifted around among different French divisions, much to the dismay of Colonel Roberts, who felt that their isolation from other regiments of the Ninety-Third Division damaged morale. In mid-August the regiment was pulled back for a rest, but when September came around it was again pressing forward. The Third Battalion, under Duncan's command, attacked the German positions in front of the Bois de Mortier and after five days of struggle pushed the enemy back across the canal. On September 16 four companies went into action in front of Mont des Signes, where they were in the thick of the action assaulting enemy positions. A sergeant named Matthew Jenkins distinguished himself by leading a platoon in capturing a large section of the enemy's works and holding it for thirty-six hours without food or water until reinforcements arrived. Another hero was Robert Ward, formerly the chauffeur for Illinois state's attorney John J. Healy. He was operating a trench mortar when he spotted a large group of Germans amassing in the front of their line. He threw a furious barrage over them, cutting them off from their rear and enabling his comrades to capture the entire unit.

From then on the regiment was nearly always on the attack, pressing forward under heavy machine gun firing and artillery shelling. It was at this time that the regiment earned two sobriquets. The Prussian Guard, who faced them across the line, called them "Black Devils." The men themselves, as well as others in the black community, clearly welcomed this nickname as a compliment. For example, the *Chicago Defender*, the prominent black newspaper, ran a story about the "brave deeds" of the "black devils," and the regimental band later toured under that name. The French Army boasted a group of Alpine fighters known as les Diables Bleus (the Blue Devils), and many black Americans enjoyed the implied comparison to those celebrated soldiers. (Duke University later named its sports mascot after the French fighters.) It might be that the Black Devils nickname had something to do with the regiment's relieving the French Blue Devils at a battle near Laon in September 1918. The French called the men of the 370th "Partridges," a title that was meant to be complimentary. According to W. Allison Sweeney, the author of a history of black American soldiers in World War I, the name was probably given "on account of their cockiness in action (a cock partridge is very game), and their smart, prideful appearance on parade."[46]

The 370th also acquired a reputation for expertise with the bayonet. When Denison was in Chicago in October, he was given a reception at the Appomattox Club and said, "Our boys are just natural bayonet fighters and have established such a reputation for themselves that the Germans let them come within a few yards of their trenches on patrol duty without molesting them. They have learned that that is the safest course."[47] During September, the regiment steadily advanced—Penancourt, Anizy-le-Chateau, Cessières, Grandloup. The 370th was pulled back from the front on October 6, but it returned to battle in early November. On November 3, as the soldiers of Company A lined up for mess, a German shell scored a direct hit, killing thirty-five and wounding forty-one. Within two days the regiment had crossed into Belgium. The 370th was the first Allied regiment to enter the Belgian town of Petit-Chapelle, and the inhabitants welcomed the men with an ovation. Half an hour after the armistice was signed on November 11, but before the regiment knew about it, the 370th captured a German combat train of about fifty vehicles—an action that has been called the last battle of World War I.

After the War

The regiment remained in Europe for another month, repairing villages and roads, and then began to withdraw on December 12. On Christmas Day the men arrived in Le Mans, and by January

10, 1919, they were back at the Pontanezen Barracks. Delous-
ing was a large part of their readjustment procedure (lice were
a major problem for all combat troops in the Great War), but
by the second week of February they were at Camp Upton in
Long Island, New York. The entire 370th Regiment was awarded
the Croix de Guerre by the French authorities for gallantry in
action, and eighty-three individual soldiers, from captains to
privates, were individually cited for bravery. On December 8,
1918, the French general Vincendon had paid them a florid tribute, which read in part, "We at first, in September . . . admired
your fine appearance under arms, the precision of your review,
the suppleness of your evolutions that presented to the eye the
appearance of silk unrolling its wavy folds. . . . The blood of your
comrades who fell on the soil of France, mixed with the blood
of our soldiers, renders indissoluble the bonds of affection that
unite us."[48] Blood was indeed shed. When the regiment landed
in France, it had about 2,500 men; it returned with only 1,260.[49]

Chicago welcomed the regiment home on February 17. After
arriving at LaSalle Street Station, the men proceeded to the
Chicago Coliseum for a banquet. The loudest cheers of the
event erupted when Colonel Denison, who had been separated
from his comrades for seven months, entered the hall. After
the lunch, the soldiers, "clad as if ready for the trenches—with
helmet, cartridge belt, service overcoat, and rifle," marched in a
victory parade down Michigan Avenue and through the Loop.
As the *Tribune* described it, "Negroes of all shades, sizes, ages,
and sexes waved the Stars and Stripes or the French tricolor, and
the whites waived the color line and sent up cheer after cheer."
The reporter, however, couldn't resist relating the soldiers' remarks in a crude dialect. "Boss," one told him, "we-all has been
Frenchified." And a corporal reportedly remarked, "Saw plenty
of France, plenty of Belgium, and plenty of Germany. Don'
wanna see nothin' mo' 'cept Chi."[50]

After the war, Otis B. Duncan took to the lecture circuit
and became a popular traveling speaker. The thirty-two-member
regimental band, now billed as the Black Devils Band, went on
a concert tour, traveling in a special Pullman car. After playing
in Detroit in April, they went on to Philadelphia. The following
month, they played at the Colonial Theater in Suffolk, Virginia. In
addition to some classical numbers, the ensemble demonstrated

their jazz chops in several pieces, including the "Memphis Blues" and the widely popular "Livery Stable Blues." In August the Black Devils Band played before four thousand paying customers at the Lexington Fair in Kentucky.

Denison, along with his partners, S. A. Watkins and James E. White, formed a law firm in May 1919, with its offices at 36 West Randolph Street. Denison retired from the military in 1922, when he was promoted to brigadier general, the highest rank attained by a black man up to that time. Denison died on April 14, 1932, and six thousand mourners attended his rites at the Eighth Regiment Armory. Ten days later the Illinois House of Representatives passed, without a dissenting vote, a resolution honoring Denison as "a military hero and a political leader who possessed the highest degree of courage and a type of honesty that is seldom found."

Erected in 1927, the Victory Monument in Chicago's Bronzeville neighborhood commemorates the city's black soldiers who died in World War I. Photograph by the author

After a long lobbying campaign by the *Chicago Defender* and George T. Kersey, a black state representative from Chicago, a monument to the men of the "Old Eighth" was erected in 1927 at Thirty-Fifth Street and South Parkway (now Dr. Martin Luther King Jr. Drive). When Denison died, the *Defender* complained that some "politicians" had "conspired to leave his name off the monument," which is confusing because the monument listed only the names of those who died in the war. But Denison's name is there now. It is inscribed on one of four plaques commemorating black military figures that have been placed on the walking court that extends north from the monument.

One Chicagoan's War

John T. McCutcheon. Author's collection

John T. McCutcheon
The Candid Cartoonist

John T. McCutcheon of the *Chicago Tribune* was one of the greatest cartoonists in American history. He was also one of the greatest adventurers. As an author who knew McCutcheon described him:

> There is probably no person living who has had more exciting adventures than McCutcheon . . . for McCutcheon has hunted lions in Africa with Roosevelt; he was on the dispatch boat *McCulloch* in Manila Bay when Dewey won his famous naval battle; he explored Siam, Cochin-China, Burma, and India; he joined the Boers as war correspondent in the Transvaal; he was with the Belgian and German armies in 1914 as war correspondent and with the French army in France, Saloniki, and the Balkans; he knows or knew nearly every crowned head, nobleman, statesman and military man in Europe; he has sailed the

Spanish Main in his own sloop; and he owns Treasure Island.
. . . He has been almost everywhere and seen almost everything
and known almost everybody.[1]

Contemporary profiles of McCutcheon unfailingly report his good
nature, his wit, and his modesty. His cartoons could be judgmental,
but they were never nasty, and his most famous, "Injun Summer,"
which appeared in the *Tribune* in 1907, reveals a sentimentality that
places him in the same school of romantic nostalgia as two fellow
Hoosiers, the poet James Whitcomb Riley and the songwriter Paul
Dresser, composer of "On the Banks of the Wabash."

McCutcheon was born in Tippecanoe County, Indiana, on May
6, 1870, and graduated from Purdue University in 1889. He went to
Chicago and landed a job as an artist on the *Chicago Morning News*.
In 1903 he moved to the *Tribune*. One of McCutcheon's college pals
was the writer, humorist, and Chicago newspaperman George Ade.
McCutcheon's illustrations for Ade's books *Artie* (1896), *Pink Marsh*
(1897), and especially *Fables in Slang* (1899) made him nationally
famous. In addition to his flair for illustration, his editors found him
to be an effective reporter, probably because of his love of travel and
ingratiating way with sources.

When World War I broke out, McCutcheon was covering the revolution in Mexico. He hurried to Europe and was in Brussels when the
Germans invaded Belgium. McCutcheon was frustrated by his inability
to get to the front, but the U.S. consul gave him and three other reporters an impressive document with a lot of big red seals on it. It meant
only that they were American citizens, but the Germans at the barricades were impressed enough to let them pass. They got as far as Louvain, where, as McCutcheon later recalled, "I had been worrying about
not getting to the front in this war. Now the front had come to us."[2]

The reporters watched as thousands of German troops, "singing in
great choruses," flowed like a gray river into the Grand Place. They
disclosed their identities to a German officer, who laughed and said
they were free to go about the city. "It was a pleasure," McCutcheon
wrote, "to find that the invaders were not the maddened barbarians
we had been led to believe. . . . I never saw a single exhibition of
rudeness or discourtesy from a German soldier or officer to a citizen."[3] After two days McCutcheon and his colleagues were permitted to retrace their steps back to Brussels. They saw many shattered
buildings but no "wanton destruction."[4]

In Brussels they witnessed the same inflow of German troops that they had seen in Louvain. As an American newspaperman with the German Army, McCutcheon realized he was in a unique position, and in his dispatches, he said, "I endeavored to give both sides."[5] A German general gave McCutcheon and some other American reporters passes that allowed them to travel to the French border, and somehow they found a couple of carriage drivers, who took them as far as Nivelle. One of the reporters, suffering from tonsillitis, went back to Brussels; the others continued on foot, determined to reach the battle ahead. At Binches they obtained a horse and cart and two bicycles. At Beaumont an intractable German officer ended their trek and put them on a train to Aix-la-Chapelle, where the American consul turned out to be an old friend, Robert J. Thompson of Chicago.

All this time the reporters had been wondering, where were the German atrocities described in the London newspapers? Convinced that such lurid tales had been "intentionally exaggerated," they collaborated on a joint statement so stating and sent it back home by way of Berlin. They reasoned that British censors would block it if it went through London, and with good reason: a reporter for the Curtis Brown bureau was arrested for pro-German remarks and threatened with jail before being released after three days.[6]

The Germans arranged for McCutcheon to be flown out of the battle zone in a biplane, and he worked his way back to London, where officials were eager to hear his descriptions of the German forces. He was back in Chicago on November 1, 1914, and the next day the *Tribune* carried a story in which McCutcheon predicted that the war would not be short, as many thought, but would last at least two or three years. He wrote a long article repeating that he had found no evidence of the many reported atrocities committed by Germans in Belgium and that some of the stories were demonstrably false. "It is well to remember," he said, "that in a great war, as in a great political campaign, there are astute masters in publicity at work in every country and that they are vitally interested in seeing that you hear only good of their side and only bad of the other."[7]

McCutcheon returned to France in 1915, and from there the *Tribune* sent him to Greece to interview the prime minister. He returned to the States, got married, and bought an island in the Bahamas that he nicknamed "Treasure Island." The birth of his first son made McCutcheon decide to remain in Chicago, but despite his growing family, he couldn't tame what he called his "wanderlust," and each contract he signed with the *Tribune* reserved him the right to take four months' leave every year. The titles of some chapters in his autobiography indicate his many exploits: "The Papuan Chief," "Across the Gobi Desert," "Hazards over the Andes," "Hurricane," and "Aboard the Graf Zeppelin." McCutcheon died at his home in Lake Forest, Illinois, on June 10, 1949. Toward the end of his life, he expressed gratitude that he was able to combine two careers, as a cartoonist and foreign correspondent, but he figured that ultimately, simple good fortune was the reason for his success: "Since there have been few disappointments in my life to act as a spur, the lion's share of any credit must go to chance, to the number of lucky breaks that have come my way."[8]

Samuel J. "Nails" Morton
The Mobster as War Hero

One of the most colorful war heroes to come out of Chicago was Samuel J. "Nails" Morton. Born as Samuel Marcowitz in 1893 in New York City, he and his family moved to Chicago's Maxwell Street neighborhood when he was very young. It was here that his father, Frank Marcowitz, changed his name to Morton, borrowing it from one of the bosses at Hannah & Hogg, a whiskey distributor that gave the boy one of his first jobs. Morton grew into a tall, strong, handsome Jewish kid who was esteemed in his community for organizing a protective crew of hardy young Jews, patrolling the streets with a baseball bat, and clobbering anti-Semitic members of rival gangs, usually Polish. It was then he acquired the colorful nickname "Nails," which testified to his toughness.

Because he was something of a legend, it's difficult to sort out fact and fiction in his biography, but the story is that Nails was arrested in 1917 for beating up two Polish gang members. According to one source, this fracas was known as the "Battle of Humboldt Park," and afterward Morton was given the choice of prison or the military.[1] He opted for the latter and was sent overseas. Most accounts, including one provided by his great-niece Lisa Safron, place him as a member of the 131st Infantry, which was the identification given in the

Chicago Tribune when he died, but his name is not listed in the roster in that unit's official history. His most thorough biographer, Walter Roth, says he was a member of the 132nd Infantry, and although his name is not in the history of that unit either, the name of his commander, Abel Davis, is.[2] During World War I, it was not unusual for enlistees to enter under an assumed name; maybe that's what Nails did. Or perhaps the lists in the histories are incomplete.

Samuel "Nails" Morton.
Courtesy of Lisa Safron

But that Morton did go overseas and did become a medal winner is unarguable; the encyclopedic *History of the Jews of Chicago* (1924) lists him on its Honor Page of war heroes.[3] In September 1918 a Chicago Jewish newspaper called the *Sentinel* ran a story relating that Morton, a member of "the 132nd infantry, prairie division," was well known before the war as a "boxer and sport lover" and went by the name "Kid Nails." It went on to tell how he went out on patrol with eight men. The sole survivor of the foray, he was brought back "with a rifle bullet hole in an arm and a shell wound in the leg." Once his wounds had healed, he asked to return to combat, but his officers would not permit it. Morton was awarded the Croix de Guerre and ordered to attend an officers' training camp. "He is undergoing schooling there now for a commission," the story continued, "and expects to send word home before long that he is sporting bars in Uncle Sam's great army."[4] (He did, in fact, return from France as a first lieutenant.) According to historian and crime writer Jay Robert Nash, "His superiors noted in his files that 'in addition to possessing natural leadership qualities, and coolness under fire, Lieutenant Morton has an unusual aptitude for weapons.'"[5]

On his return to Chicago, Morton became a member of Dion O'Bannion's mob, acting as a distributor of illicit booze and a partner in O'Bannion's florist shop. Morton owned a restaurant, operated a couple of gambling joints, and, always stylishly dressed, carried a sword cane. To Nails has been attributed the immortal phrase "Take him for a ride."[6] In 1921 he was accused of murdering two policemen, but he pleaded self-defense and was acquitted; it was said that the clout of certain Jewish politicians greatly helped his case.

But Nails's luck ran out. He had become an aficionado of horse-back riding, and on the morning of May 13, 1923, accompanied by O'Bannion, Mrs. O'Bannion, and a businessman named Peter Mundane, he went for a ride at the Lincoln Riding Academy. Morton was mounted on a horse that was said to be "particularly nervous and mettlesome." As the party proceeded along Clark Street, the mount reared up. The stirrup leather broke, Morton fell, and the horse's hoof struck him in the head. Morton never regained consciousness.[7]

Rabbi Felix Levy presided over Morton's funeral, which was attended by five thousand Jews grieving the loss of their protector. His war record was extolled, and no unlawful endeavors were even insinuated. After his death, Morton's legend continued to grow. As the story goes, Louis "Two Gun" Alterie took it upon himself to whack Nails's murderer. It is said that he and a couple of chums stole the steed from its stable and proceeded to throw a few slugs into it. Alterie then phoned the owner of the riding academy and said, "We taught that horse of yours a lesson. If you want the saddle, go get it."[8] The story might not be entirely factual (some accounts say that Hymie Weiss was the triggerman), but it was unforgettable—so much so that Hollywood couldn't resist it. In the James Cagney classic *The Public Enemy*, the protagonist, Tom Powers, exacts identical revenge on the horse that killed his pal "Nails" Nathan.

Robert R. McCormick
The Colonel

One famous forebear would gratify most people. Robert R. McCormick had two. His grandfather on his mother's side was Joseph Medill, founder of the *Chicago Tribune*, and his great-uncle on his father's side was Cyrus McCormick, the Chicago-based inventor of the McCormick horse-drawn reaper. Fittingly, such an heir had a distinguished education: Ludgrove School in England, Groton Prep in Massachusetts, Yale, and Northwestern University Law School. He was then a Chicago alderman for two years but quit politics in favor of journalism, especially after the death of *Tribune* editor Robert W. Patterson in 1910. McCormick became president of the Tribune Company in 1911.

When World War I began, McCormick's formidable mother, Kate, coaxed the Russian ambassador into getting her son an invitation to tour the Russian front. Before leaving, McCormick prevailed on the governor to grant him an honorary commission as a colonel in the Illinois National Guard. Now he would at least bear some military rank, and a natty uniform, to flourish before important people. Standing six feet, four inches, and naturally imperious, he was an imposing sight. McCormick met the tsar, watched the Russian forces in action, was

Robert McCormick. Wikimedia Commons

forced home by a sinus infection, and speedily published two books: *With the Russian Army*, and a collaborative effort, *1917*, a fantasy novel describing a German invasion of the United States that isn't stopped until stalwart Midwesterners make a stand at the Mississippi. When President Woodrow Wilson decided to punish Pancho Villa's incursion into New Mexico, McCormick, campaigning with his guard unit, got as far as the Texas side of the Rio Grande, caught dengue fever, and returned home. When Germany resumed unrestricted submarine warfare in February 1917, he quickly rescinded the *Tribune*'s opposition to American involvement in the war and pushed for preparedness and the draft.

When the United States entered the war, the McCormick family's ability to pull strings again served the ambitious "Bert," and he was appointed a liaison officer on the staff of General John J. Pershing, commander of the American Expeditionary Force (AEF). In Paris, McCormick helped launch the *Chicago Tribune Army Edition*, which he expected would net a hefty sum from its advertisements. But he itched to get into battle, and despite the army's dislike of "civilian soldiers," McCormick used his connections once more to become an artillery officer. He now added a monocle and walking stick to his outfit, and he grew the pencil mustache cultivated by many World War I brass that later became popular among Hollywood's leading men, such as Clark Gable and Errol Flynn. McCormick's division, the First Division, or "Big Red One," moved into the trenches, but he got leave to go to Paris to oversee the establishment of a *Tribune* news service staffed by the best reporters—unlike the drunken "bums" he had seen working for other papers. McCormick reportedly said, "I'll be a bigger man in the Army with the paper going in Paris."[1]

McCormick did return to the front, however, and helped set up and operate artillery batteries in the Ansauville sector. In one instance, he defied orders not to open fire and bombarded a German attack; fearing a reprimand, McCormick was delighted when General Charles Summerall said, "Thank God there is one man in this outfit who knows when to disobey an order."[2] In March 1918 the First Division was sent to the outskirts of Cantigny, the scene of the first American offensive. The outfit withstood crushing German fire, and an exploding shell knocked McCormick unconscious. When the American attack began, McCormick was recovering from the Spanish flu worsened by a whiff of poison gas, but he directed his unit's artillery fire with skill, sometimes giving instructions by telephone from his sickbed. Cantigny was taken with unexpected ease; maintaining it against German counterattacks was another matter, but the Yanks held fast. McCormick then collapsed and was transported in an ambulance to the American hospital at Neuilly.[3]

Soon after, McCormick was thrilled to hear that he was being promoted to full colonel. Now he was no longer an honorary colonel; he was the real thing. But even higher rank beckoned. Pershing promised him that if he would agree to go back to the United States to train soldiers, he would return to Europe in 1919 as a brigadier general. McCormick must have been one of the few soldiers disappointed by the armistice: by quitting the fight, those darn Germans had checked his ascent.

During his tenure as head of the *Tribune*, McCormick helped found the Medill School of Journalism, oversaw the prestigious architectural competition that led to the building of the Tribune Tower, and bought a radio station to which he gave the call letters WGN (for the *Tribune*'s nickname, "World's Greatest Newspaper"), personally broadcasting a weekly program. A stout right-winger, he and his editorial page fulminated against labor unions and the New Deal and preached isolationism (he opposed American entry into

World War II, mostly because he hated the British). He was also an advocate for a massive Chicago convention center, and McCormick Place is named after him. In 1937 he returned to Cantigny and spoke at the dedication of a monument. In Wheaton, Illinois, he established Cantigny Park, which contains world-famous gardens and two museums—one dedicated to the First Division and one dedicated to McCormick.

McCormick ran the *Tribune* until his death in 1955. For more than fifty years, he was one of the most famous people in Chicago. But once he had been to war, he was always referred to as Colonel McCormick or just "the Colonel." Many veterans understate their war service; not Robert McCormick—*Colonel* McCormick, that is.

Floyd Gibbons
The Reporter Who Lost an Eye

About a year after the American Expeditionary Forces began fighting in France, a dispute broke out over which soldier had had the distinction of firing the very first shot at the enemy. The matter was settled by war correspondent Floyd Gibbons, who explained that he had accompanied the Sixth Field Artillery for six weeks and had been there when the opening salvo went off. The soldier who had put the shell into the cannon and pulled the lanyard was Alexander Arch, "a swarthy gunner from South Bend, Indiana."[1]

That ended the debate, because Floyd Gibbons of the *Chicago Tribune* was about as authoritative as anyone could be on such an issue. Gibbons always seemed to find a way to be at the center of important events. As the *Tribune* put it, "Gibbons did not get his stories behind the lines. He went where shells were bursting."[2]

Floyd Gibbons was born in Washington, D.C., on July 19, 1887, and attended school there and in Des Moines and Minneapolis. His father, E. T. Gibbons, was a pioneer in the development of the chain-store business in the Midwest. Gibbons attended Georgetown Law School but decided that he preferred journalism and found a job on the *Milwaukee Daily News* in 1907. He then moved on to the *Chicago Tribune*, which was at the height of the golden days of the

Floyd Gibbons. Author's collection

reportage immortalized in the hit comedy *The Front Page* by Chicago reporters Ben Hecht and Charles MacArthur. Like some U.S. soldiers, Gibbons's first experience with armed conflict was in revolutionary Mexico, where he went to report on the U.S. Army's efforts against Pancho Villa.

In 1917 Gibbons was sent to England. He sailed on the liner *Laconia*. He could have traveled on the ship that was carrying Germany's ambassador to the United States, but he figured that that vessel would never be in danger, and he preferred to sail on one that might be a target for torpedoes. He chose the right ship. On the night of February 25, a German U-boat scored a bull's-eye on the *Laconia* about six miles off the Irish coast. Twelve people were killed, including two Americans from Chicago. Along with other survivors, Gibbons huddled in a lifeboat, was picked up by a British minesweeper, and the next day reached the Irish port of Queenstown (now Cobh). His four-thousand-word dispatch became legendary. Breathlessly describing the explosions, the commotion, and the anxious hours before rescue, he began, "I have serious doubts whether this is a real story. I am not entirely certain it is not all a dream."[3] The *Laconia* piece became so celebrated that it was a main feature of Gibbons's obituary in both the *New York Times* and the *Chicago Tribune*.

Gibbons thus had become a celebrity even before getting near the front. Once he did, his legend only grew. Witnessing the first shot of the war got him arrested because regulations barred his being there; the order of arrest became one of his proudest possessions. The *Tribune* bankrolled a fast car and a chauffeur for Gibbons, and in June 1918 he sped to Chateau-Thierry, where American troops were pressing forward. On the evening of June 6 Gibbons and two officers decided to try to crawl across a field in order to inspect some advance machine gun emplacements. Machine gun fire flew over their heads "like a swarm of bees." One officer was hit in the arm, and a bullet struck Gibbons in the head, gouging out his left eye. With his eye dangling on his cheek, Gibbons lay in the grass for three hours before the firing stopped and his companions were able to take him to a dressing station and then to a hospital. When someone asked him how it felt to be shot, he said, "Just as though someone pressed a lit cigarette to my skin."[4] For the rest of his life, he wore a white patch over his empty eye socket, which added the perfect touch to his swashbuckling image.

Gibbons returned to Chicago on September 27 and was met at the train station by his parents, his sister, a brass band, a host of politicians and military brass, the lieutenant governor, a band of police, and a spirited crowd. The French consul presented him with the Croix de Guerre, and everyone formed a parade on Michigan Avenue. "I am thinking that it's rather funny," Gibbons quipped. "Here I am with all those police ahead of me. In the old days they used always to be behind, chasing."[5]

After the war, Gibbons went on to cover the rebellion in Ireland, the revolution in Russia, the Spanish Civil War, the Italian invasion of Ethiopia, and the Japanese attack on China. In the 1920s NBC hired him as a radio broadcaster; he moved to New York and became one of the most famous voices of radio's early days. He was especially known for his rapid-fire delivery; it was reported that in one broadcast, he averaged 217 words a minute. Gibbons died of a heart attack at his Pennsylvania farm on September 24, 1939.[6]

PART THREE

Life on the Home Front

5

Wheatless, Meatless, and Coalless: Patriotic Chicago

Once war had been declared and the nation was committed, most residents of the city, like citizens around the country, rallied to aid the war effort. For Chicagoans dealing with food shortages and days without coal, singing "The Star Spangled Banner" at ball games, visiting the Allied War Exposition, and viewing superpatriotic movies in the city's theaters, the Great War, so distant in miles, seemed close at hand.

Food and Fuel Shortages

One way civilians could strengthen the war effort was to conserve food. Both American troops and the beleaguered peoples of Europe needed American-grown food, which became a precious commodity, and residents of Chicago, along with the rest of the country, faced a food shortage. A poignant piece published on April 30, 1917, in Chicago's *Day Book* newspaper titled "Good-bye Free Lunch!" described how the food shortage was forcing South Side saloonkeepers to abandon their revered tradition of providing midday nourishment gratis to their patrons. The federal government shut down industries deemed "unnecessary," such as brewing, and encouraged civilians to do their part by economizing any way they could, "such as recycling stale bread to extract the flour."[1] Some who took food economy seriously found themselves on limited diets, eating many wheatless and meatless meals. As historian Rae Katherine Eighmey has described it:

> While the daily calorie ration in army training camps was about 4,000 calories, citizens on the home front who observed the strongest wartime restrictions during late winter and spring 1918 consumed just over 2,000 calories. In addition, citizens cooked on a complicated wheat- and

meat-conserving regimen: Sunday, evening meal wheat-less and one meal meatless; Monday, no wheat all day and one meal meatless; Tuesday, no meat all day and evening meal wheatless; Wednesday, no wheat all day and one meal meatless; Thursday, evening meal wheatless and one meal meatless; Friday, no wheat at dinner and one meal meatless; and Saturday, no pork and evening meal wheatless.[2]

One propaganda slogan to encourage food conservation was "If U fast U beat U boats—if U feast U boats beat U."[3]

Another way to counter the food shortage was to produce more. As was also done later during World War II, many patriotic Americans planted "war gardens." In February 1918 more than two hundred Chicagoans gathered for a garden conference and began organizing activities to aid this new initiative. Harry A. Wheeler, the food administrator for Illinois, warned, "If we don't go back to the soil, we will starve."[4] Accordingly, Illinois established a War Garden Production Committee, which distributed free seeds. Again this illustrates how Chicago was a micro-

This image, produced by Edwards and Deutsch Lithograph Company of Chicago, a major printer of war posters, urges food conservation, a major issue in World War I America. Library of Congress

cosm of the United States during World War I: the city had 238,422 gardeners in 1918, and Illinois was first in the nation in wartime gardening.[5] Beginning in March 1918 the *Chicago Tribune* started running a regular column titled "The Successful Home Garden"; two months later the same newspaper published a photo of some young women of Eleanor Social Center No. 6 dressed in overalls and turning over the soil for two city gardens.

Americans were also urged to limit their use of coal, which was essential to industry and heating. Chicago observed its first "coalless Monday" on January 21, 1918—the dead of winter. Theaters closed (although some movie houses operated without heat), while grocery stores, meat markets, and bakeries were open for only half a day. Some saloon owners chose to stay open in the hope that chilly barrooms would cause patrons to imbibe more "stimulants." The order was even tougher on manufacturers, many of whom were told to shut down for five days, idling thousands of employees. The *Tribune* observed that "the city will suffer probably more heavily than any other in the country, for it stands at the top of the list of American municipalities for the amount of capital invested in manufacturing and second in point of production."[6] Mondays and Tuesdays were "lightless nights," when all nonessential lights, such as display signs, theater marquees, and those illuminating store windows and hotel and restaurant entrances, were to be turned off.

LIGHT CONSUMES COAL
SAVE LIGHT : SAVE COAL
UNITED STATES FUEL ADMINISTRATION

Turning off lights was urged as a way to save coal, which was essential to the economy. Mondays and Tuesdays were "lightless nights," when all nonessential illumination, such as in store windows and display signs, was to be turned off. Library of Congress

"The Star-Spangled Banner"

Nowadays, singing the national anthem before a baseball game is such a tradition that, as an old joke has it, a lot of people think the last words of the song are "Play ball." It wasn't always so. When the Cubs won the World Series in 1908, nobody warbled the tune. The tradition began during World War I, and it began in Chicago.

One of the first signs that the war was bringing the martial spirit to the ballpark occurred at the first game of the Cubs' 1917 season. Fans were treated to band music and "a regiment of soldiers and a display of military drilling upon the field."[7] Everyone was also given a small flag to wave. The first singing of "The Star-Spangled Banner" came during the opening game of the 1918 World Series, which matched the Cubs and the Boston Red Sox in a game played in Chicago.[8] With army planes diving over the field, the atmosphere was patriotic. During the seventh-inning stretch, the band, composed of members of a club named the Cub Claws, struck up the "The Star-Spangled Banner," and all the players removed their hats.[9] All except one, that is—Red Sox third baseman Fred Thomas, who was on leave from the navy, instead "stood at salute, facing the flag in true military fashion."[10] And then, as a sportswriter from the *New York Times* reported, "First the song was taken up by a few, then others joined, and when the final notes came, a great volume of melody rolled across the field."[11]

So inspiring was the moment that the Cubs' management realized they were on to something big and directed that the tune be played at the next home games. When the series moved to Boston, the Red Sox ordered the song played by a military band, and "a tradition was born; from then on the song was played at every World Series game."[12]

The War Exposition

One reason the city's baseball fans might have been in a superpatriotic mood was that just three days before the World Series began, the huge War Exposition opened in Chicago. On the same day that nineteen thousand people were watching the Cubs battle the Bosox, eighty-three thousand others were flocking into this huge exhibition in Grant Park, where "The Star-Spangled Banner" was played regularly.

The Allied War Exposition, as it was officially known, was a traveling exhibition organized by the Committee on Public Information. It also went to Los Angeles, San Francisco, Cleveland, Cincinnati, and Waco, Texas. In Chicago, despite rain, over 130,000 people attended the opening ceremonies. The exposition was formally opened by Mrs. Alice Gresham Dodd of Evanston, mother of one of the first three U.S. soldiers killed in France. A great white replica of the Statue of Liberty stood at the far end of the main promenade, groups of girls were dressed in the national costumes of the Allied nations, and various VIPs, including the Belgian ambassador, gave speeches.

Besides bolstering nationalistic fervor, the aim of the exposition was to give visitors an idea of what things were like on the frontlines. Miles of authentic trenches were dug by soldiers who had done the same in France, and army pilots performed aerial stunts. As the *Tribune* reported:

A mimic battle followed the speaking. Twelve hundred soldiers and sailors gave the crowd another opportunity to vent its enthusiasm. The spectators watched with breathless interest the tank Britannia as it climbed over the trenches and wandered about No Man's Land, smashing up the barbed wire entanglements. They cheered the landing party of jackies who rushed to the rescue of the hard pressed doughboys. With the rattle of machine gun fire, the sputtering of rifles, and the boom of the heavier guns, with soldiers wearing their "tin hats" and trenches half filled with water, the battle fields of rainy Flanders did not seem very far away.[13]

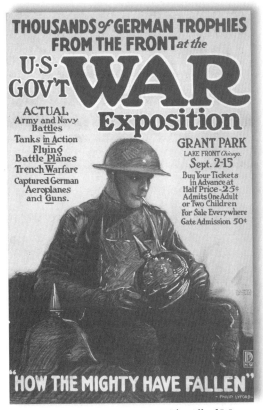

THOUSANDS *of* GERMAN TROPHIES
FROM THE FRONT *at the*

U·S· GOV'T **WAR**

ACTUAL Army and Navy Battles
Tanks in Action
Flying
Battle Planes
Trench Warfare
Captured German Aeroplanes and Guns.

Exposition

GRANT PARK
LAKE FRONT *Chicago*.
Sept. 2-15
Buy Your Tickets in Advance at Half Price - 25¢
Admits One Adult or Two Children
For Sale Everywhere
Gate Admission 50¢

"HOW THE MIGHTY HAVE FALLEN"
— PHILIP LYFORD —

The Allied War Exposition in Grant Park, which bolstered patriotism and presented scenes of life in the trenches, was the biggest event held in Chicago since the Columbian Exposition of 1893. Library of Congress

Attendees were allowed to view captured German weapons and airplanes, clamber into the trenches, inspect sandbag barricades, and view the relief work of agencies such as the Red Cross and YMCA. There were also concerts aplenty.

The War Exposition was the biggest event held in Chicago since the great Columbian Exposition of 1893. The *Chicago Tribune* said that the city's hotels had not been so crowded since that great "White City" fair and proudly reported that average daily attendance at the Columbian Exposition was 117,321, while at the War Exposition it was 139,688.[14] At the end of the fourteen days of the spectacle, the total attendance was reckoned at 2 million, far in excess of the other cities that had hosted it. (In Los Angeles, for example, the fourteen-day attendance was a mere 194,000.) If Chicago's patriotism and war enthusiasm had been in doubt before the beginning of the war, it could no longer be questioned.

Visitors attending the War Exposition were treated to impressive re-creations of World War I battles. Library of Congress

Patriotic Movies

Once war was declared, U.S. film studios, urged by the War Department, got behind the effort. Chicago's Essanay Film Manufacturing Company did not make as many saber-rattling movies as some others, but one of its most prominent was *The Man Who Was Afraid*, about a soldier who overcomes his fear of combat and volunteers for a dangerous mission. Released in July 1917, it was said to have been a big help during summer recruitment drives.[15] The following month the *Tribune* announced that the star of the film, Bryant Washburn, "a handsome young fellow . . . of athletic proportions," had been told to report to the army despite seeking an exemption as the sole support of his wife. "The man who was afraid" was apparently something of a "slacker"—his wife, who was from a wealthy family, had actually been offered a high-paying job and hardly needed his support.[16]

During the war Chicago movie theaters, like those elsewhere, stirred indignant jingoism by presenting such films as *My Four Years in Germany* and *The Beast of Berlin*. The former,

Warner Brothers' first big success, was a mix of fact and fiction purporting to portray the experiences of James W. Gerard, former U.S. ambassador to Germany. The tenor of the film can be understood from the first scene, in which a Prussian officer cuts down a disabled shoemaker. Germany's leaders come off as cartoon characters, and Belgian atrocities are vividly portrayed. The *Tribune* said it should be seen by "every man, woman, and high school student."[17] *The Beast of Berlin* was a cinematic study of the kaiser, who, according to the *Tribune*, was portrayed by Rupert Julian as a "strutting, egotistical, cunning, unscrupulous, inordinately vain, bragging bully."[18] (His generals and admirals are equally ludicrous.) "First France, then England, then America!" the raving monarch exults.

To ensure that Americans were viewing only the right kinds of movies, municipalities instituted censorship boards. Chicago's, which consisted of eleven members, was headed by Major Metellus Lucullus Cicero Funkhouser, who made national news with his handling of the film *The Little American*, directed by Cecil B. DeMille. To briefly summarize the story,

French maréchal L. Lesoil shows American sailor Clare Fetteroff a captured German airplane, one of the trophies displayed at the War Exposition. Author's collection

the heroine, played by Mary Pickford (who came to be known as "America's sweetheart"), loves a German lad before the war. She meets him again during the conflict while residing in a French chateau, where the inhabitants are subjected to unutterable degradations by the German occupiers. Even though the United States was at war, Funkhouser, sensitive to the feelings of Chicago's Germans and the antiwar sentiments of Mayor Big Bill Thompson, rejected the film as being anti-German, which obviously did not go over well with the flag-wavers. But as Funkhouser explained, "The Germans of this country didn't start the war," and the movie "would offend so many of our good citizens."[19]

A film titled *The Spirit of '76* brought out Funkhouser's pro-British side, although in a quirky way. The movie, a patriotic epic about the American War of Independence, was scheduled to open in Chicago on May 7, 1917, but Funkhouser banned it because it "might serve to arouse bitterness and sectional feeling against England, now one of the United States' Allies in the present war." He also claimed the violent battle scenes might harm military recruiting.[20] An attempt to screen the film at Orchestra Hall on May 14 was shut down by the Chicago police.[21] Thus a film about the American Revolution was rejected as anti-British. There can hardly be a better example of wartime hysteria that the conviction under the Espionage Act of the movie's producer, Robert Goldstein, who received a ten-year prison sentence (later commuted to three by President Wilson).

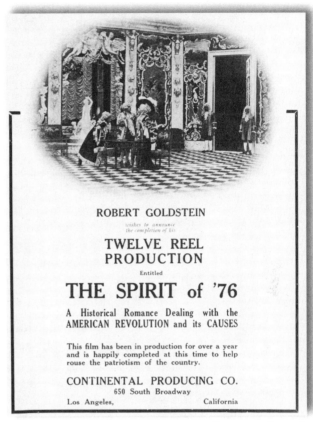

ROBERT GOLDSTEIN

wishes to announce
the completion of his

TWELVE REEL
PRODUCTION

Entitled

THE SPIRIT of '76

A Historical Romance Dealing with the
AMERICAN REVOLUTION and its CAUSES

This film has been in production for over a year and is happily completed at this time to help rouse the patriotism of the country.

CONTINENTAL PRODUCING CO.
650 South Broadway

Los Angeles,   California

After the U.S. declaration of war, Chicago's film censors banned *The Spirit of '76*, a movie about the American Revolution that they considered anti-British. Wikimedia Commons

6

Chicago's Bright Ideas: The Four Minute Men and the American Protective League

Two Chicago businessmen devised schemes in aid of the war effort that spread across the United States and recruited thousands of citizens. One of them created an association known as the Four Minute Men, which unleashed seventy-five thousand amateur orators on the nation. The other assembled a huge army of amateur spies under the umbrella of the American Protective League, which caused some of the worst civil liberties violations in U.S. history.

The Four Minute Men

The people of Chicago contributed to the war effort in many ways, but one of the most unusual was the creation of an organization called the Four Minute Men. Not everyone loved it, but it certainly made life easier for George Creel.

Creel's new job was either terrific or terrible. And for the same reason: no one had ever done it before. On the one hand, Creel was free to decide everything about how it should work. On the other, he had no guidelines, no rules, no instructions. If he succeeded, the glory would be shared with all who helped him. If he didn't, the failure would be his alone.

One week after Congress declared war, President Woodrow Wilson issued an executive order establishing a new agency called the Committee on Public Information (CPI) and placing Creel, a longtime Wilson backer and the muckraking editor of the *Rocky Mountain News*, in charge. Its job was to spread information (Creel disliked the word *propaganda*) about the war aims of the United States and to convey to Americans as well as the world "the full message of America's idealism, unselfishness, and indomitable purpose." As Creel put it, "We fought prejudice, indifference, and disaffection at home and we fought ignorance and falsehood abroad."[1] Those with a more cynical view might argue that he used the techniques of modern advertising to brainwash Americans people into supporting a conflict that they initially questioned and to stoke a hyperpatriotism that shredded the Bill of Rights.

Creel constructed an organization that eventually employed more than 150,000 people.[2] They used every means of persuasion available: "the printed word, the spoken word, the motion picture, the telegraph, the cable, the wireless, the poster, the signboard."[3] The CPI worked with advertising agencies and public relations firms to produce pamphlets, billboards, and posters, and it inundated the nation's newspapers with six thousand press releases. The agency produced movies, including *Pershing's Crusaders* and *America's Answer*; study guides for teachers; and two hundred thousand "lantern slide shows" that were screened in churches, schools, and chambers of commerce and at the meetings of fraternal societies and professional and business groups. To ensure the loyalty of the nation's workers, who tended to flirt with socialism, the CPI set up the American Alliance for Labor and Democracy, which had, in the agency's words, "the special responsibility of keeping labor industrious, patriotic, and quiet."[4] Lest fearful mothers discourage their sons from enlisting, the agency made an effort to kindle women's patriotism. It sent representatives abroad to explain and extol American policy; it reached out to the foreign language–speaking population at home through the establishment of Loyalty Leagues in ethnic communities; and it made a special effort to spread its message among black citizens, with mixed success. It supplied the soldiers with literature meant to boost their spirits, and it bombarded the Germans from the air with material meant to weaken morale.

Every day, in the interests of transparency, the agency issued the *Official Bulletin*, a newspaper listing the activities of the federal government, sending it out to all the nation's newspapers and to post offices, military establishments, and government agencies.

George Creel was the head of the Committee on Public Information, which had the task of persuading the public of the rightness of America's war aims. Library of Congress

Although it purported to be a candid report of current events, it curiously contained only good news. The CPI's reach was so long that at least one historian has raised comparisons to the Ministry of Truth in George Orwell's totalitarian fantasy, *1984*.[5]

The British had perfected a propaganda agency, headquartered in London's Wellington House, that was largely responsible for the image of the hideous "Hun" and his megalomaniacal kaiser. Although Creel did not know about this organization because it was a secret, he and American newspaper editors were steady recipients of their products. As the novelist and World War I veteran Laurence Stallings put it, "No one who believes in a free press wants to say that front-page war bulletins of 1915–16–17 were mainly a tissue of lies, but such was censorship in Europe that they were all tinged with mendacity."[6]

The Four Minute Men organization was the innovation of a young Chicago businessman named Donald M. Ryerson. In 1842 his grandfather had established Joseph T. Ryerson & Son, which became one of the country's leading processors and wholesalers of steel products, with its headquarters in Chicago. Donald, who had graduated from Yale in 1907, entered the family firm soon after his graduation and became a vice president, as did his two brothers.[7]

Ever since the United States broke off diplomatic relations with Germany in February 1917, there was a growing presentiment among Americans that hostilities were inescapable. One manifestation of that feeling was the enactment of the National Defense Act, which expanded the army and the National Guard and was part of the "preparedness" movement. When Congress adjourned in March 1917, it had been debating a measure that would institute universal military training. It never passed, but it attracted fervent supporters, Ryerson among them.

Ryerson was a member of the exclusive Saddle and Cycle Club, which had its own private Lake Michigan beach in the North Side Edgewater neighborhood. One evening, an informal discussion took place about the best way to support preparedness and the military training bill. In addition to Ryerson, the participants included Congressman (later Senator) Medill McCormick, financier William McCormick Blair, and Arthur G. Cable, son of a prominent businessman.[8] They came up with an idea that turned out to be a blockbuster. One of them considered how many millions of Americans were going to the movies—between ten and thirteen million people, 10 percent of the population, every day—and wondered how that huge audience might be reached. As Blair later reminisced, "In less time than it takes to tell it was agreed to enlist the support of movie managers in Chicago and get together a body of men who would speak during intermission."[9]

At that time full-length movies were just becoming popular. The first American features date to 1912, but many theater managers were screening one-reel films lasting about fifteen minutes and were unconvinced that audiences would sit still for longer. Consequently, projectors capable of showing long films without interruption were only just catching on, and as the club members learned, it took about four minutes for a projectionist to change reels—creating, in other words, a ready-made four-minute intermission that the speakers could use to make their patriotic pitch. They would be called the Four Minute Men.

Ryerson conferred with some of his affluent acquaintances, found enthusiasm for his plan, and made arrangements with the Strand Theater to host a trial speech, which was given on March 31, 1917. It went over well, and two days later Ryerson held a luncheon at the University Club and fleshed out his scheme. An organization was formed with Ryerson as president, and a call went out for volunteer orators. The new association now began meeting almost every day, and a committee was appointed to make contact with theater owners and arrange a schedule of speeches. It was also decided that the orator should receive guidance on the topic to be covered, although each speaker should be free to compose the text of his discourse. This assistance was provided through a bulletin outlining what should be discussed; the first two bulletins were about the draft. To prepare the audience, Ryerson arranged for a slide to be projected onto the screen declaring that someone was going to "speak for four minutes on a subject of national importance."[10]

No sooner had the Four Minute Men fanned out among Chicago's hundreds of movie theaters than war was declared. Ryerson's group decided that it needed some sort of official sanction, so the men agreed that Ryerson should go to Washington and talk to the new Committee on Public Information. The CPI had been established on April 13; Ryerson was on the train on April 15.

4 MINUTE MEN

A MESSAGE FROM WASHINGTON

INDEPENDENCE HALL

COMMITTEE ON PUBLIC INFORMATION

Independence Hall in Philadelphia provides the backdrop for a message from the Four Minute Men, a patriotic organization created in Chicago.
Library of Congress

Creel described his meeting with Ryerson this way: "In the very first hours of the Committee, when we were still penned in the navy library, fighting for breath, a handsome, rosy-cheeked youth burst through the crowd and caught my lapel in a death-grip. His name was Donald Ryerson. He confessed to Chicago as his home, and the plan that he presented was the organization of volunteer speakers for the purpose of making patriotic talks in motion-picture theaters. He had tried out the scheme in Chicago, and the success of the venture had catapulted him on the train to Washington and to me."[11] Creel later reflected that if he'd had more time to think about it, he might have rejected this wild idea of turning "loose on the country an army of speakers impossible of exact control," but he made a snap judgment, and within a flat ten minutes he had created a new national organization with Ryerson as its director.

The national Four Minute Men organization came into being on June 16, 1917, when Creel posted a memorandum explaining its mission. Other government officials came on board, and William A. Brady, president of the Motion Picture Industry and the World Film Corporation, reported that the executive committee of the Motion Picture Industry had agreed to recognize the Four Minute Men as authorized government speakers, which meant that all the nation's theaters were now available to Ryerson and his men.

Ryerson, however, would not take advantage of this offer or any others. He had already accepted a commission in the navy, and he was on a two-month leave when all this activity was going on. He relinquished control to William McCormick Blair, a young investment banker from a well-established Chicago family.[12] Blair oversaw the Four Minute Men for most of its existence, although he later enlisted in the artillery, and on

September 1, 1918, control of the agency passed to its third and final director, a New York executive named William H. Ingersoll.

A decision was made very early to move beyond movie theaters and reach people in a much wider range of venues. Churches, schools, and union halls were obvious locations, as were meetings of fraternal organizations and women's groups. But as war fever rose in the country, the ambitions of Creel and Blair ascended with it. No matter what one did or where one lived in the United States during World War I, it was next to impossible to escape being harangued somewhere, sometime by a Four Minute Man. A Yiddish-speaking garment worker in New York would hear a speech in his synagogue. An Italian baker in New Orleans would hear a speech in his church. No matter what someone's language, the Four Minute Men were sure to have orators in the area who spoke it.

When it was realized that most moviegoers at matinees were women, a special army of female speakers were sent to the theaters during the day. In many parts of the country a Colored Division reached out to African Americans in cities and on farms. Among the Colored Four Minute Men of Brunswick, Georgia, for example, were teachers, preachers, doctors, a gardener, a paper hanger, a carpenter, a shoemaker, and a barber.[13] Four Minute Men fanned out across Indian reservations, into logging camps, down into mines, and into factories. Farmers were hard to reach, but the Four Minute Men found them in churches and at public sales. One California orator delivered his speeches on trains, streetcars, and ferry boats. In Alaska a troop of some three hundred speakers, including three women, trekked by dogsled and paddled in boats to reach native Eskimos. Nearly four hundred speakers canvassed the island of Puerto Rico, and Four Minute Men even journeyed to Hawaii, Guam, American Samoa, and Panama. They set up booths at state fairs, and they even reached those who were just out for a walk in the park when the Four Minute Men of Chicago came up with the idea of providing orators for park band concerts and the idea spread to other cities.

Many theater owners welcomed the Four Minute Men, and some reported that they sold more tickets on nights that a speaker was to appear. But indications of dissatisfaction arose. One letter to the national headquarters complained that in a certain city, the audiences "have been most disrespectful of these speakers, and it is most discouraging to these men to have practically half of their audience get up and leave the theater as soon as the slide announcing the speaker is shown." In Olympia, Washington, an audience member rose up and called out, "Cut out the bunk on the Red Cross and go on with the show!" Organizational leaders advised that the way to prevent such episodes was to find speakers with "punch and power."[14]

By the time their organization was disbanded on December 24, 1918, seventy-five thousand Four Minute Men orators, operating in 7,448 cities and towns, delivered more than 755,000 speeches to a total audience of approximately 315 million (the population of the United States was then about 103 million).[15]

The national headquarters issued forty-six *Official Bulletins*, ranging from the first, "Universal Service by Selective Draft," to the last, "A Tribute to the Allies." Other titles included "Food Conservation," "The Income Tax," and "Farm and Garden."[16]

Wartime paranoia caused many to imagine a host of secret agents infiltrating American life.

Some topics were to be used for a few days, others for nearly a month. Each bulletin sketched out the material to be covered and contained facts and figures. Although the orators were supposed to compose their speeches, it must have been tempting to borrow some passages from the bulletins, such as these words urging audiences to purchase Liberty Bonds: "Are you going to stand by and suffer defeat? Are you going to look timidly at long processions of conquering troops tramping down our streets?" The Four Minute Men liked to think that they were largely responsible for the success of the government's Liberty Loan drives, and the secretary of the treasury was inclined to agree with them.

The topic of the first bulletin, the Selective Service, was chosen at a delicate time. Congress was debating a bill to inaugurate universal military conscription, and the idea was controversial. It could not be said that the efforts of the Four Minute Men caused the conscription bill to be passed on May 18, 1917, but they might have had an effect on its acceptance. Resistance and evasion did occur, but for the most part draft registration went smoothly, even in Chicago, with its large foreign-born population.

The speeches of the Four Minute Men give insights into what Americans believed they were fighting for in World War I. The lofty rhetoric of Wilson's call for a new world order based on democratic principles was fine, but most Americans preferred an uncomplicated message with more punch. Wartime paranoia caused many to imagine a host of secret agents infiltrating American life, whispering defeatist messages. Consequently, two bulletins were meant to get the speakers to counter what was seen as a flood of German propaganda. One of them, "Why We Are Fighting," offered a neat summary of the war aims, at least as conceived by Creel and Blair. Feudalism, it said, still reigned in Germany, a nation that was "inventing more horrible cruelties to inflict upon the spirit and body of man."[17] Although 4,660 miles separated Berlin from Chicago, Americans had no trouble imagining Prussian troops striding down Michigan Avenue. *Official Bulletin* No. 31, titled "Danger to America," flatly stated, "The American soldier at the front in France is fighting in 1918 for the safety of his home in America just as surely as his forefathers fought for the establishment of those homes in 1776."

In early February 1918 a bulletin went out cautioning speakers not to indulge in "hymns of hate." Some statements that had actually been used were given as examples of what *not* to say: "We must keep those goose-stepping, baby-killing educated gorillas away from our shores" and "There are only two classes of people on earth today—human beings and Germans." A belief based on emotion, the bulletin said, is not an "abiding conviction," because emotions "may wave and surge," but a belief based on "profound convictions" and "fundamental fact" is not swayed. Many Four Minute Men grumbled that it was difficult to make their points without stirring up loathing; they were reminded to make a distinction between the German government and the German people. The German soldier, they were advised, was only following orders, like any soldier. The February bulletin even argued that soldiers in the field were "good sports" who "respected their foe" and that "the greater hatred is among civilians."[18]

Once the national Four Minute Men organization took form, the original Chicago group became just one of many local branches, although because of its priority, it remained the model. Ryerson appointed George R. Jones, an executive with the Public Service Company of Northern Illinois, to head Chicago's Four Minute Men. Jones, however, was also placed in charge of the entire state, which required too-frequent absences from the city, and in March 1918 he was succeeded by Ernest Palmer. The powerful entrepreneur Samuel Insull donated office space and equipment, and the Four Minute Men of Chicago continued their tradition of Monday luncheons to discuss the organization's activities. Nineteen committees were set up; among them were panels on admitting speakers to the group, assignments, publicity, speaking, and Liberty Loans (which arranged for speakers during Liberty Loan drives). Separate committees provided orators for public schools, parks, churches, amusement parks, fraternal societies, labor union meetings, and conventions (even out-of-towners could not escape Chicago's Four Minute Men). And a special Wabash Avenue Section "arranged for speaking by colored men to colored audiences."

Reporting on how Chicago's Four Minute Men were expanding beyond the movie theater circuit, in May 1918 the *Chicago Tribune* stated, "Before the summer is well underway the 400 or so regular speakers of the Chicago group expect to be speaking to at least 1,000,000 people every week." It noted that on the previous Wednesday evening at Riverview amusement park, "no less than seven Four Minute Men were on the job," and religious leaders, including Roman Catholic archbishop George Mundelein, were opening their churches to the speakers. To reach ethnic communities, the Four Minute Men "enrolled capable speakers in almost every tongue which is used in the city," and it was hoped that their efforts would aid in the "Americanization" of this populace. One Four Minute Man was the anti-German Anton Cermak, the Czech-born politician who was later elected Chicago's mayor in 1931. The *Tribune* commented that the orators of the Wabash Avenue Section were "speakers of unusual power" and were "expected to do a great work, especially among their fellows who have so recently come to Chicago from the south."[19]

Every once in a while Chicago's Four Minute Men would stage a special banquet to honor some dignitary. On Christmas Eve 1917 they hosted Captain Paul Perigord, a representative of the French government, and on the following February 5 they feted their founder, Donald M. Ryerson, at the Stevens Building Café. A truly special occasion was the luncheon on May 29, 1918, in honor of 103 members of the French Blue Devils, a celebrated group of soldiers visiting the United States on a morale-raising tour. Former president William Howard Taft was the guest at an Armistice Celebration Luncheon on November 11. The speaker at another luncheon was Samuel Insull.

The activities of the Four Minute Men did not abruptly cease with the signing of the armistice. The orators spoke on four more subjects—"Red Cross Home Service," "What We Have Won," "Red Cross Christmas Roll Call," and "Tribute to the Allies"—and then the organization went out of business on Christmas Eve 1918. Creel's Committee on Public Information was still on the job, boosting Wilson's peace plan, but the Republican-controlled Congress cut off its funding on June 30, 1919, and the CPI passed into history.

Today the American public is readily reachable by means of television, radio, and the Internet, but none of those existed in 1918. The speeches of the Four Minute Men therefore might be considered to be analogous to television commercials or public service announcements (PSAs), perhaps the first ever. Filling a break between films with information is not much different from inserting messages between television programs.

During the war, Ryerson commanded vessels on the Atlantic Seaboard, instructed submarine crews in Chicago, and then served aboard a destroyer, becoming a lieutenant commander by war's end. After the war he returned to his business career, and when his father died in 1928, he became chairman of the board of the firm of Joseph T. Ryerson & Son. On the morning of May 8, 1932, his wife walked onto the beach behind the family mansion in Lake Forest, Illinois, and found her husband lying on the sand with a bullet in his heart. According to newspaper reports, he had "ended his life as the result of a nervous breakdown due to overwork." He was only forty-seven years old and left behind a sixteen-year-old daughter and a fourteen-year-old son.

William McCormick Blair, the second national director, also returned to Chicago. In 1935 he cofounded an investment banking firm. He was president of the Art Institute of Chicago from 1956 to 1964, and he also served as president of the Chicago

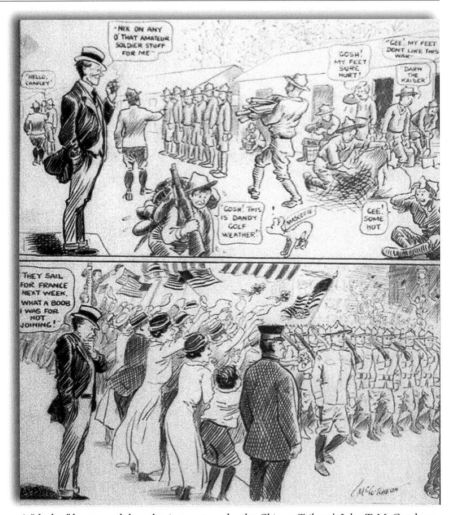

A "slacker" has second thoughts in a cartoon by the *Chicago Tribune*'s John T. McCutcheon titled "Somewhere in Fort Sheridan." One of the main activities of the American Protective League was catching "slackers," men who evaded the draft. Library of Congress

Historical Society. As late as 1980 the still vigorous Blair helped found the David Adler Music and Arts Center in Libertyville, Illinois. He played tennis and golf until he was ninety and drove to California every year for a vacation. At ninety-three he flew aboard the supersonic Concorde jetliner because he was curious to see what it was like. When he died at age ninety-seven in 1982, the *Tribune* hailed him as a "notable example of how to age with distinction and grace."[20]

The American Protective League

On July 11, 1918, a small army of Secret Service agents, police officers, and servicemen began grabbing men off Chicago streets and sending them to detention camps. Men escorting their girls to dances were taken off streetcars; other men were removed from movie theaters, amusement parks, beaches, and hotels. In the Loop, agents swarmed into pool halls and hauled players away, and at the Barnum and Bailey circus, the raiders took in 120 spectators. More than 160 men were seized from the Crane Company plant on Forty-First Street. In Grant Park, where a crowd had gathered to watch the feats of a French aviator named Lieutenant Flachaire, at least 400 men were taken. More than 1,000 of the abducted men were held overnight at the Municipal Pier, where they had to sleep on the concrete floor. Over the next day and a half about 16,000 men were taken into custody.[21]

It was a "slacker raid" intended to round up draft dodgers. One had previously been staged in Pittsburgh, and other cities that would experience them included Minneapolis, Philadelphia, Detroit, St. Louis, Boston, Cleveland, Atlantic City, and New York.[22] Not that the raids did much good. The number of genuine draft dodgers apprehended was tiny: "Questioning in Chicago yielded some 20,000 detainees . . . , of whom 1,200 alleged draft evaders were turned over to army authorities; nearly all were hastily released. These dismal results would be reproduced in cities across the country during the summer of 1918."[23]

It didn't take much to become a suspicious person during World War I. If you were a man between eighteen and thirty and didn't wear a uniform, you might be suspected of being a "slacker." The term could apply to anyone who didn't demonstrate wholehearted support of the war, but it generally defined men who were evading or resisting the draft.

Before the draft began, the government warned that resistance would be treated harshly. Even before draft registration day, June 5, 1917, seven men in Texas were arrested for "planning to resist conscription by force." Other arrests occurred elsewhere, and in New York three men were arrested for passing out antidraft literature, two of whom were sent to prison.[24] But although registration was not resisted with violence, government officials estimated that as many as 3 million men managed to avoid registration; in addition, about 338,000 men who were drafted either didn't show up at a training camp or deserted after arriving.[25] With most of the population in a superpatriotic frenzy, slackers were considered almost as bad as Huns, so it was thought justifiable to round up anyone who might be one. And a lot of patriotic citizens were willing to take part. As historian Christopher Capozzola has put it, "Americans reported their neighbors as draft dodgers, food hoarders, or subversive 'pro-Germans.' Such events filled newspaper pages nearly every day."[26]

The "secret agents" who helped round up suspected slackers in Chicago were not paid employees of the federal government. They were civilian volunteers, armed with nothing more than badges and a desire to aid their country. Their story begins with an inspiration born in the brain of a Chicago advertising man named Albert M. Briggs.

Toward the end of 1916, even though the United States had not declared war, the Department of Justice, acting through its Bureau of Investigation (the precursor of the FBI), was already looking for German agents and spies. There had already been indications of plots, such as the discovery of a scheme to persuade Austrians to quit working in American munitions plants.[27] On July 30, 1916, several huge explosions destroyed a munitions depot on Black Tom Island in New York Harbor. At first it seemed as if it might have been an accident, but German agents were suspected (it actually was a German plot, although proof was not found until years later). Congress voted to increase funding of the Bureau of Investigation, headed by A. Bruce Bielaski, and the number of agents rose from one hundred to three hundred between 1914 and 1916.[28]

However, three hundred agents was not a lot for the entire nation, and branch offices of the bureau griped about the lack of resources. One such complainer was Hinton D. Clabaugh, the superintendent of the Chicago office, whose jurisdiction extended over Illinois, Wisconsin, and Minnesota. Every day, Justice Department officials were asking him to look into yet another matter, and letters were flooding in from private citizens reporting suspicious activities by local Germans. For all this he had fifteen detectives—and no automobiles, meaning

The explosions that destroyed the munitions depot on Black Tom Island in New York Harbor in July 1916 reinforced widespread fears that a network of German spies and saboteurs was active in the country. Wikimedia Commons

that suspects had to be tailed by streetcar. So when in January 1917 Albert Briggs entered his office to offer help, Clabaugh was eager to listen.

Briggs, vice president of a firm named Outdoor Advertising, suggested that a volunteer organization might be a big help, and he would be happy to coordinate it.[29] Clabaugh was interested, but he cleared the idea with the chief of police first. He then got back to Briggs and suggested that the first thing he might help with was the acquisition of automobiles. Within weeks Briggs reported that under his direction, Chicago businessmen had collected three cars for the Chicago office and offered to supply others for New York and Washington—as many as seventy-five. Clabaugh quickly contacted the Bureau of Investigation. Bielaski was at first suspicious that the automobiles might somehow be used for advertising, but once Clabaugh allayed his concerns, Bielaski, apparently without asking anyone higher up, accepted the gift. On March 22 Briggs met with Bielaski in Washington. Briggs then wired Clabaugh, "Very satisfactory interview. Chief has approved. Organization, our original plan, to be formed immediately." Thus was born the American Protective League (APL), a secret investigative agency that engaged thousands of volunteers to, in effect, spy on their fellow citizens. And as Clabaugh said proudly, "Chicago was the first city in the United States to have such an organization."[30] Fear of German spies and saboteurs was a national phenomenon, but it was only in Chicago that a citizen created the APL. While

Chicago was a microcosm of the United States during the Great War, in this one instance, at least, the city was not reflecting a national trend; it was leading it.

Bielaski's boss was the attorney general, Thomas Watt Gregory, a Texas lawyer and backer of Woodrow Wilson. Gregory was engaged in something of a turf battle for power. Two government agencies were responsible for gathering intelligence and combating subversive activities: Bielaski's Bureau of Information, an agency of the Justice Department, and the Secret Service, an agency of the Treasury Department, which was headed by William McAdoo. In 1915 President Wilson ordered the Secret Service to begin probing espionage in the United States, and McAdoo figured that was the job of his men alone. When he learned about Gregory's creation of what McAdoo termed a "miscellaneous horde" of untrained volunteers, he was appalled. "I greatly fear," McAdoo wrote, "that . . . suspicion will be engendered among our people, smoldering race antagonisms will burst into flame, and the melting pot of America will be a melting pot no longer, but a crucible out of which will flash the molten lead of suspicion and dissension."[31] To Attorney General Gregory, however, this "miscellaneous horde" was just what he needed. It would give him a source of manpower that McAdoo could not dream of, and Gregory, not McAdoo, would become the nation's chief spy catcher.

Gregory also understood the mood of the country. Popular opinion was reaching the point where spies were feared to be penetrating into every corner of life. And not only spies from Germany, but German-Americans as well. Gregory warned, "There are a very large number of German citizens in this country who are dangerous and who are plotting trouble, men from whom we must necessarily expect trouble promptly of a sinister sort."[32] But the volunteers who joined the APL were not inspired solely by dread. Many of them, like Briggs, were ineligible to join the military and wanted to help. And with the memory of Black Tom Island fresh, anxiety about espionage and disloyalty, although largely unjustified, was not irrational.

Things happened fast. Briggs knew a lot of people around the country and asked them to form local units. The members were given ranks—chief, captain, lieutenant. They were directed to seek out employees of banks, business enterprises, and industrial plants and enlist them to monitor their workplaces. The lower-level operatives were kept in the dark about the organization and scope of the league. As far as they knew, they were working only for a higher-up in the institution they were assigned to monitor. In fact, the organization became so amorphous that neither Briggs nor Bielaski had a complete list of members. The officers were also counseled to advise the local police of their activities. In some areas local watch committees had already been organized; most of them were merged into the APL.

Officers were supplied with badges and told to produce them only to prove their membership in the APL. However, the badges indicated that the bearer was a member of the "Secret Service," and many members made that claim, some thinking it was true. This gave the wearer a lot of authority, but the claim was false and McAdoo, who headed the real Secret Service, was livid. Briggs therefore sent out bulletins reminding his agents that they were not to assert that they were Secret Service agents, had no power to make arrests, and were not to break the law when acquiring information. New badges were issued and McAdoo calmed down, although he never was happy about the APL.

On August 25, 1917, the *Chicago Tribune* ran an article titled "200,000 U.S. Agents Cover Nation," which was probably the first public announcement of the existence of the APL. It explained how Briggs had conceived the organization and how it had been "federalized" under the Justice Department: "Its scope covers every city, town, and hamlet in every section of the United States. It has a membership of 200,000 with a million intelligence agents or operatives active in the field of service. Bank presidents, railroad hands, judges, lawyers, and other captains of industry are zealous workers in this national army of detectives. They have also enrolled the services of their employees from household to office. No one is overlooked from office boy to nurse maid." And just to make sure that readers knew that they were being watched, the article added, "Your own banker is just as likely to be a secret agent of the government as your haberdasher or chauffeur."[33]

As the war went on, many of the APL's younger members went into the military. Most members now were, as historian Joan M. Jensen has put it, "men who had been born before the 1880s and reared in the atmosphere of nationalism and militarism that permeated the late nineteenth century."[34] They were proud that they were doing something to defend their country, they felt the exhilaration of carrying a badge, and they got to experience a kind of an adolescent thrill by playing spy. Emerson Hough, author of the official history of the APL, explained, "Each operative discovered that the badge he wore bred a feeling of respect or fear." The exhilaration of authority can be seen in the experience of a Chicago agent who sent the vice president of his bank to look into a draft-dodging case. "The man holds the mortgage on my home," he crowed, "and I am bossing him around as though he were my office boy!"[35] The agents were all men. Admitting women was discussed, and many members' wives were eager to join, but the directors foresaw problems—men would be angered if their wives were rejected, especially if a colleague's wife was admitted.

The first order of business for the APL—the reason it was created—was the apprehension of spies, either foreign agents or German-American traitors. To put things bluntly, in Jensen's words, "For two and a half years the APL searched for spies but found none."[36] On June 15, 1917, Congress passed the Espionage Act, which, despite its name, was directed more at punishing antiwar activity than it was at finding spies. It "provided for imprisonment up to twenty years and/or a $10,000 fine for individuals found guilty of aiding the enemy, obstructing recruiting, or causing insubordination, disloyalty, or refusal of duty in the armed forces."[37] The Sedition Act, an amendment to the Espionage Act, made punishable any remark or publication that was disrespectful to the military or the Constitution or that might be interpreted as supporting the enemy. In June 1918 the socialist leader Eugene V. Debs made a speech in which he decried "the gentry who are today wrapped up in the American flag, who shout their claim from the housetops that they are the only patriots, and who have their magnifying glasses in hand, scanning the country for evidence of disloyalty."[38] Although he didn't mention the APL by name, it's obvious what he was referring to. This oration was found to be in violation of the Espionage Act and earned Debs a ten-year prison term. Today the Espionage and Sedition Acts are considered some of the most blatant violations of civil liberties in U.S. history, but at the time the APL saw them as indispensable authorization to report even the slightest hints of disloyalty. As a result, although APL agents never caught any spies, they harassed a lot of people. It has been estimated that the APL conducted at least three million inquiries into the loyalties of individuals who were suspected of disloyalty.[39]

One of the APL's major activities was dealing with "enemy aliens"—Americans of German or Austrian birth or heritage whose loyalty might seem questionable. Once the APL identified a suspected enemy alien, that person could be sent to a concentration camp; the APL helped the government put sixty-three hundred "enemy aliens" into such camps during the war.[40] Many of them suffered "overcrowded and unhealthy facilities, where military and police guards often treated them with contempt and inflicted demeaning and often dangerous punishments."[41] Most of them, however, were put on parole with the proviso that they periodically report to a local APL office. APL members were especially zealous in scrutinizing aliens working in defense plants. They got so many fired that the Labor Department became worried about losing essential workers and Bielaski asked the APL to ease up.

Most of the members of the APL were politically conservative, which influenced their choice of targets.[42] For them the Chicago-based labor organization named the Industrial Workers of the World (IWW) was nearly as terrifying as saboteurs. The IWW, also known as the "Wobblies," had been founded in Chicago in 1905. The organization consisted of trade unionists, socialists, and anarchists who advocated workplace democracy, the abolition of the wage system, and the overthrow of the employer class. Although the Wobblies opposed the war, they cautioned their members neither to resist draft registration nor to use illegal means to demonstrate their opposition. Even so, the Justice Department and the APL put the IWW in the crosshairs. According to Hough, the organization "had men shadowing the suspects, men intercepting their mail, men ingratiating themselves into their good graces, men watching all their comings and goings, men transcribing and indexing their reports, men looking into the law in all its phases as bearing on these cases."[43]

The IWW leadership left the decision to register for the draft up to the individual members; some refused to do so. When

Bielaski ordered the APL to search for nonregistrants, the APL took it as a directive to step up its hounding of the IWW. Clabaugh opened a secret office in Chicago, where he had a group of agents working with the APL who were dedicated to gathering evidence against the Wobblies. On September 5, 1917, Clabaugh's agents and a band of APL members raided the IWW headquarters on Madison Street, as well as a Wobblie print shop and the homes of several of the organization's leaders, including its head, Big Bill Haywood. Meanwhile, similar raids took place in IWW offices throughout the country. The Justice Department was vague on the nature of the evidence it believed the agents had collected, but according to Hough, "the I.W.W. was at last found with sufficient goods to warrant the movement of the law's forces."[44]

On April 1, 1918, the redoubtable judge Kenesaw Mountain Landis opened the trial of ninety-seven Wobbly suspects in a Chicago courtroom. The trial went on for five months, at the time the longest trial in U.S. history. Haywood and fourteen of his aides were sentenced to twenty years in Leavenworth Penitentiary. Thirty-three others were sentenced to ten years, another thirty-three got five years, and twelve other Wobblies received sentences of a year and a day. Two got ten-day sentences in the county jail, and the case against two others was continued. According to the *Tribune*, the combined sentences added up to 807 years and 20 days, and the fines totaled $2.3 million. The only black defendant, Benjamin Fletcher, offered a widely quoted joke: "Judge Landis is using poor English today. His sentences are too long." Landis explained, "When the country is at peace it is a legal right of free speech to oppose going to war and to oppose even preparation for war. But when once war is declared, this right ceases."[45]

By this time the APL had moved its headquarters to Washington, and the number of national directors had increased to three. Joining Briggs at the top were two other Chicago APL men: Daniel Frey, an advertising executive, and Victor Elting, an attorney. But the heart of the APL was still in Chicago. After all, it was the home of the Wobblies and other leftist groups, as well as a large German population. Hough described the dangerous city in this way: "Among the unassimilated rabble who make a certain portion of Chicago's polyglot politik-flutter, there are perhaps more troublemakers than in any other city of America. . . . Bolsheviki, socialists, incendiaries, I.W.W.'s, Lutheran treason-talkers, Russellites, Bergerites, all the other-ites, religious and social fanatics, third-sex agitators, long haired visionaries and work-haters from every race in the world—Chicago had them and has them still, because she has invited them, accepted them and made them free of the place."[46]

The APL's Chicago branch served as the prototype for offices in other cities and throughout the war it remained the country's largest. An idea of the APL's operation can be gathered from the *Tribune* article on the league: "The achievements in Chicago alone may be summarized in this way: In the short period of organization 3,000 persons have been investigated. This covered every known form of federal disloyalty, including slackers. Nearly 5,000 agents are at the instant command of the league by the telephone system. As an illustration: If Dr. Black, an agent of the league, is conversing socially over the telephone and is wanted in an emergency by the league headquarters, the exchange telephone operator will disconnect Dr. Black's party and cut his line into headquarters."[47] By January 1918 the number of agents in Chicago had grown to seventy-five hundred; by the war's end there were some thirteen thousand.

Chicago was divided into zones, each one overseen by an inspector. Most of the work came from directives from Bielaski's Bureau of Investigation; the APL received at least 175 such requests every day. Chicago agents also independently reported instances of suspected disloyalty, and letters from concerned citizens steadily came into the office. When, for example, it was reported that during a Red Cross fund-raising drive, "many rumors and derogatory statements concerning the work of the Red Cross" began circulating, the APL had many of those who had made such utterances sent to jail.[48] The Justice Department came to rely on the APL more and more, and by July 1918 APL members were handling 75 percent of the cases assigned to the Bureau of Investigation in Chicago.[49]

The league was especially proud of its work in enforcing federal energy-saving measures. For example, the United States Fuel Administration instituted what were called "lightless nights," ordering that all nonessential lights be turned off on Mondays and Tuesdays, including those in shop windows, theater marquees, display signs, and restaurant and hotel entrances. When the chairman of the local conservation committee made a tour of downtown Chicago, he found violations "almost everywhere." Within a day 457 of members of the APL were out looking for glowing lightbulbs. It was reported that a certain jeweler refused to turn out his window lights, but when an APL agent was called to the scene, he began busily unscrewing the bulbs.[50] When it was ordered that gasoline should not be used for Sunday pleasure trips, the APL was on the case, as it also was in enforcing wheatless and meatless days.

The APL kept careful records of its activities in Chicago, as can be seen in the following table provided by Hough:

Neutrality cases investigated 43,026
War Department—all branches
    Character and loyalty investigations 3,739
American Red Cross
    Character and loyalty investigations 115
Illinois Volunteer Training Corps
    Character and loyalty investigations 141
War Risk Insurance cases 230
U.S. Bureau of Naturalization cases 3,905
Draft investigations 30,440
Food Administration cases
    Food investigations 12,637
    Sugar investigations 179
Fuel Administration cases
    Coal investigations 3,263
    Lightless Night investigations 1,500

The statistics also showed 200,000 men detained during the slacker drive in July 1918, 44,167 "delinquents apprehended and forced to appear at local Draft Boards," and 1,900 deserters sent to military camps.[51]

The APL's Chicago office required $7,000 a month in funding, plus extra money for eighteen satellite offices. Some of this money came from the federal government, but Congress was hesitant about funding secret investigations, and federal funds were insufficient. This was not a problem for the Chicago division, which secured backing from business leaders and corporations. The organization's willingness to prosecute Wobblies and harass socialists proved that they were on management's side.

The APL liked to think of itself as a "web." At the top was the executive committee, and below that were the chief and assistant chief. They oversaw the work of six divisions: Finance, Administration, Membership, Law, Investigation, and Motor Service. The Investigation Division was by far the largest, containing about half of the Chicago members. There was also an intelligence branch called the Eyes and Ears, which placed agents in positions to keep watch on enterprises in a range of categories: Real Estate, Financial, Insurance, Professional, Hotels, Transportation, Public Utilities, General Merchandise, and Industries, which covered metal trades, lumber trades, munitions, packers, grain, and so on.

Many tales were recorded of the deeds of the plucky agents of Chicago's APL. One of them might be called "The Case of the Broken Cross." One night a Polish man came home and, before his horrified wife's eyes, angrily pulled down the crucifix from the wall and broke it over his knee. The wife learned that he had joined a new church run by followers of Charles Taze Russell known as the Russellites (which later evolved into the Jehovah's Witnesses). The church was on the APL's blacklist for preaching nonresistance and pacifism, and she reported her story to an agent. The APL visited the new church, and the entire congregation was arrested. Seven of the leaders, along with Joseph Rutherford, the head of the International Bible Students Association, went to prison—and all because of the fortuitous fracturing of a cross. In another case, a deserter was being protected by his large, varied family. APL agents interviewed family members and friends, but "nothing could be learned, except that the various members of the family, male and female, were so mixed in their sex relations that apparently no two of the opposite sex were living together in a legally permissible way."[52] Eventually, agents interviewed a couple living about ten miles outside Chicago and learned that they had received letters from Norfolk, Virginia. Agents in Norfolk were quickly alerted, and the deserter was apprehended.

The APL's methods were often questionable and sometimes illegal. Members engaged in tapping phones, breaking and entering, and theft. Agents who worked for gas and electric companies used their credentials to enter suspects' homes and search for evidence. Some members got information by telling people they were reporters or insurance agents or the like. Some even put on army uniforms and posed as soldiers—a clear violation of the law. Some were moles who joined suspicious organizations; others were decoys who practiced entrapment, recommending criminal undertakings to people under suspicion. "The League," as the historian David M. Kennedy has written, "in fact constituted a rambunctious, unruly *posse comitatus* on an unprecedented national scale. Its 'agents' bugged, burglarized, slandered, and illegally arrested other Americans. . . . They always operated behind a cloak of stealth and deception, frequently promoting reactionary social and economic views under the guise of patriotism."[53] Advocates for civil liberties complained, and some called for the abolition of the APL, but Gregory defended his agents and Wilson quietly backed his attorney general.[54]

Because APL members were unable to discover any real spies, the indictments they succeeded in getting under the Espionage Act were for people who either opposed the war or criticized the government's method of fighting it. A person who opposed the war on religious grounds or thought it was being fought in the interests of capitalism was "disloyal" and liable to be locked up. Many reports of the APL's activities stressed that its work mostly involved "silencing disloyalty." When Hough boasted that the league had "brought to judgment three million cases of disloyalty," the number, based on APL estimates, was probably correct, but the great majority of these cases were either the identification of "slackers" or simple violations of the right of free speech.[55]

Once the guns fell silent, it seemed to many that the role of the APL was finished. But not to everyone. The United States was entering the First Red Scare. Russia had become Communist and was an inspiration for many western radicals. This horrified the APL, and members argued that they should continue their exertions in order to fight the Red Menace. A January 4, 1920, article in the *Tribune* reported that the Department of Justice had estimated that some 60,000 radicals were at loose in the United States and that half of them were "actually dangerous." "Chicago, according to the best estimates," the article went on, "has between 2,500 and 3,000 extremists who are dangerous enough to bear constant watching."[56] Veterans of the APL believed they were still needed and had only to redirect their scrutiny. And "as usual, the Chicago division was the most ambitious in its plans."[57]

APL administrators, however, did not agree. In December 1919 Briggs said, "Frankly, we do not believe that there is any place in American life for a volunteer espionage system."[58] Attorney General Gregory believed the same and ordered the disbanding of the APL, which was announced in the league's official newspaper, the *Spy Glass*, on December 21, the same day that Bielaski resigned as head of the Bureau of Investigation. Most APL members went along with the decision, but a hardcore group felt rejected and resentful, especially in Chicago, where the head of the local division kept asking for reports from field agents about "Socialist-bolshevik agitators." At a meeting of Chicago members, however, the majority voted for dissolution. As good Americans, they argued that to continue without government approval would be tantamount to defiance—in a way, they would be "disloyal" too. And thus the American Protective League went out of business in Chicago, where it had begun.

One Chicagoan's War

Charles Merriam. Wikimedia Commons

Charles E. Merriam
The Professor in Italy

It's safe to say that if it had not been for World War I, Professor Charles E. Merriam would not have had an affair with an Italian countess.

Merriam was on the faculty of the University of Chicago. A leading Progressive, a founder of the new field of political science, and a reformist Chicago politician, he was a man of many abilities. Although a Republican, he came to admire Woodrow Wilson's reformist ideals, and his admiration for the president was mutual, leading to Merriam's appointment as a special representative in Italy. There it was his job to explain U.S. war aims, cultivate insiders and report on Italian politics, and strengthen ties between the Italian working class and Italian-Americans.

Merriam did not come from a cosmopolitan background. He was a small-town boy, born in Hopkinton, Iowa, on November 15, 1874.

He attended Lenox College in his hometown and then went to the University of Iowa and Columbia University, where he received a PhD in political science. Political science was then a new field, and its early practitioners tended to be reformers who hoped that scientific research would lead to practical civic betterment.

Merriam joined the faculty of the University of Chicago in 1900 and eleven years later was named head of the political science department. In 1903 he was one of the founders of the American Political Science Association. He quickly became one of Chicago's leading voices for reform. He believed that the best way to study politics was to take part and became a scholar-politician in the mold of Wilson. In 1906 Merriam became chairman of a committee on taxation and produced a nationally influential report on urban revenue. Three years later he was elected alderman of the Seventh Ward and in 1911 was the Republican candidate for mayor, losing narrowly to Carter Harrison II. He was elected alderman again in 1912 and held the post until the war.

The ascension of the antireform Republican Big Bill Thompson disheartened Merriam, who found himself excluded from the Republican leadership. When the war broke out, Merriam was commissioned a captain in the Signal Corps and made an examiner at a Chicago aviation board. The job was too small, and by working his Chicago connections, he found a job with the Committee on Public Information, which was establishing bureaus in thirty-two foreign countries. Merriam was given the Italian assignment and in March 1918 set up his office in Rome.

Merriam carried out his duties with vigor and imagination. He put together a speakers bureau, supplied Italian newspapers with pro-American articles and pictures of Italian-American neighborhoods, and organized Fourth of July celebrations. He brought colorful Americans to Italy—for example, the violinist Albert Spalding played concerts and a young aviator named Fiorello La Guardia buzzed around the landscape in his plane. Many of the visiting Americans, most notably labor leader Samuel Gompers, turned out to be more interested in *la dolce vita* than in Italian politics. One southern senator was horrified that the Germans had apparently flooded the beautiful city of Venice. Merriam's greatest coup was persuading the eminent Italian poet Gabriele D'Annunzio to write a poem in praise of Italian-American friendship. Merriam's efforts were part of the Wilson administration's campaign to influence the politics of other countries by encouraging factions that would support Wilsonian ideals of democracy and progressivism. That campaign was at its most intense in Italy, where one Italian historian called Merriam's efforts a "propaganda bombardment."[1] The United States already had an official ambassador in Rome, Thomas Nelson Page, and Page and his staff resented what they considered to be Merriam's diplomatic operations outside official channels, calling Merriam the "black pope."

Most helpful to Merriam in making high-level contacts was the glamorous and accomplished Contessina Maria Loschi, a writer, journalist, and leader of the Italian women's movement.[2] An article in the *Red Cross Bulletin* of December 16, 1918, tells of her "flashing, far-seeing eyes and picturesque broken English,"[3] and a photograph of the countess in the May 10, 1919, issue of the *Woman Citizen*, an American journal, shows a strikingly youthful, elegant, intelligent woman. It was well known back at the University of Chicago that Merriam's marriage was not happy. Merriam, a Presbyterian and a Republican, had married a Catholic and a Democrat who also happened to be jealous and distrustful. Not without reason. As Merriam's biographer, Barry D. Karl, has explained, "Merriam was a warm, sociable man who enjoyed flirtation . . . women whose intelligence he admired found him attractive." That was the case with the countess, and the pair enjoyed what Karl has called "a romantic adventure." As Karl went on to write, "It was not to be the last such occasion in his life, although each would provide him with the self-romanticization he needed. His wife always 'discovered' and punished; his students always seem to know and in any case to gossip."[4]

Merriam returned home in October 1918. The mayor's race of 1919 was heating up, and Merriam was eager to take on Thompson in the Republican primary. This effort was a failure, and Merriam quit politics to return to the much safer academia. He published many more books and was an influence in shaping the New Deal and establishing the Social Security system. He died in 1953, two years before his son ran for mayor and lost to Richard J. Daley.

Contessina Maria Loschi made a tour of the United States in 1919 to study the public schools, and she served as chief interpreter at a conference of women physicians in New York. She then went on to become a distinguished personage in Mussolini's Italy. In the 1920s she was a professor at the University of Bologna, and her essay on women in the Italian labor movement was published in

1926. She was also a visiting lecturer at the University of Southern California in 1929. As far as is known, she and Merriam never met again. The story of fleeting love set against the backdrop of war is not uncommon, almost a cliché, but when it's real, it makes for a poignant memory.

Ernest Hemingway
The Adventurous Writer

When Archduke Franz Ferdinand was assassinated on June 28, 1914, fourteen-year-old Ernest Hemingway of Oak Park, Illinois, had just ended his first year of high school. When the United States declared war in April 1917, Hemingway was finishing his senior year. A little over a year later, he was an ambulance driver on the Italian front.

Few writers have done so much as young as Hemingway. He married at twenty-one, traveled in Europe and settled in Paris, and his *Three Stories & Ten Poems* was published when he was twenty-four. *The Sun Also Rises* brought him international fame at twenty-seven. He became only more celebrated as the years went on, and journalists loved covering his exploits. He was just fifty-five when he won the Nobel Prize, at which time he was the most prominent and admired writer in the world. He was the first "celebrity artist," and no writer of fiction today can claim a fraction of his fame.

Hemingway was a man in a hurry—and therefore one who went to war with enthusiasm. He spurned college

Ernest Hemingway. Wikimedia Commons

and took a job as a cub reporter with the *Kansas City Star*. He eagerly joined the Missouri Home Guard, biding his time until he could get overseas. Rejected by the army because of poor vision in his left eye, he heard that the Red Cross needed ambulance drivers and jumped at the chance. The ship on which he sailed in May 1918 was named, appropriately enough, the *Chicago*. Shortly after he arrived in Milan, a munitions factory exploded, and Hemingway helped collect the bodies. He was especially upset to find women among the dead.

As a writer assigned to ambulance duty, Hemingway was not alone. Many literary figures drove ambulances during World War I. From the United States also came E. E. Cummings, John Dos Passos, Malcolm Cowley, Louis Bromfield, and Dashiell Hammett (who never made it to the front because of tuberculosis), while British ambulance drivers included Somerset Maugham and John Masefield, among many others. Some, like Hemingway, were unfit for the army; others just didn't want to be ordinary doughboys in the trenches. Most probably got a much grimmer view of the war than they had bargained for.

Hemingway found his assignment too tame. He was stationed in Schio, a town far from the action. So he volunteered for canteen duty, delivering food to troops on the frontlines. Now he could see some real fighting, and as it turned out, he got too close. On July 8 an Austrian artillery shell shattered his knee and foot with 227 pieces of shrapnel. While attempting to carry another wounded man away, he was hit by machine gun fire. His misfortune brought him a long stay in a Milan hospital, several operations, and two Italian medals. It also led to a romance with a nurse named Agnes von Kurowsky, an affair on which Hemingway based the novel some consider his masterpiece, *A Farewell to Arms*.

Back home, Hemingway was a hero—the first American wounded in Italy—and he played the role with zest. Why not? He was a young, tall, good-looking guy with a flattering uniform. He proudly showed off his war mementos and talked about doing his duty, saying, "My country needed me." But as his biographer Michael Reynolds has expressed it, Hemingway was "nineteen going on thirty."[1] The bitterness of such characters as Nick Adams and Frederic Henry was there, waiting to be brought out, and in the early 1920s, when Hemingway became increasingly sour on Progressivism and European politics, it emerged.[2] One gets a hint of this in the Nick Adams story "The End of Something" (1924). The war veteran protagonist, Hemingway's alter ego, says, "I feel as though everything was gone to hell inside of me."

Later in life Hemingway confessed that the war had indeed damaged him. He wrote to his editor Malcolm Cowley in 1948, "I was hurt bad all the way through and I was really spooked at the end."[3] In his short story "A Natural History of the Dead" (1933), Hemingway assured readers that "Humanism" was an "extinct phenomenon."

For the rest of his life, Hemingway was fascinated by war; he didn't glorify it but viewed it as the ultimate confrontation with death.[4] In "Notes on the Next War," a piece he wrote for *Esquire* in 1935, he said, "They wrote in the old days that it is sweet and fitting to die for one's country. But in modern war there is nothing sweet nor fitting in your dying. You will die like a dog for no good reason."[5] In dealing with war and death, he both created and became "the Hemingway hero," a resilient fellow of few words and, in Hemingway's case, a fan of marlin fishing, bullfights, and big game hunting, not to mention booze and women. He later reported on the Spanish Civil War and covered World War II for *Collier's* magazine. His courage was never lacking; neither was his exaggeration of the dangers. Literary critics, analyzing the effect of World War I on the modern psyche and its spawning of disillusionment, regularly turn to Hemingway's conflicted personality, with its combination of bravado, nihilism, and the latent despair that finally resulted in his suicide in July 1961.

As Hemingway wrote in one of the most famous passages from *A Farewell to Arms*:

> I was always embarrassed by the words sacred, glorious, and sacrifice and the expression in vain. We had heard them, sometimes standing in the rain almost out of earshot, so that only the shouted words came through, and had read them, on proclamations that were slapped up by billposters over other proclamations, now for a long time, and I had seen nothing sacred, and the things that were glorious had no glory and the sacrifices were like the stockyards at Chicago if nothing was done with the meat except to bury it. There were many words that you could not stand to hear and finally only the names of places had dignity. Certain numbers were the same way and certain dates and these with names of the places were all you could say and have them mean anything. Abstract words such as glory, honor, courage, or hallow were obscene beside the concrete names of villages, the numbers of roads, the names of rivers, the numbers of regiments and the dates.[6]

Clarence Darrow. Wikimedia Commons

Clarence Darrow
Defender of the War—and Its Opponents

World War I was a major interruption in the career of Clarence Darrow, who was then, and probably still remains, America's most famous lawyer. To many, his conduct during the war was more than disappointing; it was detestable.

Clarence Darrow was born in Kinsman, Ohio, in 1857 and was admitted to the bar at age twenty-one. He moved to Chicago in 1888, became a corporate counsel in the city government, and came to know nearly all the leading politicians and officials. Darrow seemed to be on the path to becoming a wealthy corporate lawyer, but when the American Railway Union called a strike in 1894, he sympathized with the workers and defended union leader Eugene V. Debs for no fee. Four years later the woodworkers went out on strike in Oshkosh, Wisconsin, and Darrow defended the union's leaders, who had been charged with conspiracy. The jury's quick acquittal made Darrow famous as the champion of labor; it established the right of a union to strike without exposing its leaders to arrest.

Darrow had early been drawn to socialist doctrines, although neither to the movement's methods nor to its political party. Now he was becoming a hero of labor and Progressivism. In 1911 he took part in a messy labor trial of two California brothers. When he was charged with attempted bribery of a juror, the brothers' hopes for a plea agreement were dashed. Darrow henceforth fell somewhat out of favor with labor leaders and focused on criminal and civil liberties cases, although he continued to be an advocate of unions and a popular orator at union events.

In 1902 Darrow published *Resist Not Evil*, which argued the cause of pacifism and nonviolence. The book asserted that governments were responsible for violence and that "in this historic age, given to war and conquest and violence, the precepts of peace and good will seem to have been almost submerged."[1] Darrow had thus aligned himself with thinkers such as Chicago's Jane Addams, whom he knew and admired. One therefore might have expected that, like Addams, Darrow would have opposed American entry into World War I. He did not. "When Germany invaded Belgium," he wrote, "I recovered from my pacifism in the twinkling of an eye. . . . I had exactly the same reaction that I would experience if a big dog should attack a little one."[2] Many of Darrow's friends and associates were offended, none more than Debs. Austin Willard Wright of Chicago, the author of *War's Folly and Futility* (1913) and once Darrow's friend, slammed Darrow as a "prostitute."[3]

Once the United States entered the war, Darrow began to equate pacifism with treason and gave prowar speeches in the United States and abroad. In October 1918, speaking before fifteen thousand people at a Loyalty Day rally in Chicago's Grant Park, he warned against antiwar agitation: "This country is at war and this country will win and you are playing with fire when you fight us in the rear."[4]

Although Darrow sounded so jingoistic, by 1918 "misgivings," as he called them, had begun to surface. The slaughter of trench warfare appalled him. He suspected that German atrocity stories were "manufactured to create public opinion," and he grew uncomfortable with anti-German sentiment in the United States. In addition, his old socialist suspicions that capitalism bred war came creeping back: "I began to suspect that Big Business was unanimously enlisted on account of the vast financial interests involved."[5] Most of all, the

Espionage and Sedition Acts, along with the imprisonment of conscientious objectors, struck at the heart of his passion for civil liberties. However, he still largely held his peace. When twelve famous lawyers signed an open letter to the American people protesting the administration's curtailing of civil liberties, Darrow was not among them.

Once the war ended, however, Darrow immediately condemned government oppression, perhaps out of a sense of guilt—"the prison doors should now be opened!" he thundered.[6] Now he claimed that the war had brought to the United States "an era of tyranny, brutality, and despotism that, for the time at least, undermined the foundations upon which our republic was laid."[7] When the Red Scare of 1920 arrived, Darrow spent a great deal of time defending imprisoned Communists. He became so indignant at government suppression of free speech that he said, "If I had believed that that would flow from this war, perhaps I would not have believed we should have gone into it."[8]

By the time of the Red Scare, Darrow was pushing sixty-five. Rather than consider retirement, however, he went on to participate in some of the century's most memorable trials. In 1924 he was the attorney in the sensational case of Nathan Leopold and Richard Loeb, two wealthy young Chicagoans who had murdered a boy just to see if they could get away with it. A year later, in the Scopes Trial, he defended a biology teacher who had been arrested for teaching evolution. And in the Sweet Case of 1925–26, he successfully defended a black family who had used firearms to protect themselves from a mob trying to expel them from a white neighborhood in Detroit. By the time Darrow died in 1938, his high-profile criminal cases had practically erased memories of his wartime chauvinism, which merited only three brief, judicious sentences in his lengthy obituary in the *New York Times*.

Darrow was hardly alone in abandoning pacifism during the war. Socialists on both sides of the Atlantic jettisoned their belief that international worker solidarity would trump nationalism and instead took up arms. Perhaps tribal instincts all too easily crush high ideals. However, the phenomenon, as Darrow showed, can sometimes be temporary.

PART FOUR

Chicago Women and the Sexual Revolution

7

"The Work Is There to Do": Chicago Women in Wartime

Soon after the U.S. declaration of war in April 1917, it became evident that the country was going to face a worker shortage. One writer said, "The sun shines on the fertile land, the earth teems with forests, with coal, with every necessary mineral and food, but labor, labor alone can meet our necessities." The author was Harriot Stanton Blatch, daughter of the feminist Elizabeth Cady Stanton, and she added, "Man-power unaided cannot supply the demand. Women must answer their country's call." Her book was *Mobilizing Woman-Power*, a plea to the nation to emulate Britain and France and take advantage of the abilities and willingness of millions of women—women who could make the difference between victory and defeat.[1]

In the years leading up to the war, "woman-power" had already been asserting itself. In October 1911, for example, a column titled "Supremacy of Man Threatened in World of Brains and Action" appeared in the *Chicago Tribune*. The author was Belle Squire, whose book *The Woman Movement in America* had just been published. She explained that women were going to get the vote and that their achievements would soon equal those of men "in the world of science, intellect, art, and all the higher avenues of thought." This would happen because of "the growing feminist movement."[2]

The words *feminist* and *feminism* first began to appear in print in the early 1890s, but they gained wide usage in the second decade of the twentieth century. A major reason was that with the large corporations coming to dominate the economy, new technologies were creating jobs requiring skills that women were well suited to perform. Previously, American women usually worked on farms or as servants, but by 1910 they were working in department stores, offices, and factories.[3] One example of a new technology was the telephone, which created a job classification—telephone operator—that became almost entirely held by women. American feminists actively sought equality before the law and in the rights to own property, gain admission to higher education, and be granted access to jobs traditionally held by men. Many Americans opposed or even feared these changing roles. But when the war came, it was no longer a question of permitting women to move into new fields. Now they were needed. Even before the declaration of war, the National American Woman Suffrage Association had adopted a prowar stance, anticipating that the conflict would accelerate progress toward equality.

In addition to women finding new jobs, many served as volunteers to aid the war effort. Others joined the military; 11,000 went into the navy, another 250 joined the marines, and the army recruited women as telephone operators. Still other American women served in Europe in a wide range of positions; some did not come back.

Volunteers

Just two days after the U.S. declaration of war, the *Tribune* was reporting that "college girls are ready to take the places of men who are called from their regular duties to go to the front." One of them, it said, owned a motorboat and wanted to "operate it in connection with coast defense duty," while two others were

An enthusiastic Chicago woman does her part in the war effort by encouraging onlookers to sign up for Uncle Sam.
Author's collection

Thousands of Chicago women volunteered to do all kinds of war work, ranging "from the humblest tasks to the most arduous ones." Here Mrs. James L. Kirkland plows a field on vacant land in the city. Chicago History Museum DN-0068001, cropped and cleaned; *Chicago Daily News* photograph

offering their home to be used as a day-care center. Many other college women were signing up for technical and manual training in order to take over men's jobs.[4] A month later, the same newspaper reported that some two hundred representatives of women's organizations throughout Illinois had gathered at a club in Chicago to coordinate "all feminine wartime activities." An idea of their plans can be determined from the names of some of the committees: "Red Cross," "Allied Relief," "Local Charities," "Women and Children in Industry," and "Thrift and Conservation."[5] In the superpatriotic atmosphere that was emerging, volunteering was not always as selfless as the term might suggest. The social pressure to take part was intense. As one historian has put it, people were "obliged to volunteer in a culture of coercive voluntarism."[6]

In the first months of the war, food conservation appears to have been the main preoccupation of the women's organizations. Food prices were going up, and large society dinners were becoming bad form. On April 24, 1917, Mrs. John Dickinson Sherman, chairman of the conservation department of the General Federation of Women's Clubs, spoke at the Auditorium Hotel. She told her audience that the U.S. secretary of the interior was urging women to "raise their own vegetables, can their own fruit, prevent waste in their homes, and give impulse and enthusiasm to the men of the land."[7] In July 1918 a "housewives' parade" marched down Wabash Avenue, bringing "the message of conservation to every woman in Chicago."[8]

While men were required to register for the draft, women were urged to register for war work, and by July it was reported that "already 1,500 women have registered in Chicago from the humblest tasks to the most arduous ones."[9] Many private groups organized registration efforts, but eventually the Woman's Committee of the Council of National Defense drew up a national registration form. This form, which was used

WOMAN'S COMMITTEE—

No. ....
(Sign only one of these cards)
Name in full ....
               (Last name)   (First name)
                                         Tel.
Address .... No. ....
          (City or town)   (No. and street or R. D. No.)

Age (in years) .... Married or single ....

Color or race .... County of birth ....

Citizen: By birth .... By naturalization ....

Persons dependent upon you, if any.............................

Service offered (specify whether volunteer, expenses only, or paid)...

....

Time pledged for service ....
If training is wanted,
specify line .... paid or free........
                                      Tuition

TRAINING AND EXPERIENCE (ENCIRCLE NUMBER TO LEFT OF ONE IN WHICH YOU WISH

I. Agricultural
1 Dairying
2 Farming
3 Fruit raising
4 Gardening
5 Poultry raising
6 Stock raising

II. Clerical
10 Accountant
11 Bookkeeper
12 Cashier
13 Clerical work (gen.)
14 Filing
15 Office assistant
16 Office manager
17 Private secretary
18 Typewriter
19 Shipping clerk
20 Stenographer

III. Domestic
30 Care of children
31 Cleaning
32 Cooking
33 Housekeeping
34 Industries by home employ't

35 Knitting
36 Laundress
37 Practical
38 Trained attendant
39 Seamstress
40 Waitress

IV. Industrial
50 Baker
51 Boarding house
52 Buyer
Cook:
53   Camp
54   Institutional
55 Dressmaker
Factory:
56   Needle trades
57   Food trades
58   Leather trades
59   Hat trades
60   Metal trades
61   Munitions
62   Paper and printing
63   Wood trades
64   Textiles
65 Forewoman
66 Inspector
67 Janitress (cleaner)

68 Laundry operative
69 Manager
70 Manicure and hairdr.
71 Messenger
72 Milliner
73 Retail dealer
74 Restaurant
75 Saleswoman
76 Waitress

V. Professional
80 Actress
81 Architect
82 Artist
83 Author
84 Chemist
85 Dentist
86 Dietician
87 Draftsman
88 Engineer
Handicrafts:
89   Metals
90   Textiles
91   Woods
92 Journalist
93 Laboratory worker
....

by women seeking both volunteer and paid work, listed 154 areas in which women could help. Among them were "poultry raising," "bookkeeper," "laundress," "munitions," "textiles," "messenger," "saleswoman," "author," "architect," "chemist," "lawyer," "physician," "police patrol," "aviatrix," and "dietetics." To judge from this list, not many areas were off-limits to women.[10]

COUNCIL OF NATIONAL DEFENSE

. . . . .Division. . . . . .Unit

Present occupation . . . .

By whom employed . . . .

Where employed . . . .

References . . . .

Education (graduate or length of time attended):

    Grammar. . . . . .College (give name). . . . .
    High or   Specialized
    private. . . . . .training . . . .

Emergency service (specify whether volunteer, expenses only, or paid)

. . . .
Will you go
anywhere?. . . . . . .Home town only?. . . . . . .In United States?. . . . . . .

How soon can you start? . . . .

OCCUPATION IN WHICH YOU ARE TRAINED. <u>UNDERLINE</u> SERVICE OR TRAINING

94 Languages (foreign):	116 Telegraphy	**VIII. Red Cross and**
	117 Wireless	**Allied Relief**
Read well.	118 Telephone	Instruction:
	Transportation:	150 Surgical dressings
Speak well.	119 Aviatrix	
95 Lawyer	120 Horse	151 Dietetics
96 Lecturer	121 Motor car	152 Elementary hyg.
97 Librarian	122 Motor cycle	153 First aid
98 Musician	123 Power boat	154 Garments—
99 Osteopath	124 Railroad	Hospital
100 Pharmacist		Civilian
101 Photographer	**VII. Social Service**	
102 Physician	130 Camp work	**IX. Miscellaneous**
103 Publicity	131 Charities—Which?	. . . .
104 Statistician	. . . .	
105 Surgeon	132 Club executive	**X. Contributions**
106 Teacher (subject):	133 District nursing	A. Ambulance
	134 Hospital	B. Driver for car
	135 Industrial welfare	C. Duplicating mach.
Of adults		D. Funds
	136 Investigator	E. Home for convalescent hospital
Of children.	137 Playgrounds	
	138 Protective assoc'n	F. Hospital
VI. Public Service	Recreational:	G. Laboratory
	139 Dancing	H. Motor boat
110 Inspector	140 Music	I. Motor car
111 Institutional mgr.	141 Reading aloud	J. Typewriter
112 Mail carrier	142 Relief visiting	K. Share home with
113 Police patrol	143 Settlement	widow or children
114 Postmistress	144 Social clubs	L. . . . .
115 Signaling		

Many private groups organized registration efforts for women volunteers, but eventually the Woman's Committee of the Council of National Defense drew up a national registration form that gave women a great many choices. Author's collection

Chicago newspapers ran articles with titles such as "What Are You Doing to Help Win the War?" and published stories about women who were doing their bit. One told of a fifty-five-year-old widow with three sons. Two were in the army, but the third was entitled to an exemption as his mother's support. She wouldn't hear of it but sent the third son to the front as she rented out her house, keeping one small room for herself, and spent her evenings knitting at the Red Cross. The *Tribune* lamented, "If you make a round of tea rooms in hotels, cafes, and restaurants you'll find the waster there, overdressed more likely than not, bejeweled and leading the same life she had before the war. . . . How can these women be made to see the light?" It advised female slackers, "The work is there to do, and you'll be an infinitely happier woman for the doing of it!"[11]

In Chicago many women volunteers went to the Comfort Shop at 76 East Madison Street and purchased khaki material from which to fashion sturdy sacks. They then bought items to fill the sacks—tobacco, playing cards, toothpaste, and so on—and the store shipped them to the soldiers. Other forms of volunteerism were what were considered "women's work," such as knitting sweaters, making surgical dressings, sewing hospital shirts and pajamas, and providing lunches and dinners for soldiers passing through. One clever Chicago woman won national recognition for inventing the "flag hospital," a place

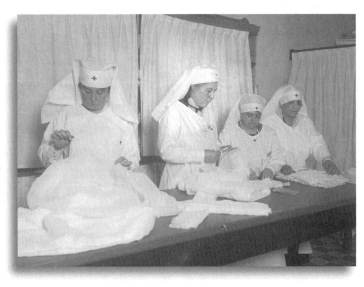

The Red Cross attracted many women who were eager to do their bit. Here four Chicago Red Cross volunteers roll bandages and fold linen. Chicago History Museum DN-0067784, cropped, cleaned, and sharpened; *Chicago Daily News* photograph

for the "cleaning and mending" of national banners. The Red Cross naturally attracted many women; in June 1917 it was reported that eight thousand women had already signed up for Red Cross courses in Chicago.[12]

On the Job

Stitching comfort bags was undoubtedly gratifying, but with so many men going into the service, Chicago women would have to do more than that. Tasks such as making pajamas were reported in society columns because they were mostly carried out either by middle- or upper-class single women who didn't need to work or by married women who were supported by their husbands.

Women's employment during World War I was mostly a matter of class. If the contributions of middle- and upper-class women were volunteer efforts, many lower-class women—mostly single, but not all—needed and sought paid jobs. And the labor shortage also opened up jobs that women had never held. The fame of "Rosie the Riveter" of World War II suggests that wartime factory work for women began in the 1940s, but Rosie had thousands of predecessors during the Great War, when women worked as crane operators, truck drivers, railroad laborers, ice deliverers, and even barbers. And Chicago, being the capital of the industrial heartland of the United States and a leading center of entrepreneurialism, is the perfect place to examine this phenomenon.

In June 1918 the *Tribune* published an article titled "Women Must Be on the Job as Men Go to War," by Lucy Calhoun, who reported extensively on women's wartime activities. It began "Jobs for women! Jobs of every variety under the sun—jobs which pay beginners from 10 to 50 per cent more than they ever paid before with increase in wages of 30 to 50 per cent after two months' service!" According to Calhoun, "All the employment bureaus are being swamped with calls for women workers and it is difficult to meet the demand for trained help." She reported that the large downtown department stores were rapidly losing male employees; that women were needed as floor walkers, wrappers, janitors, elevator operators, and clerks; and that the manager of Marshall Field's insisted that the store "stand[s] for the 'equal pay for equal work' scale." The superintendent of employment at the Western Electric Company told Calhoun that he expected to lose five hundred men in the next draft and that he was finding the women already hired to be "very capable." The Chicago Telephone Company was hiring seventy-five to one hundred women every week, and wages there had already gone up 10 percent. Government contracts had increased business for the clothing manufacturers; at Rosenwald & Weil the workforce had increased from eight hundred to one thousand, and wages had gone up as much as 50 percent. That company, too, pledged equal pay for women. Calhoun related that some Chicago women were so patriotic that they had volunteered to work in factories without pay, but union leaders considered that going a bit too far.[13]

In July 1918 Florence Schee, manager of the employment department of the women's committee of the State Council of Defense, reported that Chicago enterprises were seeking women to fill some "really large and important positions." One firm desired a "first class employment manager," and another was searching for "a steel expert with engineering experience."[14] Jobs such as these, which required education, were obviously not for lower-class women. Harry H. Merrick, vice president of Chicago's Association of Commerce, gave a speech in which he complained about the difficulty of finding educated women employees: "There is a hanging back among the middle class women. They don't want to go into the trades. It's up to us to make them."[15] Mary King of the *Tribune* pointed out that a married woman who gets a job "releases two men for combative service—her husband and the man whose job she fills."[16] A song of 1918 warned American men that women were moving into jobs previously closed to them. The title tells it all: "You'd Better Be Nice to Them Now."

Many women, both white and black, found employment in munitions plants . . .

Black women benefited greatly from the labor shortage, especially in Chicago, which was so greatly affected by the population shift of the Great Migration.[17] Commercial laundries were some of the main sources of employment. They had previously hired mostly immigrant women, but those women had moved on to the factories. Laundry work was hard, but most black women preferred it to domestic service, where jobs were abundant but the hours much longer. By 1917 the great Chicago packinghouses had hired more than ten thousand African Americans, and nearly one-third of them were women.[18]

In other factories black women took the lowest-paying jobs as white women moved up the ladder; such was the case in glass factories, commercial bakeries, and waste-processing factories. However, for many black women the only way to get a factory job was as a strikebreaker; when, for example, the International Ladies' Garment Workers Union called a strike in 1917, hundreds of black women were hired to replace the strikers.[19]

Many women, both white and black, found employment in munitions plants; one reason was that the owners came to believe that women handled explosives more carefully than men.[20] In May 1918 the *Tribune* announced that munitions jobs were open to women in a factory in southern Illinois and that those interested were to apply at the office of the Federal Employment Bureau on Wabash Avenue.[21] Munitions work for women was controversial, however, because of the dangers of the chemicals. A newspaper columnist warned women that "the fumes and acids rise up and hurt the eyes and skin, and ruin the complexion."[22] However, the threat was even worse than that. "Canary girls" was the term used in Britain for the women whose skin and hair were turned yellow by the chemicals in the munitions plants.[23] Dr. Alice Hamilton, a special investigator of dangerous occupations for the U.S. government, said in June 1918 that the government would try to find ways to limit exposure to the chemicals.[24] To oversee the work of women in munitions plants and in other factories producing cannons, shells, fuses, rifles, and so on, the federal government created a special Women's Branch of the Bureau of Ordnance in January 1918.[25]

Even before the war, the nation's railroads had problems with poor maintenance, underpaid and dissatisfied workers, overcrowded stations, and not enough railroad cars. The wartime labor shortage worsened these difficulties and emboldened railroad workers to threaten a strike. The Wilson administration followed the examples of the Europeans and took over control of the railroads, which until 1920 were run by the United States Railroad Administration (USRA). For women this government action made railroad work attractive: the USRA established an eight-hour day, efficient grievance procedures, and higher wages.[26] The USRA also set up a special Women's Service Section to oversee the working conditions of women on the railroads.

During World War I jobs once held only by men, such as working on the railroad, suddenly became available to women. National Archives and Records Administration via Wikimedia Commons

Railroad work was not exactly ideal; male workers were not welcoming, and women suffered from job discrimination, sexual harassment, and a lack of union protection. One of the fears of male workers and their unions was that women would work for less, which would lead to a general lowering of pay. In November 1917 a *Tribune* article titled "Women Making Good in Track Repair Labor" described a group of "sturdy, stalwart, rough looking" women carrying pickaxes, crowbars, and shovels as they did track work. The reporter was told that they learned the work faster than men and said, "Some of 'em can cuss as good as men too."[27]

The same page carried a picture of Mrs. Harry H. House of Glen Ellyn, Illinois, holding a stop sign at a railroad crossing as a steam locomotive rumbled by. She had taken the job after her husband was drafted. By the following November seventy thousand more women were employed as railroad workers than there had been a year before.[28]

The federal government established organizations to monitor workplaces employing women to ensure that they were clean and safe. These agencies employed women reformers who were determined to see that women got equal pay, weren't harassed or exploited, were matched to suitable jobs, and were given effective training. As assistant director of the Women in Industry Service, a division of the U.S. Department of Labor, Mary Anderson of Chicago was one of the most prominent women in these efforts. Born in Sweden in 1872, Anderson came to Chicago in 1892 and found work in a shoe factory. She became involved in the labor movement and by 1911 had become a paid organizer for the Women's Trade Union League (WTUL), which represented women who were barred from men's unions.

Called to Washington during the war, Anderson, along with her boss, Mary van Kleeck, fought for better wages and working conditions. Her attempts to inspect manufacturing plants met with resistance from the owners, and at one point she felt as if she just wanted to "pack up and go back to Chicago."[29] When she went to a factory that made hand grenades, she was told that although the women, who worked at night, were superior employees, they earned 25 cents an hour while the men got 40 cents. When she asked about the difference, she was told that the women "had no family responsibilities." She exploded, demanding, "Do you really know that? And what family responsibilities have the men?" She related the case as one typical of "two of the most difficult problems we had to deal with—unequal pay and night work for women." Anderson wrote, "The question of the substitution of women for men in various occupations was one that we had to watch very closely. If the jobs were desirable there was usually a good deal of opposition to women's employment by the men in the industry, but if the jobs were low grade and no one else wanted them, there was much enthusiasm about women taking them over."[30] In 1920 Anderson replaced van Kleeck as head of the Women in Industry Service.

Military Service

It was one thing to allow women to take jobs that had previously been held only by men; women had been working in factories for a long time and on farms even longer. But what about serving in the military? Would the United States allow women to put on a uniform? Women nurses had served with the army during the Spanish-American War, but they were under contract with the army and not in it.[31] But World War I was a war on a totally different scale.

The army had created the Army Nurse Corps (ANC) in 1901, but although it claimed that its members were "officers without rank," during the Great War it gave nurses neither uniforms nor equipment, preferring to leave that task to the Red Cross. Nurses were auxiliaries, not bona fide members of the army. Many officers, however, complained of a shortage of clerical workers, argued that many men who could be fighting were holding support jobs that women could do perfectly well, and pointed out that the British had established a Women's Army Auxiliary Corps. But even though General John J. Pershing, commander in chief of the AEF, sympathized, the War Department resisted the pressure to form a women's army corps.

Although the army was not willing to admit women, the navy was. This was because of Secretary of the Navy Josephus Daniels, "generally credited with being the first U.S. official to approve enlistment of women in the armed forces."[32] His order to admit women actually went out a month before the declaration of war, and by the time the United States entered the conflict, the navy had already signed up two hundred women. Although Daniels didn't like the term, they became known as yeomanettes. Many were trained in military drill and carried rifles, but nearly all were employed in stateside clerical work. And although they were not allowed to serve on ships, a few did get to France to work as nurses.

One of the earliest navy enlistees was a Chicagoan named Daisy Pratt Erd. Her work as chief yeoman in charge of women employees at the Boston Navy Yard so impressed the local congressman that he asked Secretary Daniels to make her an officer; the secretary sympathized but replied that he lacked the authority to do so. Erd was also something of a songwriter and composed several World War I tunes, including "Uncle Sam's Ships" and "We'll Carry the Star Spangled Banner through the Trenches." Una Perin of Chicago was acclaimed as the youngest yeomanette; she was accepted on her eighteenth birthday. Although yeomanettes could not go to sea, at least one managed to climb aboard a navy plane. In April 1919 Marthe Ballot, who was assigned to the Great Lakes Naval Training Station north of Chicago, took a ride in a seaplane. The lake was rough, the air was choppy, and Yeoman Ballot found the flight a bit nerve-racking, but after it was over she said, "If I ever get a pension I'm going to buy myself a plane, all painted pink, and go sailing for the rest of my life." It was reported that she was the first woman ever to fly in a navy plane.[33] In all, more than eleven thousand women served in the navy during the Great War, and what had begun as a controversial experiment ended as a universally acknowledged triumph—and more important, as proof that there were no convincing reasons to bar women from the military.[34]

Overseas Service

Helen Burnett Wood of Evanston was one of the first army nurses to die in the First World War. She was sailing to France in May 1917 when a gun test-fired a faulty shell that exploded as soon as it left the barrel. A shell fragment slammed into Wood's chest, killing her instantly. Also killed was Edith Ayers of Ohio. An eyewitness said, "We were all more or less expecting to be torpedoed, but this accident took us off our feet—coming so soon and from such an unexpected source. . . . I understand that the gun had not been tested before."[35] Wood's funeral was held in Evanston. Fifty sailors and the Great Lakes Training Station band accompanied the cortege, along with fifty automobiles bearing Red Cross and Medical Reserve Corps representatives. At the church, the casket passed through a long line of Red Cross and hospital nurses, female students from Northwestern, and twenty-five Civil War veterans.

Twenty-five thousand American women served overseas in World War I. They went as nurses, physicians, dentists, physical therapists, statisticians, decoders, accountants, secretaries, laboratory technicians, architects, Red Cross volunteers, telephone operators, canteen workers, and more.[36] Well before the United States declared war, the military began preparing for the

About eleven thousand women served in the U.S. Navy as yeomanettes during the war, proving that there were no convincing reasons to bar women from the military. Library of Congress possibility of combat, although funds were lacking. The army arranged with the Red Cross to establish fifty base hospitals in case they should be needed, and by the time the war came twenty-five hospitals were ready. The nurses for these hospitals came from the ANC. By the time of the armistice, the ANC had reached a size of 21,480, and most of the army nurses were supplied by the Red Cross Nursing Service.[37] The Red Cross also recruited its own nurses for overseas hospital duty, but the organization placed women in many other capacities. One of the most welcome sights for the doughboy was a Red Cross portable kitchen staffed with women volunteers who brought sandwiches, coffee, lemonade, and other refreshments. No American nurses were killed by enemy action, although 102 died overseas from disease, most of them victims of the influenza epidemic of 1918.

One Chicago woman attracted a good amount of attention because she didn't just volunteer—she started her own hospitals. Mary Borden Turner, a wealthy socialite, had married a Briton and in 1914 had established two large field hospitals in France. In January 1917 her sister in Chicago set up a booth at a fund-raiser at the Chicago Coliseum and supplied the *Tribune* with descriptions of the war from Mary's letters. Mary wrote of the French wounded, "We shall need many, many things for the care of them—night shirts, bedsox, bed jackets, towels, handkerchiefs, water pillows, air cushions, bed rests, hot water bottles, large pillows, and fracture pillows. It is for this reason I appeal to you."[38] Mary Turner was a writer and a friend of some of the leading modernist authors, including Gertrude Stein. In a bitter poem titled "Where Is Jehovah?" Turner lamented that God had apparently abandoned those suffering on the battlefield.[39] To her was dedicated an extraordinary book, *The Backwash of War* (1916) by Ellen N. La Motte, an American who served as a nurse in one of Turner's field hospitals. This bitter, disillusioned, and unflinching appraisal of the carnage of war was so dispiriting that its publication was banned in France and Britain. It sold well in the United States until the declaration of war, when it was censored there too. One of the book's most chilling passages describes the return to his father in Paris of a veteran with all four limbs amputated, "a hideous flabby heap, called a nose," and no eyes. The first words of the sobbing boy to his father were "Kill me, Papa." "However, Antoine couldn't do this, for he was civilized."[40]

Mary Curry Desha Breckinridge, a nurse affiliated with a Chicago hospital unit near the frontlines, returned to Chicago with a souvenir album that included this watercolor drawing by a French artist.
Library of Congress

Several prominent Chicago women volunteered for YMCA canteen work in France. One was the writer Maude Radford Warren, who was made an "honorary major"; a prominent judge reassured doubters that "it was entirely legal for a woman to hold such a commission."[41] One of the most interesting of these Chicago women was Kathryn M. Johnson. The YMCA was especially noted for its "Y-huts," where soldiers could go for recreation. To serve the black soldiers, the YMCA created separate Y-huts, and these segregated venues allowed a handful of American black women to make it overseas. Kathryn Johnson was one of them. Before the war she was an associate editor at *Half-Century Magazine*, which had been founded in Chicago in 1916 by the black entrepreneur Anthony Overton. In 1918 she volunteered, and just when it seemed that the wishes of black women to serve overseas would be routinely denied, she later recalled, "the Paris Headquarters of the Young Men's Christian Association cabled as follows: 'Send six fine colored women at once!'"[42] Johnson was one of the first three women given permission to go—"two hundred thousand colored soldiers and three colored women in France!" was how she put it; eventually the total reached nineteen. She spent nine months in Camp Lusitania, where was located the largest YMCA hut in France, one built for black soldiers. "The work was pleasant and profitable to all concerned," she wrote, "and no woman could have received better treatment anywhere than was received at the hands of these 9,000 who helped to fight the battle of St. Nazaire by unloading the great ships that came into the harbor."[43] She later coauthored *Two Colored Women with the American Expeditionary Forces*, an invaluable source of information on this neglected aspect of the war.

Although the army refused to enlist women, it did accede to at least one of General Pershing's entreaties. The telephone system in France was conceded to be deficient—the joke among U.S. soldiers was "If you want to get hold of a friend to talk, the phones are there, but it's quicker to walk." Consequently, in November 1917 Pershing asked the War Department to send him 100 female French-speaking operators. Advertisements were placed in newspapers across the nation, and more than 2,400 women applied; eventually, over 7,000 women applied, and 223 were sent to France.[44] Chicago was one of seven cities chosen to be a training center for the operators; instruction began in January 1918. The course ran for four to six weeks, and the primary requisite was "a thorough knowledge of idiomatic French." In March the *Tribune* published pictures of fifteen young Chicago women who were being trained and reported that four of these "Hello Girls," as they were now known, had already left for the front. "When in service the telephone girls will wear a special uniform," the article said. "The rate of pay ranges from $60 a month for operators to $125 a month for chief operators, with allowances for rations and quarters when those are not provided by the army."[45] By May three units of Hello Girls trained in Chicago were already in France, and another was preparing to leave. A signal corps captain remarked, "These girls are going to astound the French by their efficiency. In Paris it takes forty to sixty seconds to complete one telephone call. Our girls are equipped to handle 300 calls an hour."[46] Pershing's "switchboard soldiers," as he called them, mostly worked in city offices, but they occasionally reached the frontlines. During the Battle of Saint-Mihiel, for example, women operators wearing gas masks and helmets worked feverishly just behind the trenches and endured shelling and bombs that kept cutting the telephone lines.[47] About two dozen Hello Girls received citations for their wartime bravery.

Kathryn Johnson, a magazine editor from Chicago, served as a volunteer in a segregated YMCA hut built for black U.S. soldiers.
Author's collection

After the War

Less than two weeks after the armistice, the *Tribune* was reporting that women workers were already beginning to lose their wartime jobs and having difficulty finding civilian employment: "With soldiers coming back to their former positions and the dropping of many war activities 1,000 or more girls have been ousted. The prospect that fighting will not be resumed has put an end to the work of several organizations that employed many women and girls and has limited the activities of others." An appeal from Washington for five thousand stenographers had been canceled, and twenty women had been let go by the Military Training Camp Association. The chairman of the Chicago branch of the Red Cross, however, remained optimistic: "I do not know that we face any immediate problem with reference to our young women employees. . . . Our regular work requires a large force . . . so I do not expect we will have much of a problem

Hello Girls were women who volunteered to work as telephone operators on the frontlines. Chicago was one of seven cities chosen as a training center. Library of Congress

regarding paid workers." Similarly, the head of the woman's committee of the State Council of Defense said, "We will take care of our employees some way. It is more than possible that some of our branches will remain in existence and in that case, of course, the girls will stay, too." It was hoped that many soldiers' wives who were working would soon give up their jobs and create some openings, and some business executives were optimistic that a business revival would "furnish employment for all who wish it."[48]

However, the economy entered a recession in August 1918, and a year-and-a-half-long depression began in January 1920. Nevertheless, one of the beneficial developments of the war was that the issue of women's workplace rights had moved into the mainstream and wasn't forgotten. The Woman in Industry Service in which Mary Anderson operated was transformed in 1920 into the Women's Bureau of the Department of Labor.

By the end of July 1919 all the yeomanettes had been released from active duty. Two months before, Lucy Calhoun had reported that "several hundred of these girl sailors who enlisted from Chicago will soon descend upon their home town looking for jobs." The woman in charge of the women's division of the Federal Employment Bureau in Chicago said she would try to persuade local businessmen to hire the yeomanettes, but she warned that some "unreasonable girls" who were "spoiled by wartime salaries" would have to accept realistic wages. "I do not see," she said, "why Chicago should have to shoulder the burden of giving jobs not only to soldiers, sailors and women war workers, but to everybody else. But these navy girls are surely deserving of good positions and we shall try to get them."[49] The Hello Girls faced less challenge in finding employment because switchboard operation was already considered "women's work." Women working for the railroads resisted their dismissals, but the trend was overpowering. Some women were kept on in clerical jobs and as telegraphers and telephone operators, but by the end of 1919 twenty thousand were gone.[50]

At the end of 1918 Mary van Kleeck reported that about 12 million American women were gainfully employed, compared with 8 million in 1910.[51] However, according to the U.S. Department of Labor, by 1920 the number was back down to 8 million. The women who went to work during World War I understood that in most cases their work would be temporary.[52] Many of the women war workers, as historian Carrie Brown has written, "married, stopped working, and had children. Such had been their plan all along."[53]

However, if the World War I years are put into a wider perspective—the half century between 1880 and 1930—the dimensions of the change in women's occupations are clearer. The numbers of women who were living on their own and supporting themselves without the help of husbands or fathers expanded enormously. The swelling of the female labor force during the Great War might have been a temporary anomaly, but the female labor force grew from 2.6 million in 1880 to 10.8 million in 1930, and "the number of women gainfully employed grew almost twice as fast as the adult female population."[54] By 1930 over half of all single adult women, and one-fourth of all adult women, in the United States had paid jobs. These are impressive numbers, but they are even more striking when one looks solely at Chicago. There the female labor force skyrocketed from 35,600 in 1880 to 407,600 in 1930, an increase of more than 1,000 percent—three times that of the nation as a whole. By that year 67 percent of the single women in Chicago were working.[55]

During the war, employment of women declined in traditional women's jobs, such as laundresses and domestic servants, and increased in jobs such as factory workers and clerks. As historian Robert H. Zieger has written, "During the Great War, about 400,000 women joined the ranks of semiskilled manufacturing operatives and common laborers, and more than 750,000 began employment as office, clerks, typists, stenographers, cashiers, and telephone operators. Meanwhile, more than half a million women left domestic service, nonfactory dressmaking and sewing, and personal laundry work. . . . Wartime employment boosted the economic status of hundreds of thousands of women."[56] In a *Tribune* article published at the end of 1919, an official of the Illinois Free Employment Bureau said that many women had quit working when their husbands returned home but that many others had kept their office and factory jobs. "This doubtless accounts," she said, "for the feeling of independence which is keeping women away from domestic work." The article gave the clear impression that although the number of women workers was declining, many of those who were working were holding jobs that were unlikely to have been available to them before the war.[57] By 1940 the female labor force in the United States was back to 12 million—the same number employed during the First World War. In the years between the wars, more and more women graduated from high school, and jobs opened up in factories using new technology, such as the manufacture of radios and electric appliances.

An even greater impact of the war was a change in attitudes. As historian Maurine Weiner Greenwald has explained, "Working women took advantage of their new strength. They seized opportunities for changing jobs, petitioned the government for fairer labor policies, struck at their workplaces for better pay and conditions, joined trade unions, and challenged the authority of their bosses in a myriad of ways to say no to exploitation."[58] Another historian, Lettie Gavin, wrote that "the war, in fact, marked the beginning of a new era in the history of women. . . . Many believed that those four years of war liberated women from old molds and stereotypes, provided new opportunities for them, and made them economically independent.

Women working diligently and efficiently laid the foundation for higher wages, better jobs, improved working conditions, and a more competitive status in the labor market."[59] Even women at the time recognized the irreversible trend. In 1920 Frances Donovan observed, "There is now no talk of 'back to the home.' The war has made conclusive a revolution that had already begun."[60]

The Hello Girls came home believing that they were veterans and entitled not only to honorable discharges and service medals but also to veterans' benefits. The army had other ideas—to the brass, the switchboard operators had been civilian volunteers. For half a century representatives of the Hello Girls battled to have their military status recognized, and it was not until 1978, sixty years after the armistice, that President Jimmy Carter signed legislation giving them veterans' status. An army general visited each surviving switchboard soldier in her home and gave her an honorable discharge. The youngest was eighty.[61]

8

"Sex O'Clock in America":
Chicago and the First Sexual Revolution

On August 1, 1913, readers of the *Chicago Tribune* discovered an article titled "A Study in English Slang." In the piece, a young British woman was described as a "flapper." This odd new word would catch on fast. Just two years later another *Tribune* article, "Fetching Indeed Are Fashions for the Flapper," featured illustrations of four smartly dressed young women, noting that "the flapper flits hither and yon, dressed in fashion's giddiest extremes."[1]

Few things are associated with the Roaring Twenties more than the flapper, that convention-defying, sexually liberated, bobbed-haired, female rebel out for a good time, riding in a Tin Lizzie with her beau and a flask of bootleg gin. But the *Tribune* articles show that the flapper phenomenon appeared well before the 1920s. Although bathtub gin appeared only with prohibition, flappers and Tin Lizzies were around before World War I, and use of the term *flapper* increased during the war as more women entered the workforce.

Today we talk about the sexual revolution as something that happened in the 1960s. That phenomenon, though real, was not unique. Historians and sociologists have come to recognize that another sexual revolution began in the second decade of the twentieth century and that it was accelerated—even made irreversible—by the First World War. In fact, observers in the 1960s knew of the precedent. In January 1964 *Time* magazine ran a cover story titled "Sex in the U.S.," in which it spoke of a "second sexual revolution." The writers were entirely aware that the sexual revolution of the 1960s was the second of the twentieth century and that the first had occurred in the World War I era.[2] And the epicenter of the first sexual revolution, for many reasons, was Chicago.

A 1928 book by a physician named Lee Alexander Stone, *It Is Sex O'Clock*, provided a sympathetic view of flapper mores, explaining that rebellion was usually the result of "too much

Comparing what the well-dressed woman wore in 1904 with the flashy garb of the flapper demonstrates the revolution in women's clothes that occurred during the war years. Library of Congress

parent" and arguing the need for sex education. By then the phrase "sex o'clock" was more than a decade old. In 1917 *The Marriage Question*, by Chicago playwright Ralph T. Kettering, successfully toured the country billed as "The Play That Strikes Sex O'Clock." As historian Thomas Fleming has observed, "The modern woman strode onto history's stage, not in the Roaring Twenties, but in the Tempestuous Tens."[3] Another historian, Joshua Zeitz, has explained:

> As early as 1913, social commentators observed that the bell had tolled "Sex o'clock in America," signaling a "Repeal of Reticence" about matters both carnal and romantic. Writers noted with disapproval that "making love lightly, boldly, and promiscuously seems to be part of our social structure" and that a new set of concerns like "'To Spoon' or 'Not to Spoon' Seems to Be the Burning Question with Modern Young America." They lamented that it was now "literally true that the average father does not know, by name or sight, the young man who visits his daughter and who takes her out to places of amusement," a practice that grew ever

more common as more men acquired automobiles, which a disapproving Victorian scorned as the "devil's wagon."[4]

As for those "devil's wagons," as a historian of the automobile has explained, "As early as the first decade of the twentieth century, the automobile was equated with adventure, including and perhaps especially sexual adventure."[5] An 1899 tune by songwriter Alfred Dixon was called "Love in an Automobile," and the huge 1905 hit "In My Merry Oldsmobile" ended with the suggestive lines, "You can go as far as you like with me / In my merry Oldsmobile." And Chicago was no exception to America's love affair with—and in—the automobile. As early as 1909 Michigan Avenue south of Congress Street in Chicago was known as "Automobile Row" because of the large number of showrooms.

According to John D'Emilio and Estelle B. Freedman in their history of sexuality in the United States, "Among the many changes during this period, two stand out as emblematic of this new sexual order: the redefinition of womanhood to include eroticism, and the decline of public reticence about sex."[6] In fact, a 1913 article by Agnes Repplier in the *Atlantic Monthly* was titled "The Repeal of Reticence." The flapper was the manifestation of this new attitude, and Chicago made a singular contribution to the flapper phenomenon. The city was home to the *Flapper*, a racy magazine that billed itself as "The Official Organ of the National Flappers' Flock" and carried such articles as "Why Does a Flapper Flap?" and "How to Edjimicate a Sweet Daddy."

Jazz, like the flapper, is linked with the zeitgeist of the 1920s, but in Chicago it reached its greatest popularity during, not after, the war. This novel music was shocking to many; one Chicago critic, for example, brought the war into the discussion by comparing jazz's enfeebling quality to healthful patriotic music: "the difference between the incantation-crazed fanatics and the patriot or soldier stirred to noble actions by music is a difference in the music itself."[7] For guardians of sexual restraint, the new styles of dancing that were performed to jazz were signs of creeping immorality. Chicago jazz musicians played for dancers, and many were the laments about the immorality of the steps; leg-to-leg dancing was considered especially horrifying.[8] The turkey trot, bunny hug, and other "animal" dances were denounced, but one

THE FLAPPER

Not For Old Fogies

November, 1922

p. two

Flappers Here to Stay, Says Colleen Moore

By GLADYS HALL, in the Chicago
Daily News

One day, not so very long ago, Colleen Moore and I had luncheon together. I don't suppose I ever met anybody so enthusiastic as Colleen. Even about the subway, upon which — or rather, within which—she had been spending most of her New York visit, frequently getting lost, but gallantly persisting, none the less.

Flappers came up—in conversation, I mean—and I found Colleen as enthusiastic for the maligned misses as most doleful individuals are against them!

"Why," said Colleen, with her head slightly to one side, an alert little manner, sort of characteristic of a humming bird, "Why, I'm a flapper myself!" Colleen is twenty-one, correct flapper age, at any rate —but somehow, until she mentioned it, I really hadn't catalogued her as precisely that. Flappers don't generally do as much as Colleen, and they are more blase — about the subway.

"A flapper," Colleen went on, with wisdom, "is just a little girl trying to grow up—in the process of growing up.

"She wears flapper clothes out of a sense of mischief — because she thinks them rather 'smart' and naughty. And what everyday, healthy, normal little girl doesn't sort of like to be smart and naughty?

"Little Lady Flapper is really old-fashioned; but in her efforts not to let anyone discover that her true ideal is love-in-a-cottage, she 'flaps' in the most desperately modern manner.

"Left to her own devices she would probably dance and flirt just as girls have always done — but honest, I don't think she'd wear her skirts so short!

COLLEEN MOORE
IN GOLDWYN PICTURES

"She likes her freedom, and she likes to be a bit daring, and snap her cunning, little manicured fingers in the face of the world; but fundamentally she is the same sort of girl as grandmamma was when she was young.

"The chief difference is that she has more ambition, and there are more things for her to wish for, and a greater chance of getting them.

"She demands more of men because she knows more about their work.

"She uses lipstick and powder and rouge because, like every small girl, she apes her elders.

"She knows more of life than her mother did at the same age because she sees more of it.

"She knows what she wants and what she is doing, all of the time— and she meets life with a small and an eager, ardent hope. She's a trim little craft and brave!

"The flapper has charm, good looks, good clothes, intellect and a healthy point of view. I'm proud to 'flap'—I am!"

Chicago was home to the *Flapper,* a racy magazine that called itself "The Official Organ of the National Flappers' Flock." Wikimedia Commons

New dances such as the turkey trot and the toddle scandalized guardians of traditional morality, as shown in this drawing by illustrator Gordon Ross titled "The Dance of Death."
Library of Congress

of the most appalling was a dance called the toddle. At the end of 1916 a *New York Times* article explained that an organization called the Inner Circle, which was "devoted to the development of the modern dance," had designated the toddle as the incoming craze.[9] Chicago's *Day Book* newspaper picked up the news and published an item telling readers they had better learn the new dance.[10] By 1921 the toddle was considered so salacious that Northwestern University had banned it from the prom and the Chicago superintendent of schools had forbidden it at school dances, saying, "We do not believe the shimmy and the toddle are proper dances for school entertainments."[11] Although the toddle was a national mania, a version called the Chicago toddle was considered particularly naughty. The fad was on the mind of songwriter Fred Fisher when he wrote the song "Chicago" (1922). Many people still know the words but don't know their meaning. It's one of the more obscure facts of Chicago history, but that's how the metropolis got its nickname "that toddlin' town."

Liberated Women

The war years quickened a trend that was bringing women into the workplace in unprecedented numbers. Unsurprisingly, analysts of the era's sexual revolution have posited a link between the two phenomena.

The women who took the new jobs were usually from rural areas and small towns. They left for a variety of reasons, including inadequate family finances, brutal fathers, or a love of adventure. When they arrived in Chicago, they commonly settled in "furnished room districts," areas near the city center where the owners of conventional buildings and houses divided their interiors into spaces with one- or two-room apartments. Chicago had three of these districts. The one on the South Side centered on Michigan Avenue from Sixteenth Street to Thirty-Third Street; the one on the West Side was bordered by Washington, Halsted, Harrison, and Ashland; and the one on the North Side ran along Wells Street from the river to Division Street. Here singles of both sexes lived side by side. Newly arrived working women forged bonds with other women in the same circumstances, and they easily formed liaisons with single men, while the landlords largely kept their noses out of their tenants' business for fear of losing them. In 1917 a visitor to a female renter's apartment gave this description: "A decrepit double bed sagged in the middle of the floor, a dresser with its mirror half hidden by gay neckties, appeared to be sliding towards one window, a rusty stove attempted to warm the dingy atmosphere, and a ragged strip of carpet tried to hide the splinters in the worn floor."[12]

A term was coined to describe these new urban dwellers: "women adrift." A U.S. Bureau of Labor report from 1910 defined women adrift as "practically without homes in the city and entirely dependent upon themselves for support."[13] At first sociologists and reformers viewed them as women in peril, helpless in the wicked city and in danger of falling into immorality. However, when reporters and reformers took a closer look, they found an awful lot of women who were not at all helpless and passive, but instead were tough, assertive, and resourceful. Although some young women became the prey of unscrupulous men, others played the "sex game," in which they craftily enticed their wooers to buy them dinners and gifts while refusing sex. Some even went further by trading sexual favors for gain in an arrangement that was similar to prostitution but not at all the same. Meager salaries made these affairs nearly imperative. As one of them explained, "If I did not have a man, I could not get along on my wages."[14]

The possibilities of meeting men were much greater than these women were used to back home: "The growth of sexually integrated workplaces and new entertainment industries provided settings in which the steadily increasing number of wage-earning women could make friends and meet men."[15] Each furnished room district had what was called a "bright light" area filled with cabarets, restaurants, dance halls, tea rooms, and so on, which became social centers for single young people. These meeting places have been called "a commercialized world of pleasure." The commercialization of urban places of amusement was one of the key elements in shaping the new morality.[16]

It was in the 1890s that the idea of dating began to take hold. Previously, it was customary for male suitors to visit young women in their homes, where a parent would be hovering nearby.

In February 1916 a committee of Chicago women organized to investigate the goings-on at movie theaters.

The new practice of dating enabled courting couples to leave the parental home and frolic in these new places of recreation. And as with so many other things in American life, Chicago was ground zero for this development. Beth L. Bailey has traced the origin of the terms *date* and *dating*, as they are used today, to the Chicago author George Ade, whose writings from the 1890s are invaluable resources for anyone studying the history of American slang. She quotes the title character of Ade's 1896 novel *Artie*, who complains to his girlfriend, "I s'pose the other boy's fillin' all my dates." In his 1893 *Fables in Slang*, Ade tells of a popular girl named Marie (a "Pippin") whose "Date Book had to be kept on the Double Entry System."[17]

Movie theaters were instrumental in the sexual revolution, because films began romanticizing the independent, spunky young woman who meets and masters the city. *The Adventures of Kathlyn* (see chapter 1) was one of the first of these; later, Mary Pickford specialized in movies about these young women. Movie theaters terrified the guardians of traditional morality. As early as 1907, when films were being shown in nickelodeons (5-cent theaters), the *Tribune* began a campaign against their "vicious" programs. Although some other Chicago newspapers mocked the *Tribune*'s prudishness, city laws were passed requiring films to have a police permit and enlarging the censorship board.[18] The lighting in theaters was considered as perilous as the pictures. Jane Addams noted, "The very darkness of the room . . . is an added attraction to many young people, for whom the space is filled with the glamor of love making."[19]

In February 1916 a committee of Chicago women organized to investigate the goings-on at movie theaters. They scrutinized films for "malicious, vulgar, lewd, and criminal acts," protested "suggestive titles and subtitles," and insisted on "light auditoriums in theaters where there is too much darkness." The women inspected 137 theaters and reported 43 of them as "dark."[20]

Students of women's history during the World War I years are especially fortunate to have Frances Donovan's 1920 book, *The Woman Who Waits*. Donovan got the idea of experiencing firsthand the life of a Chicago working woman by becoming a waitress, which she did for about nine months starting in 1917. At the beginning she notes that young women come to Chicago because "life is dull in the small town or on the farm and because there is excitement and adventure, in the city. . . . It is her frontier and in it she is the pioneer." As Donovan begins her job in a downtown restaurant, her encounter with the other waitresses is stunning: "They were putting on their aprons, combing their hair, powdering their noses, applying lipstick to their lips and rouge to their cheeks, all the while tossing back and forth to each other, apparently in a spirit of good-natured comradeship, the most vile epithets that I have ever heard emerge from the lips of a human being, and mingled with these were long oaths of obscene profanity." These women were remarkably frank about sex: "In the easy familiar contact with men, these girls had acquired in regard to matters of sex . . . the incredible candor of men." "The filthy language," Donovan concluded, "is the outgrowth of the low ideal of sex around which centers the greatest interest. There is not much that is complex about the waitress and her behavior can easily be reduced to the two fundamental appetites of food hunger and sex hunger. She is intelligent, efficient, industrious, dishonest, and dishonorable, loose in her sex relations, impatient of the restraints put upon her by the members of the group from which she came (parents, relatives) and inclined to set up new standards for herself and to make a new group life in which these standards are approved."[21]

Donovan saw how the waitresses played the "sex game," and some were pretty successful at it. A coworker said of a waitress named Daisy: "When she first came here to work, she had nothing and was glad to pick up an old pair of gloves out of the garbage can and wear them. Now she has everything, including a thousand dollars' worth of diamonds and a sealskin coat. She didn't earn them hashing at Lane's." Donovan reported that most waitresses preferred to land husbands, but "because of the economic inefficiency of the men in her world, the waitress fails to realize her ideal of domesticity and so she takes on a life of semi-prostitution. She is not, however, exploited nor driven into it, but goes with her eyes wide open."[22] Sometimes venereal disease was part of the price she paid, as was abortion, which appears to have been readily available.

In an important 1973 essay titled "The Dating of the American Sexual Revolution: Evidence and Interpretation," Daniel Scott Smith surveyed historical statistics on premarital sex, premarital pregnancy, and illegitimacy rates and concluded that the timing of the first wave of the sexual revolution can be traced to the end of the nineteenth century.[23] The major changes in sexual behavior, however, took place among "less-educated" women, which is why middle- and upper-class observers of contemporary mores either were unaware of them or ignored them. But as Smith has explained, in the first three decades of the twentieth century, "the behavior of the educated minority of women converged upon the behavior of the less-educated majority."[24] Or as historian Joanne Meyerowitz has speculated, middle- and upper-class women "may have observed and learned from the unconventional behavior of the working-class women who were their neighbors. . . . By the 1920s, young middle-class flappers romanticized and imitated the working-class women who lived on their own and socialized with men."[25] In any case, when middle-class young women began to adopt more liberal sexual attitudes, intellectuals began to take notice, and as Smith has pointed out, between 1910 and 1914 there was a notable increase in the number of magazine articles on birth control, prostitution, divorce, and sexual morals.

Chicago newspapers regularly published articles in which guardians of morality expressed horror at the activities of young people and the salacious entertainments available to them. For example, a 1914 *Tribune* article, "Women Start War on Sex Novel," described how members of Chicago women's clubs were organizing to "keep bad books out of circulation." One of the members even said that "with some publishers it has struck sex

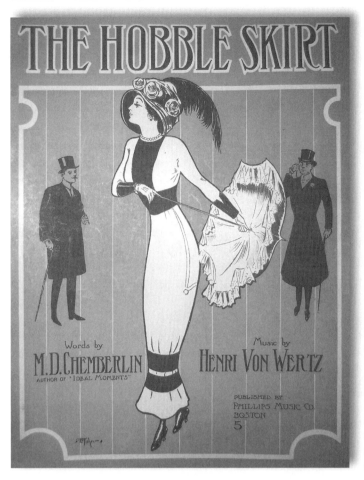

One of the more controversial fashions of the day was the hobble skirt, a slimming garment that hindered walking—but got men's attention, as seen in this sheet music cover from 1912. Author's collection

o'clock." The piece also reported laments about the immodest clothes coming into fashion. One Mrs. H. B. Burnet of Indiana stated, "I firmly believe that we should not permit the wearing of such clothing as I have seen here on the streets of Chicago."[26] As historian Alan Valentine has expressed it, "Women were discarding corsets, camisoles, petticoats, ankle-length skirts, and only heaven knows what else. Shirtwaists and blouses had become 'peekaboo,' and knees were openly exposed to public censure or approval."[27] One controversial fashion was the hobble skirt, a slimming garment with a hem so narrow as to hinder walking. In 1911 the *Tribune* reported that the owners of Riverview amusement park were replacing old wooden steps with lower ones: "It cost the park management a lot of money to

Rosalie Ladova, a well-known Chicago physician, was arrested for wearing an "indecent" outfit at a Lake Michigan beach. Library of Congress

build steps to accommodate the hobble skirt, but the concession managers again are happy and business is booming."[28]

By the summer of 1913 women's attire had become a major issue on Chicago's lakefront. One woman caused a stir when, standing knee-deep in Lake Michigan, she proceeded to unbutton and remove her skirt and then step out of the water wearing bloomers. She left her skirt on the shore and returned to the lake, but a patrol wagon quickly hauled her off. It turned out she was no flapper, but a well-known physician named Dr. Rosalie Ladova, and she insisted that her costume was more decent than those worn by the men at the beach. The next day Dr. Ladova appeared before a judge, who ruled that her beach outfit was legal. "Dr. Ladova's suit was quite modest," he stated. "No one but a prude could object to it."[29] That a woman as well educated as Dr. Ladova was challenging long-established conventions showed how the sexual revolution was creeping upward in class.

The shifting morality, however, did not come entirely from the bottom up. Chicago was home to a lively bohemian radical scene that featured free-thinking intellectuals all too happy to shed Victorian scruples. Some were leftists who derided conventional views of marriage as a bourgeois conspiracy against women; one such person was the anarchist Emma Goldman, a vocal critic of "Puritanism," who became a friend of Margaret Anderson, the Chicagoan who had founded the influential literary magazine the *Little Review*. In 1916 Anderson invited the "firebrand" to Chicago, where Goldman gave a series of lectures. Many of these leftist nonconformists preferred "free love" to marriage and studied the writings of such thinkers as Sigmund Freud and the sexologist Havelock Ellis, who argued that a variety of sex partners might be beneficial and that emotional fidelity was more important that sexual fidelity.[30] In Chicago an influential local intellectual was the sociologist Thorstein Veblen, who criticized the institution of marriage as the means by which men turned women into "property." Another Chicagoan aiding the liberationist cause was the socialist writer Floyd Dell, an advocate of free love and "companionate" marriage. In his 1913 volume, *Women as World Builders*, he praised the young modern woman: "In her endeavor to create a livelier, a more hilarious and human morale, she is doing, I feel, a real service to the cause of women. . . . And emancipation from middle-class standards of taste, morality, and intellect is, so far as it goes, a good thing." He considered their "hell-raising" attitude to be a "great moral improvement."[31]

The Sex Education Controversy

Another sign that sexual matters were coming out in the open was the high-profile sex education controversy that engulfed Chicago just before the war. When Progressives assessed urban society, they saw numerous ills, and one of the most worrisome was prostitution (euphemistically called "the social evil") and the existence of vice districts, such as Chicago's notorious Levee on the near South Side. What troubled them most was the danger to public health—specifically, gonorrhea and syphilis, which, they said, were not just confined to the wicked but also struck married women who were infected by their wayward husbands. The problem was exposed by the 1911 report of the Chicago Vice Commission, titled *The Social Evil in Chicago*. This detailed document, which was banned from the mails as obscene, estimated that Chicago housed some five thousand professional prostitutes who annually serviced five million men.

For the reformers, the most effective way to change men's behavior was through the schools, with a program teaching sexual hygiene. Leading this effort in Chicago was sixty-eight-year-old Ella Flagg Young, who was the first woman to earn a PhD from the University of Chicago's Department of Education, the first to become a full professor, the first to become president of the Illinois Teachers Association, and the first to become superintendent of a major U.S. school system.[32]

On June 19, 1913, Young announced that several "prominent physicians"—male for the boys, female for the girls—would deliver lectures on "matters of sex" in all of Chicago's twenty-one high schools in September.[33] The *New World*, Chicago's Catholic weekly, assailed the notion as "modern faddism—modern and mischievous, too."[34] The opponents of the lecture idea not only feared that exposure to sex would encourage teenage experimentation but also charged that the idea interfered with the rights of parents. Under pressure, the board of education quickly countermanded Young's decision and said it could not support sex education. Young rallied the Progressives, and a flood of mail inundated the board. When it was proposed to change the name of the course from "sex hygiene education" to "personal purity," the board approved it, 11–2.[35]

The course went ahead. Physicians tactfully explained the virtues of clean living and the dangers of promiscuity. Complaints were rare, and few parents removed their children from the classes. Nevertheless, Young's opponents were not finished. In November circulars containing excerpts from the lectures were ruled obscene, and the course was discontinued. Later advocates of sex education found it more effective to introduce the subject as part of other courses, such as biology or home economics. Yet Young's effort signaled the onset of a debate that would last for decades. As historian Jeffrey P. Moran has expressed it, "The Chicago experiment illustrates the origins of a cultural divide over questions of state action and scientific authority that would persist throughout the century."[36]

The Effects of the War

Although the sexual revolution began before the Great War, contemporary observers recognized that the conflict accelerated it. For one thing, many of the young men who went off to war received an education in much more than combat. Reformers worried about venereal disease were encouraged by the high command's closing of brothels near military bases and orders to the troops to practice sexual abstinence, but neither action seemed to have much effect. One observer said, "The fact is that the soldier is very much more unmoral than when he entered the army. . . . Shorn of modesty, morals, sentiment, and subjectivity . . . men will sit til late at night . . . and talk about women—but this talk is of the physical rather than the emotional."[37] The army inadvertently raised awareness of sex by providing soldiers with surprisingly explicit pamphlets on such subjects as prostitution and masturbation. As one historian put it, "In its own blunt way, the Army contributed to the demythologizing of erotic life by bringing sexual matters into the arena of public discourse, which was to become a characteristic feature of twentieth-century American culture."[38] The title of a popular song of 1918 sums up the effect of overseas duty on all-American country boys: "How Ya Gonna Keep 'Em Down on the Farm (After They've Seen Paree)?"

The mingling of women with male workers in wartime factories also caused concerns. In August 1917 the *Tribune* published an article titled "Immorality in War Time Work" that portrayed conditions in which "women and men have been allowed to sleep in the same cars without partitions" and "there was no dressing room or rest room for the women."[39] Elmer T. Clark, a writer who served in Europe during the war with the YMCA and as a reporter, related:

> In this war the women have shown once for all that they are abundantly able to care for themselves, so that their dependence upon the opposite sex for support is a thing of the past. In the matter of morality and the welfare of the home as an institution, however, the influence of the disparity of one sex will be felt. It will not be a good thing, either for the women or for the world, to throw the women into industry by the side of men, giving them the same wages and offering them all inducements to become cogs in the machine of industry. . . . The fact will remain that the ideal life for the woman is in the home; from this standard we will regress at our peril.

He went on to lament, "The world is also threatened with having its confidence in and respect for women undermined. . . . Their familiar association with the men, their profligate use of cigarettes, which the war has so heightened that it seems well-nigh universal, the masculinity which comes from doing the work of men, the increasing carelessness in the matter of personal appearance. . . . Then in connection with this there is the awful deluge of vice which has degraded so many thousands and resulted in so much disease."[40]

The sexual revolution of World War I was summarized by suffragist and writer Alyse Gregory in a 1923 article titled "The Changing Morality of Women." It's worth quoting at length:

> Then suddenly all was changed again. The war was over and women were admonished to hurry once more home and give the men back their jobs. It was too late. The old discipline had vanished in the night. . . . They took flats or studios and went on earning their livings. They filled executive offices, they became organizers, editors, copywriters, efficiency managers, artists, writers, real estate agents, and even in rare instances brokers. . . . However unwilling one may be to acknowledge it, girls began to sow their wild oats. Women of the aristocratic upper classes and the poorest women had never followed too rigidly the cast-iron rules of respectability because in neither instance had they anything to lose by digressing. But for the first time in the memory of man, girls from well-bred, respectable middle-class families broke through those invisible chains of custom and asserted their right to a nonchalant, self-sustaining life of their own with a cigarette after every meal and a lover in the evening to wander about with and lend color to life. If the relationship became more intimate than such relationships are supposed to be, there was nothing to be lost that a girl could not dispense with. Her employer asked no questions as to her life outside the office. She had her own salary at the end of the month and asked no other recompense from her lover but his love and companionship. . . .
>
> Profoundly shocking as such a state of affairs may seem to large numbers of people, there is no use pretending that it does not exist. There are too many signs abroad to prove that it does. Ministers may extol chastity for women from pulpit rostrums and quote passages from the Old and New Testaments to prove that purity and fidelity are still her most precious assets, but this new woman only shrugs her shoulders and smiles a slow, penetrating, secret smile.[41]

By the time the war was over, the term "women adrift" was becoming passé. Now people spoke, sometimes with dismay, sometimes with admiration, of the "gold digger," the "vamp," and the "jazz baby."[42]

The flapper not only wore provocative clothes but also flouted the law by "bootlegging" illegal liquor. Library of Congress

One Chicagoan's War

Eunice Tietjens. Photo courtesy of the Newberry Library,
Chicago; call # Midwest MS Tietjens (cleaned), box 9, folder 139.

Eunice Tietjens
The Disillusioned Poet

On the night of January 19, 1919, two young, elegant American women stood at the rail of the steamer *Lorraine* as it sailed into the Bay of Biscay off the coast of southern France. They stepped back a little. Suddenly, one of them dashed forward and plunged into the sea. The second then followed. An American soldier saw what happened, but by the time he was able to stop the ship, it was too late. The bodies were retrieved a few days later.

Also on the ship was the Chicago poet Eunice Tietjens, who was returning home from France after serving as a war correspondent. The first suicide, she later learned, was Gladys Cromwell, who was also a poet—one whose work Tietjens had published as an editor at *Poetry* magazine. The second suicide was Cromwell's twin sister, Dorothea. They had been volunteers with the Red Cross and had worked near the frontlines. Tietjens, herself depressed from her war experiences, bitterly commented, "I believe that every one of us on that boat might have done the same."[1]

The war was an equal-opportunity destroyer of illusions. Both soldiers and civilians suffered psychological trauma; both discovered despair.

Eunice Strong Hammond was born in Chicago on July 29, 1884. Her father, a banker, died when Eunice was thirteen, and her mother took her four children, of whom Eunice was the oldest, to Europe to resume her youthful dream of becoming a painter. This was an artistic family: one sister, Louise, became an expert on Chinese music and poetry; another, Elizabeth, became a professional cellist; and Eunice's brother, Laurens Hammond, invented the Hammond electric organ. Eunice was educated at the University of Geneva, in Dresden, and at the Sorbonne and the Collège de France. In Paris in May 1904 she married the composer Paul Tietjens, best known for the music for the stage production of L. Frank Baum's *The Wizard of Oz* (1902). The couple then returned to the United States so Paul could work with Baum on another theater project.

Eunice and Paul had two daughters, Idea, who died at age four, and Janet. The marriage fell apart, and Eunice took Janet to Evanston, Illinois, where both of them lived with Eunice's mother. Eunice, who had long dabbled in verse, began to take seriously the idea of becoming a writer. She became acquainted with Chicago's literary figures, such as Floyd Dell and Edgar Lee Masters, and joined the staff of Harriet Monroe's groundbreaking *Poetry* magazine, which introduced American readers to such poets as Ezra Pound, Carl Sandburg, T. S. Eliot, and Robert Frost, several of whom Eunice Tietjens befriended. Tietjens was also a supporter of Chicago's innovative Little Theater and Margaret Anderson's avant-garde literary periodical, the *Little Review*, even pawning her engagement ring to raise funds for the magazine.

When the war broke out in Europe, Tietjens's sister Louise was a missionary in China, and Tietjens went with her mother to the Far East. They spent some time in Japan and then traveled to China, which, Tietjens said, "left me a changed being."[2] Thus began a long love affair with Chinese culture. Soon after returning to Chicago, she published *Profiles from China* (1917), which contained what became her best-known poem, "The Most-Sacred Mountain."

Early in 1917 Tietjens realized that the United States would soon enter the war. "At once," she wrote, "I made up my mind that I must go to France, and that the *Chicago Daily News* must send me."[3] To her surprise, Henry Blackman Sell, the literary editor of the *Daily News*, asked her before she asked him. In October 1917 she was on her way.

Although thousands of American women served overseas in World War I, only a handful went as war correspondents. Some of the others were Peggy Hull of the *El Paso Times*, Anna Steese Richardson of *McCall's*, Jessica Lozier Payne of the *Brooklyn Eagle*, and Sigrid Schultz, who managed the *Chicago Tribune* office in Berlin. Tietjens, like the others, was assigned to write "women's stories"—about soldiers on leave, refugees, and children—which she resented. Her boss didn't press the issue and left her free to look into other matters.

She found life at the front inspiring, admiring the resolution of both soldiers and civilians. In Paris, however, she felt that she was "wading through filth."[4] Her most satisfying achievement was organizing the distribution of donated Christmas toys to ten thousand French children in the war zone. Mostly, she said, she lived in "pain and loneliness and terror."[5] Near the end of her stay, she went with a small group of women to Rheims. The party was led by a French lieutenant and a female guide. With Tietjens were a woman reporter from the *Newark Evening News*, a writer named Elizabeth Shepley Sergeant, and the wife of an American officer. When inspecting the battlefield at Mont de Bligny, the female guide picked up an unfamiliar object and asked Tietjens what it was. Tietjens didn't know, so the guide went to ask the lieutenant, who shouted, "Put it down quickly!" It was a live grenade that went off, killing its carrier instantly, ripping off the lieutenant's arm, and wounding Sergeant in the legs. As the guide fell, Tietjens wrote, "all her entrails boiled up through the broken abdominal walls like some hideous fountain."[6] Tietjens managed to persuade a French soldier to drive her, along with the mangled corpse, back to Paris, where the body was buried with honors.[7]

After that horrific incident and the suicides of the Cromwell sisters, Tietjens returned home in a state of depression. She went on a Liberty Tour for the government, but then spent time quietly recuperating at the Indiana Dunes, where she wrote a novel titled *Jake* (1921). It was not a war novel, but Tietjens said that it purged "all the sense of human pain and futility that the war had roused in me."[8]

In 1920 Tietjens married a publisher, poet, and playwright named Cloyd Head. With her husband she wrote a play, *Arabesque*, in 1925. Set in North Africa, it failed in New York, although it was notable for featuring the recently arrived Hungarian actor Bela Lugosi.

Tietjens wrote other books on China and Japan, including some for children, and a sojourn in Tunisia resulted in 1928 in a successful book for young adults titled *Boy of the Desert*. Tietjens spent a few years working with Chicago's Goodman Theater and then lived for ten months in Polynesia. In 1933 she began a three-year stint as a poetry instructor at the University of Geneva. Her autobiography, *The World at My Shoulder*, was published in 1938, and she died of cancer six years later. Toward the conclusion of her autobiography, Tietjens wrote that her life "just goes bumbling along, falling into holes and climbing out of them." But she concluded, "Of only one thing I am reasonably certain. Whatever happens, it is sure to interest me."[9]

PART FIVE

Chicago's Changing Ethnic Landscape

9

"The Biggest Town in the World": The Great Migration

During World War I a black sergeant named Corneal Davis was serving in France when he got an unusual letter from his mother in Vicksburg, Mississippi. She related how one of Davis's boyhood friends, a lad named Hamilton, had gotten into trouble. As Davis later told the story, "One day they picked him up because some white woman said she had been raped or something, and they took that boy who was completely innocent and they hung him up on a tree." With the letter was a newspaper clipping about the lynching and a statement from Davis's mother: "Son, we are leaving." Before long, they were in Chicago.[1]

Not every black person who left the South to come to Chicago in the early twentieth century had such a chilling incentive, but every emigrant's story was dramatic in its own way. All were taking part in one of the pivotal events in U.S. history—the epic population shift now known as the Great Migration. During this exodus, so many black people left the South that historians are not even sure of the exact number, but the best recent estimate is that between the onset of the migration around 1910 and its ending around 1970, six million had made the move.[2] Black migrants fanned out into the cities of the North—St. Louis, Cleveland, Pittsburgh, Philadelphia, New York, Boston, and many other places—but for so many black southerners, the word *Chicago* was a kind of magic. Chicago meant a place where a black man could be considered a man, a worker could earn an honest wage, the Jim Crow laws did not apply, and the lynchings and daily insults and condescension did not occur. One black Mississippian summed it up: "You could not rest in your bed at night for *Chicago*."[3] In this context Chicago was more than a microcosm of the United States; it was the prime example of a dynamic and transformative national trend.

Few developments changed the face of modern Chicago more than the Great Migration. Chicago was not a city with a major black presence before World War I. But after the war, it was impossible to think of it any other way. The vast black South Side was taking shape, and Chicago's culture was being stamped with attributes that still characterize it today—from powerful black politicians, civil rights leaders, sports stars, entertainers, and writers to soul food, barbecue, jazz, and blues. For many visitors to Chicago, a trip to the city is incomplete without an outing to a Chicago blues club. And the blues, like jazz, came to Chicago with those who arrived in the Great Migration.

Emmett J. Scott, one of the earliest analysts of the Great Migration, calculated that in just the eighteen months beginning in January 1916, some fifty thousand black people arrived in Chicago, an estimate, he said, that was "based on averages taken from actual account of daily arrivals."[4] Although some of these travelers went on from Chicago to other cities, census figures show that Chicago's black population increased by 65,355 between 1910 and 1920.[5] According to historian Christopher Robert Reed, in just two years (1916–18) the black population of Chicago doubled, from 58,056 to 109,594.[6] African Americans made up only 2 percent of Chicago's population in 1910 and 7 percent by 1930, but by the end of the twentieth century there were "more blacks living in Chicago than in the entire state of Mississippi," constituting one-third of the city's population.[7] Most of the newcomers to Chicago came from four states: Mississippi, Alabama, Georgia, and Louisiana. (Migrants from the Atlantic Seaboard tended toward cities in the Northeast and Mid-Atlantic, particularly Philadelphia and New York.)[8]

The main reason that the war initiated the Great Migration can be summed up in two words: labor shortage. After the war in Europe started in 1914, the flow of immigrants to the United States nearly ceased. In 1914 immigrants numbered 1,218,480; in 1915 the number was 326,700; and three years later it was a mere 110,618, and many of those were from Canada.[9] A contributing factor to the decrease was the Immigration Act of 1917, which mandated a head tax of $8 from each immigrant and included,

The main reason that the war initiated the Great Migration can be summed up in two words: labor shortage.

for the first time, a literacy requirement (see chapter 12). The act also barred all Asians except Japanese and Filipinos. There was also an outmigration—the *Chicago Tribune* reported that in 1916 "66,000 aliens left the United States" and that in November 1917 alone 4,500 more aliens left the United States than entered it.[10]

Because of a brief economic downturn, the effect of the dwindling immigrant stream was not felt strongly at first, but by 1916 U.S. businesses were experiencing increased demand both from overseas and from a reviving domestic market. And once the United States entered the war, four million young men left the nation's farms and factories for the military.[11] The factories of the North found themselves desperate for workers, which opened up jobs that underpaid and oppressed black people in the South were eager to take. In 1916 the black-owned *Chicago Defender* newspaper explained, "It is a fact that the north holds out a hundred opportunities to every one that the laborer will find in the south. Not alone will he find an abundance of work, but the housing and living conditions are so superior that there is no comparison. The wages are so much higher for workers of every kind, the pennies paid laborers in the south land would hardly interest a bootblack of the north."[12]

It takes a lot to compel people, white or black, to leave homes that they've known for generations. Circumstances on the native turf affect their choices perhaps even more than the attractions of the new place. In the Great Migration, factors that were luring workers to the North, such as higher wages, superior schools, and an absence of Jim Crow laws, were matched by developments in the South that were driving workers away from conditions that were never that congenial in the first place—the arrival from Mexico of the cotton-destroying insect known as the boll weevil, devastating floods in 1915 and 1916, and a tightening of credit.[13] And most important, there was the omnipresent racism, which could be lethal. In January 1917 the *Defender* published an article titled "Why They Leave South." The subtitle explains it all: "The Lynching Record for 1916." The report went on to state that fifty black people had been lynched in the South in that year, three of them women. The crimes included "hog stealing," "insult," and "brushing against girl on street." A later *Defender* article clarified that "fear of mob violence, peonage, low wages and poor educational facilities

187

for the children are the principal reasons for the steady trend Northward."[14] The Chicago Urban League reported that after a lynching, "colored people from that community will arrive in Chicago inside of two weeks."[15] This helps explain why predictions that the migration would taper off when the war ended turned out to be wrong. The Great Migration only got stronger.

Contemporary interviews draw a clear picture of what the migrants liked about the North. Nearly always at the top of the list was "freedom"—freedom "to do anything I please," "freedom of speech and action," "freedom allowed in every way," "freedom and liberty," "freedom and opportunity to acquire something."[16] But there were more specific factors, such as the right to vote, the ability to put money in the bank, "better houses

This dramatic cartoon from the March 1920 issue of the *Crisis* powerfully illustrates how southern violence helped drive the Great Migration.
Author's collection

and furniture," "more places of attraction," even "the friendliness of the people." Some migrants expressed satisfaction that they were allowed to try on clothes in stores. One man said his wife could try on a hat and "if she doesn't want it she doesn't have to keep it." And one of the biggest surprises came when a black passenger nervously boarded a streetcar. Many were afraid to sit next to a white passenger, but when they did, nothing happened. Finally, better schools were crucial. It's not that the schools in the North were ideal—white teachers often viewed black children as incapable of learning, lacking in self-discipline, or even "retarded." But compared with the schools in the South, where class sizes could be as high as 125, northern schools were fine.[17] In 1910 less than half of the black children under ten in Louisiana, Alabama, and Georgia went to school at all.[18] A Mississippi politician said, "The only effect of Negro education is to spoil a good field hand and make an insolent cook."[19]

Chicago as a Destination

Chicago was the first choice of many black southerners for several reasons. Some twenty years before the Great Migration began, the city had hosted the Columbian Exposition, and word of that spectacular fair had penetrated into just about every corner of the nation, including the Deep South. And although it's doubtful that sharecroppers made the journey to the White City, some black visitors did come. One was Louis B. Anderson, who made the trip from Petersburg, Virginia. He felt the pull of Chicago, and by 1919 he was the alderman from the second ward.[20] After the Columbian Exposition, Chicago was not just another metropolis, it was the capital of the "Inland Empire," the "Second City," with designs on becoming the first.

Another asset was Chicago's many industries, especially the packinghouses, which required enormous numbers of workers. Because so much of the labor was unskilled, these huge killing factories offered a job to just about anybody who wanted one, and black workers seized the opportunity. As one black observer put it, "A Negro could always get a job in the stockyards. They could go to the stockyards any day of the week and get a job."[21] Emmett Scott reported that "it was most widely advertised throughout the States of Mississippi and Louisiana that employment could easily be secured in the Chicago stock yards district."[22] By 1918 ten thousand to twelve thousand black men and women were employed in the stockyards, and the packinghouses were employing a "large majority" of those who had made the trip north.[23] The next-largest employer of black workers was the steel industry. One worker recalled, "They were hiring day and night. All they wanted to know was if you wanted to work and had a strong back." Illinois Steel, which employed 35 black workers in 1916, had a black work force of 1,209 in 1919.[24] One migrant wrote to a friend in Alabama, "I do not see how they pay such wages the way they work laborers. They do not hurry or drive you."[25]

Other jobs were to be found at the Pullman car shops, in tanneries and laundries, in food-producing plants, and in lumberyards. The railroads, too, hired black workers—in rail yards, on track gangs, and as firemen. According to historian Touré F. Reed, "Between 1910 and 1920 the percentage of black male workers employed in Chicago's domestic and personal service trades fell from 51 percent to only 28 percent. At the same time, the percentage of black unskilled and semiskilled workers employed in manufacturing increased five- and tenfold, respectively, as Afro-Americans more than doubled their share of manufacturing jobs and tripled their representation in trade. . . . In only ten years factory work had replaced domestic and personal service as the most significant source of employment for black Chicagoans." Most reassuring were the results of a survey that the Chicago Urban League conducted of more than a hundred area businesses; the employers reported that although turnover was higher among black workers, "blacks and whites performed equally well on the job."[26]

And the money was good: a stockyard worker could earn $3 a day and a lumber stacker could earn $4, a laborer in a rolling mill could bring home $25 a week, and a railroad worker could earn $125 a month—a sum far beyond the dreams of a cotton picker in the South. A musician could make a fat $40 a week plus tips as a sideman in a jazz band, and there were a lot of them. Music historian Richard Sudhalter has written of "the sheer numbers of regularly employed bandsmen and other entertainers, especially on the black South Side. There's nothing even roughly comparable today: sometimes it seemed every block had a theatre, a dance hall, a cabaret with a band, or some combination of all three."[27]

Some black women worked in the stockyards and a few other industries, but most found employment as servants or laundry workers. Nevertheless, black female migrants found even those jobs liberating; although they worked hard, Chicago at least offered them recreation—clubs, theaters, dance halls, and just promenading on the "Stroll," that bright, nationally famous section of State Street that one black newspaper called "the Bohemia of the Colored Folks." Such amusements were just not available in the South, where, as one historian has put it, a black "woman or girl in the South found herself in danger of being attacked whenever she walked down a country road."[28]

Migrants prized Chicago's educational facilities as places not only to send their children but also where they themselves could take night classes. At Wendell Phillips Night School, an adult could enroll in an elementary class for $1 and a high school class for $2, and the school even offered classes in African American history and culture. Segregation in Chicago schools had legally ended as early as 1874, and although the drawing of district lines kept black people out of many of the city's all-white schools, in 1920 there were no all-black schools. Despite its reputation as a haven for black students, in 1920 the black enrollment in Wendell Phillips High School was only 56 percent.[29] One migrant wrote to his family in the South, "I have children in school every day with the white children."[30] In 1922 the Chicago Commission on Race Relations reported a spirit of racial harmony between black and white students at Wendell Phillips, but it also quoted the dean of Englewood High School, which was only 6 percent black, as thinking that although there was no "trouble or prejudice," that might change if black attendance increased.[31]

Wendell Phillips High School gained a reputation as a haven for black students and also offered extensive night school courses for adults.
Author's collection

191

Another major element in drawing black migrants to Chicago was the Illinois Central Railroad, which the historian Isabel Wilkerson has called "the Overground railroad for slavery's grandchildren."[32] The black poet Langston Hughes once said, "The railroad tracks ran to Chicago and Chicago was the biggest town in the world to me."[33] The Illinois Central ran up from the South like a great steel river, with its tributaries spreading across the Mississippi Delta region. Memphis served as a crucial transfer point; no fewer than eight southern railroads converged on the city's Grand Central Station, where a migrant could transfer to the Illinois Central.[34] Not only did the Illinois Central take black passengers to Chicago, but it was also an employer. Around 1915 many northern railroads suffering a labor shortage began recruiting black workers in the South, and the Illinois Central gave free transportation to hundreds. However, the railroads soon found out that recruiting was hardly necessary—black workers were coming on their own. Railroad workers who had settled in Chicago served as advertising for the city; they found it easy to travel back to the South and spread the word about the opportunities to be found in Chicago. Chief among these workers were the Pullman porters and dining car attendants, whose coveted jobs gave them prestige and influence in the black community. Another source of information was black entertainers, who were often on the road. Finally, in 1915 fifteen to twenty thousand delegates came to Chicago for the National Baptist Convention, and a great many returned home with favorable reports. Attendees at other conventions did the same.

In addition to carrying migrants who returned home to spread the news, the railroad brought to the South two crucial Chicago publications. One was the thick catalog of Sears, Roebuck & Company, the universal "Nation's Wish Book." This widely distributed volume illustrated the abundant goods that were made available by mass production and were available to anyone—anyone, that is, who had a reasonable income, such as could be earned in the factories of Chicago. The other was the *Chicago Defender.*

The *Chicago Defender*

Robert Sengstacke Abbott was born on November 28, 1868, on St. Simon's Island off the coast of Georgia. His father died when he was young, and his mother later married Joseph Sengstacke, the biracial son of a white German-born merchant and a slave. Sengstacke was a minister, fond of books, and desired an education for his stepson. He also published a local newspaper. Abbott first went to the Beach Institute in Savannah and then Claflin University in South Carolina. Finally, he entered Hampton Institute in Virginia with the intention of studying how to become a printer, which he thought might enable a transition into the newspaper business. On his first night at Hampton, he was sitting in the chapel when a group of students began singing. He joined in, and the others discovered that the newcomer had a fine tenor voice. This led to a position in the prestigious Hampton Quartet.[35]

In 1893 the Hampton Quartet went on a fund-raising tour that included a stop at the Columbian Exposition. While in Chicago, Abbott had the opportunity to be introduced to several black leaders, such as Frederick Douglass and Ida B. Wells, as well as successful members of Chicago's black community. Abbott wrote to his mother, "Tell father if he will back me, I will come home and run a paper. If not, I will stay out here in the west and try to make a fortune." As Roi Ottley, Abbott's biographer, explained, "He undoubtedly had been impressed by the display Negroes made of their progress in Chicago."[36] His stepfather evidently was encouraging, because Abbott did return home and worked on his stepfather's newspaper. However, he returned to Chicago to seek work as a printer but found that his race barred him from full-time employment. He enrolled in law school, but even though he graduated, his foray into a legal career was a failure, and he returned to printing. The death of his stepfather in 1904 might have been the impetus for another career change. Abbott decided to run a newspaper too—not in a small Georgia town, but in the great metropolis of Chicago.

Chicago already had three black-owned newspapers, but they were, as Ottley described them, "primarily vehicles for the editors to expound their views, punish opponents, and advance their personal political ambitions."[37] Abbott explained, "I wanted to create an organ that would mirror the needs, opinions, and the aspirations of my race."[38] (The *Defender* rarely used the terms "black," "Negro," "colored," or "Afro-American," but preferred to speak of "the Race" and "Race men.") The first issue appeared on May 5, 1905, and the newspaper appeared every week for the next fifty years. Abbott's hiring of an assistant editor named J. Hockley Smiley was a key move in directing the newspaper toward sensationalism, with lurid stories about lynchings, rapes, and other assaults on the black people of the South. By 1917 it had a nationwide circulation of 125,000, was the largest black newspaper in the United States, and had a reputation for militancy.

The historical importance of the *Defender* is due to its becoming a national paper with many readers in the South. As Emmett J. Scott has expressed it, "It had a large circulation in Mississippi and the supply was usually bought up on the first day of its arrival. Copies were passed around until it was worn out. One prominent negro asserted that 'negroes grab the *Defender* like a hungry mule grabs fodder.' In Gulfport, Mississippi, a man was regarded 'intelligent' if he read the *Defender*."[39] One reader in New Orleans called the paper "a God sent blessing to the Race."[40] As they traveled through the South, Pullman porters sold subscriptions to the *Defender* for a dollar a year.

At first the Defender did not encourage black people to leave the South and head to Chicago. In fact, editorials warned them not only that there were no jobs for them, but also that Chicago's labor unions barred black workers from membership.[41] Two

The former home of Robert S. Abbott, founder of the *Chicago Defender* newspaper, was designated a National Historic Landmark in 1976.
Library of Congress

things changed that outlook. First, the war cut off immigration from Europe, the traditional source of nearly all the labor force in the stockyards and steel mills. Now Chicago's industries needed black workers. Second, Abbott began to realize that the migration of black workers didn't just help the North, but it also damaged the South—and anything that did that was a boon. The *Defender* gleefully reprinted a dispatch describing how "the white people of the extreme South are becoming alarmed over the steady moving of race families out of the mineral belt."[42] Henceforth, the *Defender* did not just advise black people to leave the South, it *implored* them. One editorial said, "I beg you, my brother, to leave the benighted land. . . . If you can freeze to death in the North and be free, why freeze to death in the South and be a slave, where your mother, sister, and daughter are raped and burned at the stake; where your father, brother, and sons are treated with contempt and hung to a pole, riddled with bullets at the least mention that he does not like the way he is treated. Come North then, all you folks, good and bad."[43] The newspaper backed up its claim that work was to be found by running a great many want ads, specifying the numbers of openings available and the salaries to be paid.

Abbott's most forceful move was what he called the "Great Northern Drive"—a mass exodus from the South. The formal date for its beginning was set as May 15, 1917, but the *Defender's* mere announcement of the event inspired thousands to set out months before. In February 1917 the newspaper said, "Thousands have left for the north and thousands are still leaving, and a million will leave with the Great Northern Drive." A month later a *Defender* article reported that people were leaving Birmingham, Alabama, "by the thousands." The exodus was already unstoppable.

Not that some southerners didn't try to stop it. Whites in the South realized that they were losing their workers, their field hands, their maids. As a Macon, Georgia, newspaper put it, "We must have the Negro in the South. It is the only labor we have, it is the best we possibly could have—if we lose it, we go bankrupt!"[44] At first the white southerners blamed "labor agents," white troublemakers who roamed Dixie enticing black southerners to emigrate. They did exist, and some northern businesses, including a few in Chicago, did recruit black southerners, but when the war came agents were not needed. The exodus was self-sustaining. White southerners tried different tactics to keep their black workers home. New Orleans was the southern terminus of the Illinois Central, and the mayor of that city telegraphed the president of the railroad and asked that he stop carrying black passengers to the North. The response was that although the railroad did not exactly encourage migration, it could not refuse to sell tickets.[45] In some cities officials closed the railroad ticket office or police evicted black people from the railroad station or even arrested them. In March 1917 the *Defender* reported that in Savannah, black would-be passengers "were NOT ALLOWED the privilege of even entering the station to wait for the train and were forced back by the bully police to the adjoining streets. The police had no respect nor regard for the women and children. They used their clubs freely and beat some people badly. . . . Many of the people took the street car and rode three miles from here, and others, fearing trouble, went eight miles to the next station. Some waited all night for the train which did not come."[46] In 1917 a Georgia newspaper estimated that nearly a hundred black people were leaving Savannah every week, "and those who are going are the better class of blacks. The worthless ones are remaining here to be cared for. . . . Just what the remedy is to prevent it we do not know."[47]

Some white employers sent agents of their own to the North to attempt to persuade black émigrés to return. The *Defender* reported one such occasion, in which a representative of a Mississippi lumber business appeared at the headquarters of the Urban League in Chicago before a group of some two hundred black émigrés. He said that he had many logs that needed sawing and needed many men to do it. "The silence was painful. Finally one courageous man spoke up and said: 'I tell you what you do; you send the logs up to Chicago and we'll saw them up here.'"[48] T. Arnold Hill, an official of the Chicago Urban League, explained that the city's black population was not responsive to the labor agents because "the promises of fairer treatment and unrestricted economic development are powerless because they are barren. Negroes know they are barren. The good intentioned white persons of the South in serious moments confess their own impotence to deal with community problems. They are, unfortunately, as helpless as Negroes themselves in changing conditions."[49]

Measures against the *Defender* were part of the antimigration effort. A Georgia newspaper denounced the *Defender* as "the greatest disturbing element that has yet entered Georgia."[50] In many southern communities, the authorities ordered copies to be confiscated and distributors took to smuggling the newspaper in. And although African Americans might have idolized Chicago, many southern whites hated the place, seeing it, as Thomas Dyja has put it, "as the capital of uppity negritude." Dyja cited the poet William Alexander Perry, who wrote, "Every black buck in the South today has gone or will go to Chicago, where it is not only possible but inexpensive to sleep with a white whore."[51]

The duties of the *Defender* did not stop once a black worker had gotten aboard a train. Migrants might not have known a great deal about Chicago, but they did know that the offices of the *Defender* were there. In February 1918 the newspaper reported the story of Robert A. Wilson of Atlanta, who said, "I landed in Chicago April 2 with one nickel and a Lincoln penny. I spent my last nickel for car fare to the Defender office and the penny for a handful of peanuts. . . . After interviewing Mr. Abbott, editor of the Defender, I was advised to see Mr. Hill of the Urban League, which would enable me to secure employment. I left with the good wishes of the Defender office 'to make good.'" The story went on to relate how Mr. Wilson eventually found a job paying an excellent wage of $7 a day, how his wife and brother came to join him in Chicago, and how he went on to acquire a bank account, a house, and an adjoining lot.[52]

When the United States entered World War I, the *Defender* advised black citizens to support the war in the hopes that their participation would lead to civil rights advances. Abbott argued for the inclusion of black officers in the army and was invited to a meeting in 1918 of thirty-one representatives of the black press to discuss black involvement in the war effort. Secretary of War Newton D. Baker had appointed a "special Negro assistant," Emmett J. Scott, who convened the assembly. According to one report of the meeting, "every man was encouraged to voice any complaint or objection that might be apparent in his section of the country. The talks gave proof of unwavering loyalty."[53] After three days the group issued a set of recommendations called a "bill of particulars," one of which included sending a black war correspondent overseas. That turned out to be Ohio newspaperman Ralph W. Tyler, but Abbott also dispatched his own man, Roscoe Conkling Simmons, who fell in love with Paris and stayed there, avoiding the front and interviewing soldiers on leave.

The U.S. Department of Justice was skeptical about the patriotic fervor of the black press, and indeed, the war proved a tough sell in the black community. Although the supposed German atrocities in Belgium were ballyhooed as a reason for war, black Americans were well aware of the bona fide atrocities committed by the Belgians in their Congo colony and saw little need to protect a people capable of such cruelty. Their feelings toward the British colonialists, who had their own African empire, were only slightly less disapproving. But the main source of discontent in the black press was the lack of civil rights and ongoing racial discrimination, both in and out of the military. Black newspapers were vigorously reporting instances of racial injustice, and some in Washington began wondering whether such protests could morph into treason. The attorney general, A. Mitchell Palmer, therefore began an investigation into the loyalty of the black press. One of the publications that most interested Palmer was the pacifist and socialist *Messenger*, edited by A. Philip Randolph and Chandler Owen, which opposed U.S. entry into the war. Randolph and Owen were even charged with treason, and although the charges were dropped, the *Messenger* lost its second-class mailing privileges. The *Defender* did not face charges of disloyalty, but government investigators did look into its affairs. An investigator was charged with assessing the *Defender*, and after doing so, he sent Abbott a memorandum explaining the government's concern. That memo has disappeared, but Abbott's lengthy reply has survived. In it he stated, "I say with absolute certainty that without a doubt," the newspaper "has never at any time spoken disloyal."[54] He pointed out that he had personally subscribed to $12,000 in Liberty Loans and had advised his employees to also support the campaign. This seemed to settle the loyalty issue as far as the *Defender* was concerned.

After the war Abbott continued to advocate for migration and civil rights. In 1923 he and his managing editor, Lucius Harper, created the Bud Billiken Club for black youth. This led to the Bud Billiken Day Parade, which remains the oldest and largest black parade in the country. When Abbott died in 1940, control of the newspaper passed to his nephew John H. H. Sengstacke. In 1956 Sengstacke turned the paper into a daily and renamed it the *Chicago Daily Defender*. He died in 1997, and in 2008 the paper returned to weekly publication as a result of financial problems. Like many other American newspapers, it struggles with the challenges of the digital age—competition from the Internet, fewer readers, and decreased advertising.

Life in Chicago

The Illinois Central station in Chicago served as a portal that often eased the migrants' transition to the city. Many migrants arranged things so they would arrive on a Sunday— that way relatives or friends would be able to meet them at the station. Inside the station were both station officers and city police available to answer questions, although many migrants, because of experiences with southern police, were hesitant to speak to men in uniform. Another option was the Travelers Aid Society. Initially, there was a problem with the society because it was staffed mostly by white women, and black men from the South knew the dangers of initiating a conversation with a white woman, but eventually the society hired a black representative. The Travelers Aid Society commonly directed migrants to either the offices of the Urban League or the black branches of the YMCA or YWCA. In addition, black porters and doormen were readily visible in the station and served as nonthreatening sources of information.

The Illinois Central Depot was the portal to Chicago for thousands of black migrants. The Illinois Central Railroad ran up from the South like a great steel river. Author's collection

Newly arrived black migrants usually went to live on the South Side, because either someone they knew had preceded them there or they were directed there by whomever they asked. A Black Belt was taking shape, stretching from just south of the Loop mostly along State Street as far as about Fifty-Fifth Street, an area that would become known as Bronzeville. Overcrowding was not yet a problem—the houses migrants found were shabby but large. In the 1920s, however, their growing numbers were squeezed into crowded housing as de facto housing segregation solidified and landlords began to subdivide large houses into small apartments. It would be a mistake, though, to label the entire Black Belt of the war years a ghetto consisting only of substandard housing. The area, as historian Christopher Robert Reed has expressed it, was rather "a constantly expanding South Side enclave with housing and lifestyles that ranged from extravagant to middle class to commonplace to deteriorating."[55]

The migrants for the most part were much younger than the black citizens already living in Chicago, and some of the old-timers saw them as being too high-spirited. Some middle-class black Chicagoans were dismayed by the appearance and behavior of their rural cousins, with their head rags and aprons and their proclivity for setting up curbside barbecue and watermelon stands. One of them said that the black people who were in Chicago before the war "were just about civilized and didn't make apes out of themselves like the ones who came here during 1918."[56] Various entities, including churches, the YMCA, and the *Defender*, counseled the newcomers on the need for good manners and proper deportment.

Although the migrants created a lively entertainment district in the Stroll, they also established businesses and organizations; many formed clubs based on the state they came from. And they went to church. The *Defender* regularly published messages from churches saying things like "newcomers are welcome." Olivet Baptist Church, along with other large churches, as historian James R. Grossman has put it, "viewed the newcomers as a challenge to their expanded programs, which included such services as employment bureaus, housing directories, and day nurseries. Others offered guidance, dynamic preaching, or 'good singing.' The migrants responded enthusiastically. Olivet, which soon claimed to be the largest Baptist church in the world, added more than five thousand members between 1916 and 1919."[57] It grew so crowded, one parishioner said, that "we'd have to stand up. I don't care how early we'd go, you wouldn't get in."[58] Walters African Methodist Episcopal (AME) Church on the South Side, founded in 1875, tripled its membership.

The Urban League was founded in New York in 1910 as the Committee on Urban Conditions among Negroes, and the Chicago branch, known as the Chicago Urban League (CUL), was established on December 11, 1916.[59] The organization concentrated on aiding the migrants, and because of the publicity given it by the *Defender*, which supported the CUL and let its readers know that it was "the society in Chicago that cares for colored emigrants," they knew it was the place to get help in finding shelter and a job. Within just the first eight months of its existence, the CUL had aided seven thousand people, and it went on to assist thousands more. In the first year of the Great Migration more than two thousand letters poured into the league's offices asking about finding work.[60]

As a civil rights organization, the CUL was unique and prestigious in that it was closely linked to the University of Chicago, where the Chicago School of Sociology was at that time pioneering the new field of sociology and sending researchers into communities to study the life patterns of inhabitants. By formulating theories of assimilation, the Chicago sociologists argued that behaviors were rooted in conditions of life and not, as racist theories of the day would have it, in inherent racial characteristics.[61] The first president of the CUL was Robert E. Park, a white professor of sociology at the University of Chicago who, having worked with Booker T. Washington at Tuskegee University, was viewed as an expert on the problems of African Americans. He believed that prejudice could foster a sense of solidarity among black people. Although Park apparently considered himself free of racism, he nevertheless succumbed to racial theorizing. He believed that black people showed a "disposition for expression rather than for enterprise and action" and went so far as to muse that a little race mixing and the introduction of white blood might make black people more "aggressive and ambitious."[62] Park outlined three major tasks for the CUL: providing black organizations with the facts they needed to function effectively, acting as an intermediary between the city's black people and its welfare agencies, and evaluating the needs of black Chicagoans and advising them on where to get help. The CUL explicitly did not want to become a welfare organization itself; its goal was to be a "clearing house" that would refer people in need to the proper agencies.

Another main area of interest of the CUL was housing—specifically, the substandard, crowded conditions that many newcomers endured. The league attributed this especially to two factors: first, discrimination from white landlords, real estate developers, and bankers; and second, the behavior of the black residents themselves, whose "unawareness of proper conduct and indifference to the upkeep of their properties" worsened the deterioration of their neighborhoods. The view was that the rural background of the arrivals was making it difficult for them to adapt to urban life, and the CUL became active in moral and educational training in what was labeled a program of "uplift" to advance the migrants. "Partly to dispel racist sentiments among whites . . . ," the CUL "offered blacks printed instructions outlining proper comportment in the city." The organization published lists of dos and don'ts that urged the newcomers "to 'bring about *a new order of living*.'"[63]

Improving industrial conditions and elevating the status of black workers were also of concern to the CUL. Many newcomers had been rural workers unaccustomed to the routines of factory work, and employers needed to be convinced that a black workforce would be efficient and reliable. The lists of dos and don'ts were part of the effort to discipline the workers; employer reassurance came in the form of direct appeal, and the CUL had a good record in placing black applicants in industrial jobs. According to historian Arvarh E. Strickland, "During its first eight months of operation, the League placed 1,792 applicants, and between November 1, 1917 and October 31, 1918, jobs were found for another 6,861."[64]

Another effective resource for the newcomers was the all-black Wabash Avenue YMCA, which was where the CUL was founded. The *Defender* went so far as to proclaim that the opening of this institution was equal in importance to the Emancipation Proclamation.[65] It boasted "102 dormitory rooms, a swimming pool, a reading room, and other amenities needed to make urban adjustment easier."[66] The Y worked with

the meatpacking industry to steer workers to their plants. The meatpackers then turned to the YMCA to help them set up recreational clubs—sports teams, singing groups, orchestras, and the like—for their black employees. Overwhelmingly, the new workers fulfilled their employers' hopes. A study done in the early 1920s found that white and black productivity were about the same, and a 1920 survey of employers reported that nearly all were pleased with the dependability and competence of their black employees.

For recreation, lodging, and help in finding work, many male African American migrants turned to the YMCA, such as this all-black one in Chicago around 1915. Library of Congress

Racial tension spiked as dwellers in the Black Belt began moving into all-white neighborhoods—a process that continued well into the second half of the twentieth century. Mainstream Chicago newspapers reported the influx of black people with such language as "peril to health." In an editorial the *Tribune* called the Great Migration a "huge mistake" and cried, "Black man, Stay South!"[67] The escalation of the black population led to an intensification of racism in Chicago, and black people who bought houses in white neighborhoods often had their properties bombed, which sometimes resulted in the inhabitants' death. In one instance a six-year-old girl was one of the victims. According to historian Thomas Lee Philpott, "By the spring of 1919, bombs were going off at the rate of two per month, and the rate was rising."[68] Bombers also struck the homes of real estate agents, white and black, who sold to black home buyers.[69] In the 1920s, with the blessing and advice of the Chicago Real Estate Board, many white neighborhoods adopted what were known as "restrictive covenants" that effectively sealed off their turf from African Americans, at least for some years.[70] In 1920, 36 percent of Chicago's black population lived in a tract that was more than 75 percent black; in 1910 none did. By 1930 nearly two-thirds of Chicago's black population lived in tracts that were more than 90 percent black.[71] As Allan H. Spear has written, "The majority of Chicago's Negroes now lived in black enclaves; the 'scattered' portion of the Negro population had almost disappeared. . . . An unprecedented influx of Negro migrants from the Deep South swelled Chicago's black belt and converted it into a solidly Negro community that cut through the heart of the South Side."[72] The mounting tensions over housing were a major cause of the race riot that flamed up in 1919. In that year, while the Black Belt suffered a housing shortage, there was an "abundant surplus" in the rest of the city.[73]

The sheer size of the new black population of Chicago meant new institutions of all kinds—banks, insurance companies, manufacturing enterprises, sports teams, restaurants, nightclubs, storefront churches—as well as more readers for the *Defender*, which made Robert Abbott a wealthy man. But the large numbers of black Chicagoans also meant that, like groups that had arrived earlier, they acquired political clout. The first black alderman in Chicago was Oscar De Priest, who served from 1915 to 1917 and went on to become a congressman. By 1983 Chicago had a black mayor, Harold Washington.

The Great Migration grew stronger in the 1920s; more than nine hundred thousand black southerners came north during that decade. The 1920s became a kind of golden age, as black people were able to move into city jobs, win electoral offices, and establish an effervescent culture. The Depression of the 1930s slowed migration, but World War II once again brought a labor shortage that launched what some historians have called a second Great Migration, which brought an additional 1.6 million north in the 1940s and 1.4 million more in the 1950s.[74] Another million followed in the 1960s, but that decade brought to Chicago, as it brought to many northern Rust Belt cities, a process of deindustrialization, as packinghouses, steel mills, and factories closed. Greater access to housing meant that black professionals were able to move to the suburbs or wealthier Chicago neighborhoods, but the loss of those professionals depleted the traditional black community, which became increasingly impoverished. Many black Chicagoans still had relatives in the South, and quite a few had selectively nostalgic memories of life there. As a result, in the 1980s a kind of "reverse migration" began to occur as black people headed to the South, which had undergone a metamorphosis in race relations since the civil rights movement. At the beginning of 2011 Census Bureau estimates showed that the black population of Chicago had fallen by about 11 percent between 2000 and 2009 and that whites were the largest racial group in the city for the first time since 1980. Some of the black decline was attributable to a decrease in black fertility and to suburbanization, but the effect of reverse migration was evident in the fact that Atlanta had replaced Chicago as the city with the second-largest black population in the United States (after New York). The Great Migration was over.

This chapter began with the story of Corneal Davis, whose family moved north from Mississippi to Chicago. There Davis attended John Marshall Law School and got involved in politics. He became a member of the Illinois General Assembly in 1943 and served until 1978. His nickname there was "the deacon." When, in the early 1940s, he threatened to withhold funds from the University of Illinois Medical School, he effectively brought about the end of racial discrimination at that institution. Working with Thurgood Marshall, he filed suit in Cairo, Illinois, on behalf of black teachers who were being paid less than white teachers and won the case. After retiring from the assembly, Davis was appointed to the Chicago Board of Election Commissioners and served from 1979 to 1986. He was an associate pastor at Quinn Chapel AME Church, the chairman of the Illinois Emancipation Proclamation Commission, and the first black Boy Scout scoutmaster in Chicago. He died in a South Side nursing home in 1995 at age ninety-four. What were the chances he would have achieved these things in Mississippi?

10

"That Was Music": Chicago Jazz

When World War I began in the summer of 1914, few Americans had ever heard the word *jazz*, much less listened to the music. But by the time the armistice was signed five years later, thousands were buying jazz records, dancing in jazz clubs, and purchasing instruments to join in the new sound. Jazz, so identified with the Roaring Twenties, really conquered America during the war years. And Chicago was at the center of it all, becoming "the jazz capital of the world" between 1915 and 1930.[1] F. Scott Fitzgerald was the first to use the term the "Jazz Age," in the title of his 1922 book of short stories, *Tales of the Jazz Age*, and in 1924 the *Chicago Defender* published an article titled "Jazz Most Popular Music of the Day."[2]

The traditional story of how Chicago became linked with jazz music goes something like this. In 1897 the New Orleans City Council, troubled by widespread prostitution, decided to restrict it to a designated red-light district called Storyville after the alderman Sidney Story, who had come up with the idea. In addition to bordellos, Storyville offered a new kind of music. Spun out of ragtime, marching band music, and the blues, it would eventually become known as jazz. The higher-class houses hired piano players, the best ones offered small ensembles, and out-of-town patrons were enthralled. But after the United States entered World War I, the secretary of the navy, fearing for the health and morality of his sailors, closed the Storyville bordellos. The famous district was no more, and the musicians were forced to find other places to work. They followed the Mississippi River north and landed in Chicago, which replaced New Orleans as the home of jazz.

It's a tidy narrative that explains a lot, but almost none of it is true. First, Storyville never really closed; prostitution was suppressed and dispersed to other parts of the city, but dance halls and saloons remained open, and jazz was still heard in New Orleans. Second, jazz was not born in bordellos. Some might have considered the music low-class, but it wasn't a soundtrack for sin. The early jazz bands played mostly in parades, on riverboats, in vaudeville theaters, at picnics, and for club groups. A musician might take a job in a sporting house when he could find nothing else, but as Sidney Bechet, one of the great early New Orleans jazzmen, once recollected, "In those days there was always some party going, some fish fry, and there was always some picnic around the lakes. . . . So how can you say Jazz started in whorehouses when the musicianers didn't have no real need for them?"[3] He concluded, "The way some people talk, you'd think we all sat and waited for Storyville to close."[4] Finally, jazz musicians began leaving for Chicago long before the Great War. One of the first was Spencer Williams, the composer of "Basin Street Blues," who arrived in Chicago in 1907. The pianist Tony (or "Toney") Jackson came to Chicago around 1912, and Jelly Roll Morton arrived in August 1914. His "Jelly Roll Blues," considered the first printed jazz composition, was published in Chicago a year later.[5] The first white New Orleans jazz band to hit Chicago was Tom Brown's Dixieland Jazz Band in 1915. The list goes on.

Although the Storyville tale doesn't stand up, World War I still was the catalyst for the emergence of jazz in Chicago. First, the war did affect the economy of New Orleans. Second, and most important, the war expedited the Great Migration, which brought thousands of black people to Chicago. They wanted entertainment, so cabarets, nightclubs, dance halls, and theaters opened to serve this new clientele, who, thanks to the jobs created by the labor shortage, now had money to spend on recreation.

Extensive research on over four hundred black jazz musicians has discovered that "about six out of seven major black jazz musicians born in the South before 1915 migrated to the North in the four decades preceding World War II."[6] The musicians found themselves in competition with the best, and as they learned from and attempted to outdo one another, this fostered an intensely creative atmosphere that allowed jazz to evolve from its rough-and-ready New Orleans roots into the sophisticated music that it became in the 1920s. Because of the Great War, it was in Chicago that this evolution mostly occurred.

Arrival of Jazz in Chicago

The first jazz musician to take the new music out of New Orleans appears to have been William Manuel ("Bill") Johnson, who was born in 1872 and lived to be a hundred. Considered to be the inventor of the "slap bass," he went in 1907 to Los Angeles (some New Orleans jazzmen headed not for Chicago, but for California). There he put together an ensemble called the Creole Band, which toured the country. Chicago bandleader Dave Peyton, a music columnist for the *Defender*, wrote that he saw the band play in Chicago well before World War I. He recalled, "How well do I remember that opening night, and at that time I predicted that the Creole style of playing music would soon grip the Middle West." In Peyton's view, it was the success of Johnson's seven-man group that inspired other New Orleans musicians to head to Chicago: "Their Creole brothers down home, learning of this success, decided to come to the land of the free and plenty money. One by one they came North, most all of them top-notchers on their instruments."[7]

In Peyton's opinion, however, the first musician "to do this kind of playing" was a Chicago-based clarinetist named Wilbur Sweatman, whom Peyton heard in 1906 at "a little picture house on S. State St." "Little did we think," Peyton wrote, "that Mr. Sweatman's original style of playing would be adopted by the great artists of today; but it is, and Mr. Sweatman can claim the honor of being the first to establish it."[8] Sweatman, however, who was born in Missouri in 1882, was hardly playing "Creole" music, and it's debatable that he was playing jazz at all—at least in 1906. He did go on to lead a true jazz band later in his career, but in the years before World War I, Sweatman, who was famous for playing three clarinets at once, was a vaudeville performer as much as a band leader. He learned from the innovators and from recordings and was quick to adapt to changing styles, and recognition of that evolution was what made Peyton praise Sweatman's priority. Music historian Tim Brooks has called Sweatman "one of the great pioneers of recorded African American music during the transitional years from ragtime to jazz."[9]

At the time of World War I, two important transitions in popular music occurred successively in Chicago: first, the evolution of jazz from ragtime, and second, the transition from early jazz, which often presented the music as a deliberately primitive, even clownish, entertainment, to a disciplined art music that highlighted the improvisational skills of gifted soloists.

Sweatman's career illustrates how a kind of proto-jazz was being played in other places besides New Orleans. Missouri, for example, was the cradle of ragtime, and the jazz bandleader Sam Wooding, who was from Philadelphia, once said that "jazz spontaneously originated all over the United States." The jazz legend Benny Carter believed that "if there had been no players coming from New Orleans, New York music would have gone on the way it did, more or less the same." The jazz played in Chicago in the World War I era *did* come largely from New Orleans. As Bechet recalled, by 1917 New Orleans musicians dominated the Chicago theater bands—the clarinet player Darnell Howard, he said, "was the only man who wasn't out of New Orleans who played with us."[10]

Sidney Bechet, who came to Chicago from New Orleans in 1917, said that by the time of the war New Orleans musicians dominated the Chicago jazz scene.
William P. Gottlieb via Wikimedia Commons

Chicago's Lively Music Scene

Even before jazz came to the Windy City, several factors had already made Chicago a dynamic musical center. Many music publishers were based there, and traveling vaudeville shows and other theater productions often began and ended their tours in Chicago. A black vaudeville circuit called the Theater Owners Booking Association (TOBA) provided a wide range of acts for Chicago's stages, and according to one jazz historian, as of December 1912 the city had 635 theaters, with 110 more being constructed[11] Additionally, Chicago had a large number of support facilities—arrangers, agents, writers, costumers, producers, musicians, and recording companies—and important recording studios were also in nearby Grafton, Wisconsin (Paramount) and Richmond, Indiana (Gennett).

A wide variety of black music besides jazz was being heard in Chicago before and during World War I. For example, a *Defender* article from October 24, 1914, tells of music ranging from "symphonic art to rag-time jollity," with Miss Caroline Lillison singing "from Johann Strauss to Irving Berlin"; "Mr. Sherwood, the great lyric tenor"; "little petite Marjorie Lorraine, the dainty of the dainties"; a group singing the choruses from Mendelssohn's *Elijah*; and "America's best unique composer, Mr. Clarence Jones, the man with the harmony idea." The orchestra at the Pekin Theater (also known as the Pekin Inn, Pekin Café, and Pekin Pavilion), a crucial venue for black music since 1904, was said to be "equally at home in rag time or grand opera."[12] The kinds of music played in black vaudeville houses included plantation melodies, country dances, minstrel tunes, cakewalks, and such prewar hits as "Darktown Strutters' Ball." It wasn't jazz, but it was popular.[13] Probably the most important black musical ensemble of the prewar era was the Society Orchestra, headed by James Reese Europe, musical director for the white dancing duo Vernon and Irene Castle, who created the social dancing craze of the early twentieth century. The Society Orchestra's rendition of the 1913 number "Too Much Mustard" (also known as "Tres Moutarde") is convincing evidence that the music of the prewar era was not sedate.[14] The tempo is frantic and the musicians are hardly less so. Chicagoans heard Europe's band when it played at the

Auditorium Theater in May 1919, and the *Defender* called it "a 'hot-stuff' musical organization."[15]

The transition from ragtime to jazz occurred against this variegated musical background. Musicians played in several styles and sometimes made little differentiation among them. Consider the titles of some of Jelly Roll Morton's compositions: "Dead Man Blues," "Frog-i-More Rag," "Black Bottom Stomp," "Georgia Swing," "Shoe Shiner's Drag," and "Mama Nita," a tango. Quite a few early recordings with "blues" in the title are not blues at all. Ragtime and jazz have some core features in common: metronomic pulse, basic two-beat meter, and lots of syncopation. In a sense, both can be thought of as treatments of basic models, as in "ragging" a march or "jazzing up" a song. But there are crucial differences. Ragtime is primarily an idiom for solo piano and uses composed pieces that are fixed before they are performed, and the forms of rags are mostly limited to two types: linear and rounded. Jazz takes a more varied approach to form. It also employs many instruments and ensemble types and relies heavily on pitch inflection—that is, bent notes or blue notes, the flattened degrees of the scale that characterize the blues.[16] Inflection enables performers to develop an individual sound and voice in a manner not available in ragtime. Jazz also blends premeditation and improvisation in a way that ragtime does not, and improvisation, like inflection, gives a jazz performer a unique musical profile.[17] This transition was worked out in several places, including New Orleans, but Chicago became the main laboratory. A local figure in the evolution of jazz from ragtime was the New Orleans–born violinist Charles Elgar, who was a leader of Local 208, the "Colored" branch of the American Federation of Musicians in Chicago.

Black Jazz on the South Side

The arrival of musicians from New Orleans made Chicagoans realize that a new sound had been born. Tony Jackson, whom the vainglorious Jelly Roll Morton considered his superior, played at the Pekin Theater. Morton believed that Jackson left New Orleans for Chicago because he "happened to be one of those gentlemens that a lot of people call them lady or sissy," and Chicago offered him "freedom."[18] When Bill Johnson's Creole Band first appeared in Chicago in 1914, it was on a vaudeville tour, so it didn't stay long. Morton, however, who also arrived in 1914, remained in Chicago for three years. He said that the reason he came to Chicago was because Jackson was there.

Listeners were unsure how to categorize this new music. Some considered it a type of ragtime. In a 1914 review of Johnson's band, for example, the *Los Angeles Examiner* said that "one has to hear them to appreciate what rag-time is."[19] As late as 1922, long past ragtime's heyday, the *Defender*, in reviewing a performance by the jazz singer Alberta Hunter, said she "has got them all beat when it comes to singing ragtime."[20] Another word used to describe the new sound was *Creole*. Columnist Peyton was so impressed by Johnson's Creole Band that he used the term to define the music in general, and he included Jimmie Noone, Manuel Perez, King Oliver, Charles Elgar, and Louis Armstrong among the "Creole" musicians in Chicago. A third term was *blues*. In 1915 *Chicago Tribune* writer Gordon Seagrove wrote a groundbreaking article titled "Blues Is Jazz and Jazz Is Blues," in which he tried to figure out what made the new sound distinctive.[21] He recounted an explanation by a piano player in a club: "A blue note is a sour note. It's a discord—a harmonic discord. The blues are never written into music, but are interpolated by the piano player or other players. They aren't new. They are just reborn into popularity. They started in the south half a century ago and are the interpolations of darkies originally. The trade name for them is 'jazz.'" The musician that Seagrove interviewed was probably referring to either the bent notes of jazz or the blue notes of the blues, or possibly to both. In any case, he made no distinction between blues and jazz; other contemporary writers groping for a word to describe the new music also referred to jazz as blues, although the two styles are distinct.

Eventually, *jazz* became the settled term. The first use of the word in the *Defender* appears to have come on September 16, 1916, in an article mentioning a performance by "Al Narcisse and his famous Jass Orchestra" in Milwaukee. Two weeks later the newspaper reviewed the appearance in Chicago of singer Estella Harris, who was accompanied by her "Jass entertainers." The group consisted only of Estella and the "famous Pekin

"The blues are never written into music, but are interpolated by the piano player or other players."

Trio," but it played Spencer Williams's "Shimme Sha Wabble," a tune that became a jazz standard.

However, by the time the *Defender* got around to using the word *jass*, Jelly Roll Morton had been performing in Chicago for nearly two years. Back in New Orleans, where he was born Ferdinand Joseph Lamothe, the flashy Morton was, in addition to being a great pianist and the first jazz composer, intermittently a gambler, pool shark, and pimp. He later claimed to have "invented jazz"; the derision that this braggadocio has drawn doesn't diminish his pivotal role, and his claim is probably as good as anyone's. In the opinion of jazz historian Gary Giddins, "He did prove to be, after all, the catalyst who transfigured ragtime and minstrelsy into a new music that adroitly weighed the respective claims of the composer and the improviser—in a word, jazz."[22] Morton traveled a good deal before he came to Chicago in 1914, and the three years he spent there were the years in which jazz took root in the city. After taking a job as music director of the Richelieu Café, Morton went to the De Luxe Café on South State Street, where he headed up a seven-piece ensemble, and then to the Elite Club, where he showcased Jelly Roll Morton and his Incomparables.[23]

"Have you heard Emanuel Perez's Creole Band?" asked the *Defender* in March 1918. "Have you not heard that wonderful jazz music that the people of Chicago are going wild about? It's gripping the dancers of the Windy City and causing people to come to the Pekin dancing pavilion, 2700 State street, and hear the music that's all the rage in the East and in the West. Chicago is not behind and never was. The jazz music is right at your door."[24] Emanuel, or Manuel, Perez was a cornet player who had been playing in New Orleans brass bands since the late 1880s. Louis Armstrong recalled hearing him play alongside King Oliver in the renowned Onward Brass Band. Perez came to Chicago in 1915 and took a job performing with Charles Elgar at the Ansonia Café before going out on his own. Elgar's ensemble was not considered a jazz group, but going by the *Defender*'s enthusiastic reports, Perez's Creole band definitely was when it performed at the Pekin Café. By all accounts, Perez was an expert musician, but his place in jazz history is minor, most likely because, although he lived until 1946, he made no records, and when jazz historians tried to interview him in the 1930s he refused to talk.

In Morton's opinion, Perez was the "perfect player": he never made a mistake. But when it came to exciting the crowd, Morton said, Perez took a backseat to Freddie Keppard, the cornet player with Johnson's Creole Band.[25] Chicagoans had many chances to hear this band because the Windy City was a regular stop on its tours. When the Creole Band was in New York in early 1916, the Victor Talking Machine Company offered to record it. The offer was refused, reportedly because Keppard thought that a record would let other musicians "steal his stuff." A second version of the story is that the group refused to make a demo record without being paid, and a third is that a test actually was made but Johnson's bass was so loud it broke the grooves.[26] Whatever the reason, it could have been the first jazz band to make a record; instead, it never made any. After the Creole Band broke up in 1918, mostly due to the alcoholic Keppard's unreliability, Keppard settled in Chicago and played with various bands, including his own. He made some recordings between 1924 and 1927, but according to John Chilton, "none of them indicates any degree of his genius."[27]

After making his first appearance in Chicago in 1917 with a touring group, Sidney Bechet returned in 1918 to join a band led by the clarinetist Lawrence Duhé at the De Luxe Café. Two clarinets were not unusual in a New Orleans band, but Bechet was "the featured hot man." Duhé once recalled that "Sidney couldn't read, but he only had to hear a piece once to be able to play it. He used his lips to get effects like chicken cackles."[28] Duhé's group soon moved to the prestigious Dreamland Café; while playing there, Bechet briefly took a second job with King Oliver at the Royal Gardens. In 1919 bandleader Will Marion Cook enticed Bechet to travel with him to Europe, and the great clarinetist left Chicago.

Nearly all of the cafés, cabarets, and dance halls in which these black New Orleans musicians performed were located on the Stroll, a brightly lit stretch of South State Street. The pianist Earl Hines found the scene there even better than in New York—"there seemed to be more night life, maybe because it was more concentrated."[29] Jazzman Eddie Condon once said, "I don't think so much good jazz was ever concentrated in so small an area. Around midnight you could hold an instrument in the middle of the street and the air would play it. That was music."[30]

It was a late-night crowd. In June 1919 the Royal Gardens Club was offering a musical comedy called "After July First," with shows at 11 P.M. and 1 A.M. According to the *Defender*, the Pekin Pavilion offered refreshments and "public dancing from 11 P.M. to 5 A.M."[31] Some black workingmen were in the habit of arising around 2 A.M. to hit the clubs for a few hours before heading off to their jobs. After prohibition became law in early 1920, many musicians played in speakeasies, where closing hours could be, let's say, flexible. Some black Chicagoans were not so enamored of the Stroll: "The *Chicago Defender* condemned the practice of strutting and of public ostentatious display of expensive clothing and other paraphernalia along the Stroll."[32] And the civil rights pioneer Ida B. Wells-Barnett lamented the vice and crime that pervaded the neighborhood.

A map of the Stroll featured in the book *Destination Chicago Jazz* shows no fewer than thirty music venues between South Twenty-Second and South Forty-Eighth Streets—most of them operated by black entrepreneurs.[33] Perhaps the most celebrated was Dreamland, at 3520 South State Street, "one of the most pleasant places of amusement on the South Side," according to the *Broad Ax* newspaper.[34] Operated by William Bottoms, one of the most admired black impresarios, it featured its own Original Jazz Band as early as June 1917. Among the performers who played Dreamland were King Oliver, Louis Armstrong, Sidney Bechet, and Ethel Waters, and the club was also the home of Doc Cook's Dreamland Ballroom Orchestra, which showcased such New Orleans musicians as Freddie Keppard, Jimmie Noone, Andrew Hilaire, and John St. Cyr. Alberta Hunter once said, "These clubs in New York haven't got a chance [compared] with what the Dreamland was. Only the Cotton Club . . . no, it didn't compare with the Dreamland."[35]

The proprietor of the Elite Café, which was first located at 3030 South State Street and then moved—as Elite Café No. 2—four blocks south, was Henry "Teenan" Jones, a South Side political strongman. Elite No. 2 featured both classical music and jazz, switching effortlessly, as one newspaper put it, from "grand opera" to "high class vaudeville."[36] Nearby was the Royal Gardens, which was renamed the Lincoln Gardens around 1921. The owner was Virgil Williams, whom the *Defender* hailed as "a public spirited man and a philosopher." In 1919 he spent over $3,000 to revamp the club in order to make it "the most beautiful place of its kind in America."[37] The Pekin Theater, or Café, at State and South Twenty-Seventh Streets, established by Robert Motts, became famous not only for musicians such as Tony Jackson, Manuel Perez, and Sidney Bechet but also as the place for a racially mixed audience to see elaborate stage shows. Motts died in 1911, and in 1916 the theater seats were replaced by a dance floor, which was the way it was when Manuel Perez played there.[38]

At most of the Chicago nightclubs of the era, a floor show with singers and dancers would commonly be presented first, and then patrons were allowed to take the floor. One much-noted feature on the South Side was interracial dancing in clubs known as "black and tans." Unsurprisingly, race mixing was a prominent cause for alarm in certain quarters. One newspaper article breathlessly described the scene at the Pekin this way: "lawless liquor, sensuous shimmy, solicitous sirens, wrangling waiters, all tints of the racial rainbow. . . . Black men with white girls, white men with yellow girls, old, young, all filled with the abandon brought about by illicit whisky and liquor music."[39] One reason for the popularity of "public dancing" was that a person could dance with a single partner for an entire evening. At conventional parties and balls, it would have been considered unmannerly not to dance with several partners, hence the request seen in novels of the time—"save the next dance for me."

White Jazz Downtown

While all this activity was taking place on the South Side, jazz was going strong in the Loop as well. Here too New Orleans musicians were in charge, but with a difference: these performers were white. Alongside the famous black jazz innovators, white band music also flourished in late nineteenth-century New Orleans. Drummer George "Papa Jack" Laine, for example, was playing in ensembles while he was still in grade school in the early 1880s. In addition, there was a strong Italian band tradition in which white jazz players were schooled. Many of these white jazz musicians later asserted that they were little influenced by black players and developed their sound on their own, although it's difficult to accept their more insistent claims because influences worked both ways. Papa Jack Laine, for one, hired Creole musicians, getting around the color line by claiming they were Hispanic.

The presence of white New Orleans jazz musicians in Chicago demonstrates that the arrival of jazz there was not due solely to the Great Migration. There were other incentives for both white and black musicians to leave New Orleans. Police harassment was one. New Orleans clubs were routinely raided, and for King Oliver a raid on the Winter Garden was the last straw that made him decide to leave.[40] But economic conditions played a larger role. Unemployment due to stagnant cotton prices had been a problem since the 1880s, and as Bechet's biographer, John Chilton, has written, "Business had been hit by various trade recessions that occurred as an aftermath of the outbreak of World War I in Europe (in 1914). Drummer Paul Barbarin said: 'The music business was at a standstill long before the district [Storyville] closed.'"[41] Although a new cotton warehouse, a new grain elevator, and an army supply base were built in New Orleans during World War I and barge traffic on the Mississippi increased, mechanization of the dock facilities led to labor disputes and strikes while the war was in progress.[42] The high cost of living was a major source of complaint; another was the effect of the wartime Shipping Act, which fixed shipping rates and which New Orleans officials protested for favoring eastern ports—it was often cheaper to ship goods to Latin America from New York than it was from New Orleans.[43] According to historian Daniel Rosenberg, the city "lost its share of national commerce during World War I, dropping from second to sixth among the leading ports between 1911 and 1918."[44]

Perhaps most important, jazzmen could make more money in Chicago. Most musicians who played in New Orleans had to take second jobs; for example, Manuel Perez and a few other Creole musicians worked as cigar makers. Southern musicians were lucky to make $5 a night, but in Chicago the union scale on the South Side climbed from $25 a week in 1920 to $52.50 two years later. By 1928 it was $75 a week, or "almost three times what Henry Ford was then paying black auto workers under his heralded 'five-dollar-a-day' wage."[45] These salaries didn't include tips, which could come to as much as $100 a week in the classier clubs. In the late 1920s, King Oliver and his musicians ranked in the top 10 percent of all American workers in earnings.

As early as January 1915 a white banjo player named Bert Kelly and his band began appearing at a club in Chicago's Hotel Sherman called the College Inn (soon to become a trendy music venue). Kelly later said he was the first bandleader to describe his group as a "jazz band." The claim isn't far-fetched, because Kelly came out of San Francisco, where the term *jazz* seems to have originated. In 1919 the *Literary Digest* quoted a jazz expert named Joseph K. Gorham as saying, "The phrase 'jazz band' was first used by Bert Kelly in Chicago in the fall of 1915, and was unknown in New Orleans."[46] In any case, Kelly's music was probably more like ragtime than classic jazz.[47] Also playing at the College Inn was an ensemble headed by saxophonist Paul Biese; his Novelty Orchestra made some recordings in 1919, and they don't sound especially jazzy either—both Kelly and Biese were playing syncopated music for dancing. Lawrence Gushee has said that the two bandleaders "are considered of no real consequence by orthodox jazz history," although the dancers surely found them plenty hot at the time.[48]

While appearing in New Orleans around 1913, a touring vaudeville comedian named Joe Frisco discovered a white band-leader named Tom Brown and his group.[49] He asked the band to come to Chicago, and in mid-May 1915 Frisco and Brown's ensemble began playing an engagement at Smiley Corbett's Lamb's Café in the basement of the Olympic Theater at Clark and Randolph Streets. At first business was slow, but once the word got out, the crowds started to pour in. The group advertised itself as "Brown's Dixieland Jazz Band, Direct from New Orleans, Best Dance Music in Chicago" and the sheer novelty of this odd new word *jazz* drew people in just to see what it was all about.[50] Soon other clubs, such as the Casino Gardens on North Clark Street, were bringing in New Orleans musicians, and white jazz had become a Chicago fixture.[51] Like the Creole Band, Tom Brown's ensemble never made records.

A group that did make records—and history—was the Original Dixieland Jazz Band. It was hardly the best jazz band of the era (although not as bad as its detractors say), but it gained an unshakable place in music annals by cutting what has been called the first jazz record—and this record rocketed around the country, setting off a jazz craze and inspiring youngsters everywhere to take up their instruments and give this new sound a whirl. This

Meet Me at the
Green Goose, Dearie

Words by
O. C. TAYLOR

Music by
EMIL CHRISTIAN

Featured by Bert Kelly's Jazz Band at the Green Goose

TROMBONE

EMIL CHRISTIAN
Composer of
'Green Goose Dearie'

CLARINET

ALCIDE NUNEZ
Composer of
'Livery Stable Blues'

BANJO

BERT KELLY
(Himself)

DRUMS

(Rag Baby)
STEVENS
America's Greatest
Ragtime Drummer

PIANO

HARRY FOSTER

Compliments of **BERT KELLY**

Phone Lake View 9261   3101 N. Clark St., Chicago

The banjo player Bert Kelly and his band began performing in Chicago as early as January 1915. One of the clubs where they played was the uptown Green Goose, the name of which gave rise to a pop song. Wikimedia Commons

FLYING HIGH in NEW ORLEANS

The first white New Orleans jazz band to come to Chicago was Tom Brown's group, which arrived in 1915. This novelty postcard, made in New Orleans just before Brown's departure, shows (*left to right*) Alcide Nunez (clarinet), Tom Brown (trombone), and Frank Christian (cornet) flying over Canal Street in a balloon. Wikimedia Commons

ensemble, headed by drummer Johnny Stein, began life as Stein's Dixieland Jass Band, which Chicago club owner Harry James discovered in New Orleans. He booked them into Schiller's Café, which was not downtown but on East Thirty-First Street and Calumet Avenue. The *Chicago Herald* described the scene like this: "The shriek of women's drunken laughter rivaled the blatant scream of the imported New Orleans Jass Band, which never seemed to stop playing. Men and women sat, arms about each other, singing, shouting, making the night hideous, while their unfortunate brethren and sisters fought in vain to join them."[52]

According to cornet player Nick LaRocca, "After the sensation we created, other café owners sent to New Orleans for men who were supposed to play our kind of music. They imported anybody that could blow an instrument, and they all had 'New Orleans Jass Band' in front of their names." Soon after, three members of the group, LaRocca, Eddie Edwards, and Alcide Nunez, left Stein's band. The remaining group members added two other New Orleans musicians, Tony Sbarbaro and Larry Shields; named their group the Original Dixieland Jazz Band (ODJB); and opened at the Café de l'Abbée in Chicago's Normandie Hotel on June 2, 1916. A month later they moved to the Casino Gardens.

The music of the ODJB has been called "nut jazz" and has been described as "frenetic," "funny-hat," "nervous," and "rowdy."

The Original Dixieland Jazz Band, the first band to make a jazz record, created a sensation at Schiller's Café on East Thirty-First Street and Calumet Avenue. Wikimedia Commons

That's just what the band wanted. They exalted their own primitivism to the point of falsely claiming that they couldn't read music. A sometimes forgotten characteristic of early jazz was just this cartoonish, comic quality. For example, a 1920 photograph of the white entertainer Ted Lewis at Chicago's Edelweiss Gardens shows him in a tuxedo but his musicians in genuine clown outfits.[53] A 1922 article in the *Defender* included this colorful description of a group called the High Brown Five: "The five members went through all the antics which Negro orchestras are noted for when they start syncopating and harmonizing. Drum sticks flew in the air, the fiddler danced, the saxophone strutted, the piano player did everything but walk on the keys, and over and above all the hilarity that went with the music there was such banjo playing as has not been heard for many a day."[54] Even Jelly Roll Morton was not above going the slapstick route; sometimes he would "dress in bell-bottom pants and cowboy hat, presenting a clownish image to listeners."[55]

The ODJB did not stay in Chicago but took its circus act to New York, where the group was a sensation. It was in New York that on February 26, 1917, the band recorded "Livery Stable Blues," normally cited as the first jazz record. However, it's an interesting footnote to jazz history that in 1916 a Chicago songwriter named Henry L. Marshall published a tune titled "That

Funny Jas Band from Dixieland," and it's likely that Brown's group or the ODJB was his inspiration. A recording of Marshall's song was actually released a month before "Livery Stable Blues." Although it tries to mimic early jazz's boisterousness, it's more of a parody.

Although the two groups that pioneered white New Orleans jazz in Chicago did not stay in the city long, their effect endured. For example, when a teenage piano player in Davenport, Iowa, named Leon Beiderbecke (better known as "Bix") heard the ODJB records, he immediately taught himself to play the cornet. Four years later he was playing in Chicago himself, and before long he was jamming in the wee hours with Louis Armstrong. It's difficult to exaggerate the importance of Bix in the 1920s, when young, usually white, wannabes coveted his sweet cornet tone and emulated his wayward lifestyle.

The ODJB was followed in Chicago by the New Orleans Rhythm Kings (NORK), a group led by cornet player Paul Mares that included clarinetist Leon Roppolo, whom jazz historian Richard Sudhalter has called "the first great jazz soloist to appear on records."[56] The NORK made history in July 1923 when they cut six sides at the Gennett Studios in Richmond, Indiana, with Jelly Roll Morton at the piano—the first interracial jazz records.

In 1923 a group of Chicago teenagers hanging out at an ice cream parlor called the Spoon and Straw listened to some of the NORK Gennett platters. As cornet player Jimmy McPartland later recalled, "I believe the first tune we played was 'Farewell Blues.' Boy, when we heard that, I'll tell you we went out of our minds. Everybody flipped. It was wonderful. So we put the others on. We stayed there from about three in the afternoon until eight at night, just listening to those records one after another, over and over again. Right then and there we decided we would get a band and try to play like these guys."[57] McPartland and his pals became known as the Austin High Gang, a group of adolescent Chicago musicians who went on to distinguished careers in jazz, the best known, besides McParland, being the saxophonist Bud Freeman and the clarinetist Frank Teschemaker. Other young Chicago musicians who were either inspired by or played with the Austin High Gang were Gene Krupa, Muggsy Spanier, Eddie Condon, and Benny Goodman, who in the 1930s became known as the "King of Swing." New Orleans musicians had sowed the seeds, but now there was a music known as Chicago jazz. And it was still called Chicago jazz even when many of its practitioners went to New York, which was where the major recordings were being made.

King Oliver and Louis Armstrong

In early 1918 the man himself came to Chicago—King Oliver, who was called "King" for a reason. According to Edmond Souchon, who was a fan of Oliver's in New Orleans, by the early 1920s Oliver was "the most important personage in the jazz world."[58] Following the breakup of the Creole Band, Bill Johnson reached out to Oliver to replace Keppard. After arriving in Chicago, Oliver eventually became the leader, and Johnson settled in as the bass player. Oliver's band played at the De Luxe Café, at Dreamland, and at the Pekin Inn. He spent a couple of years in Los Angeles, but in June 1922 he returned to Chicago and took up residence at the redecorated Royal Gardens, soon renamed the Lincoln Gardens. As the *Defender* reported in 1923, "Lincoln Gardens in E. 31st St. seems to have taken on new life and the nightly attendance has grown to close to capacity. The fact that King Oliver's Creole Jazz band furnished the music at the handsome resort no doubt has a great deal to do with its present popularity." The *Defender* said that Oliver's group was the "razziest, jazziest band you ever heard" and "the finest Negro jazz band that ever came out of New Orleans."[59]

According to music historian William Howland Kenney, Oliver "recorded sixty-six sides" and "made more records than

Clarinetist Benny Goodman, who went on to become the "King of Swing," was one of many Chicago teens who were enthralled by the new sound of jazz. Library of Congress

223

any Chicago band leader of the twenties except Jelly Roll Morton."[60] The magic of digital restoration has enabled listeners to hear Oliver's recordings with unexpected fidelity, and they demonstrate, as jazz historian Gary Giddins has written, that "as a cornetist, his impassioned playing reaches us across the decades, conveying a solitary dignity, a pain and urgency, even as it spurs his cohorts to action."[61]

By 1923 the quantity of jazz records had grown so large that young fans, such as the Austin High Gang, no longer had to hear the music live (this was a major shift in the history of music in general). And although Oliver's records were among the most influential, his band became even more celebrated after he sent a telegram to twenty-one-year-old Louis Armstrong in New Orleans asking him to come to Chicago and play second cornet. Armstrong arrived in early August 1922 and made his first recordings with Oliver's band on April 5, 1923, at the Gennett Studios. In February 1924 he married the band's piano player, Lil Hardin, and in September of that year he accepted an invitation from Fletcher Henderson to join him in New York. Armstrong returned to Chicago in 1925 and there organized the Hot Five and the Hot Seven, groups that made a series of recordings that still rank among the greatest in any musical genre.[62] Armstrong played with Erskine Tate at the Vendome Theater, with the Carroll Dickerson Orchestra at the Sunset Café, and with his own band, Louis Armstrong and His Stompers. He moved back to New York in 1929.

Pop music critics like to speculate about the "artist of the century," and because they usually base their opinions on numbers of record sales and their personal memories, they normally come up with the Beatles, Elvis Presley, or Michael Jackson. But Louis Armstrong almost certainly has the best case. First, he taught musicians how to "swing." *Swing* is a difficult term to define; it involves playing just behind or ahead of the beat and altering the duration of the notes as written, giving the music an extemporaneous quality. Second, Armstrong turned jazz into a soloist's art by expanding the concept of improvisation and making even the greatest songs a springboard for new composition. Third, despite his uniquely gravelly voice, his style of singing influenced just about every pop singer that came after him (Bing Crosby most notably). Armstrong brought

When King Oliver needed another cornet player, he reached out to Louis Armstrong of New Orleans. During his years in Chicago, Armstrong developed the style and reputation that made him the most celebrated of all jazz musicians.
Library of Congress

to vocal stylization a timing, a phrasing, and a looseness that revolutionized popular singing. Finally, he reached his musical maturity at the same time that technology was enabling him to have a global audience. Electrical recording was replacing the crude acoustic method, sound films were in development, live radio was becoming widespread, and a new group of American songwriters were creating refined melodies and harmonic structures that turned out to be perfect for jazz improvisation. Armstrong took advantage of all these developments.

As Giddins has expressed it, Armstrong's music "changed the cultural direction of America and took possession of the world."[63] Although this happened after World War I, the Great War was a crucial factor in bringing New Orleans jazz musicians to Chicago. Among them was King Oliver, who then brought Louis Armstrong, who then brought jazz to everyone.

11

"Sweet Home Chicago":
The Chicago Blues

Frommer's Chicago, one of the major guidebooks to the city, calls Chicago simply "the world capital of the blues." It urges visitors to head to one of the city's blues clubs because "if there's any music that epitomizes Chicago, it's the blues." For many visitors, a night at a blues club is as essential a Chicago experience as Millennium Park or deep-dish pizza.

The blues has been heard in Chicago for a long time—since the time of World War I, in fact. But although clubgoers seek a kind of "authenticity" in what they hear, the music a tourist finds today is much different from what was heard in 1917. Nevertheless, the presence of the crowds that pack Chicago's contemporary blues venues is a vibrant example of how events that occurred during World War I still influence Chicago today.

The Background of the Blues

The *Oxford English Dictionary* has traced the use of the word *blue* to describe a state of melancholy to as far back as 1550 and cites Washington Irving as describing someone as "in a fit of the blues" in 1807. The term "blue funk" is as old as 1861. Given that etymology, it's not surprising that blues music has been thought of as the painful cry of someone who is anxious or depressed, even suppressed. Music critics have therefore spoken of blues-like music in other cultures, such as *fado* (Portugal), flamenco (Spain), *rebetiko* (Greece), *morna* (Cape Verde), and tango (Argentina).

The idea of the blues has taken such a powerful hold on the American imagination that a mythology has grown up around it. When one journeys to the Delta Blues Museum in Clarksdale, Mississippi, and sees the remains of the cabin that once housed the bluesman Muddy Waters (born McKinley Morganfield), one is face-to-face with the romanticized version of where the blues came from—dirt-poor sharecroppers who

played mournful songs on homemade guitars, refrains with their roots in Africa, pieces based on "field hollers" or "moans" carried over from plantation days, and call-and-response refrains chanted by chain-gang prisoners. It's all the more meaningful because Muddy Waters is thought of as the most significant musician who brought the Delta blues to Chicago, plugged his guitar into an amplifier, and created the post–World War II Chicago blues sound that rules the city's clubs today.

But the idea that blues is a music born of distress is belied by this comment from W. C. Handy, the acknowledged "father of the blues": "The sorrow songs of the slaves we call Jubilee Melodies. The happy-go-lucky songs of the Southern Negro we call blues." Or this statement by bluesman B. B. King: "It angers me how scholars associate the blues strictly with tragedy."[1] Some of the earliest recorded "blues" songs are actually sprightly, even sunny.

Around the time of World War I, when the blues began to catch on nationally, it was viewed not as folk music but as pop music. Most of the musicians were professionals who were

The cabin that once was home to bluesman Muddy Waters is now in a museum in Clarksdale, Mississippi. The iconic structure is something of a symbol of the romanticized version of the origin of the blues. Photograph by the author proud of their ability to play not only blues numbers but also anything their audiences liked, including Tin Pan Alley hits, rags, old minstrel tunes, and comic vaudeville numbers. They played for dances and needed to keep things lively. The blues artists thought of themselves as projecting a new sound, a modern sound, and they dressed the part—not in overalls and homespun but in outfits as sharp as they could find: pinstripe suits for the men, sequined gowns for the women. As blues historian Elijah Wald has expressed it, "If someone had suggested to the major blues stars that they were old-fashioned folk musicians carrying on a culture handed down from slavery times, most would probably have been insulted."[2]

Although some performers became identified primarily with the blues and specialized in it, in the 1910s and 1920s blues was not thought of as a genre, as it is now. It was a certain kind of song that a versatile performer might have in his or her repertory. For example, Bessie Smith, the "Empress of the Blues," recorded several pop standards and at the end of her life was moving into swing. It's unlikely that anyone attending a Chicago blues club today will hear a rendition of "After You've Gone," which Bessie recorded in 1927 with a band that included Fletcher Henderson on piano and Coleman Hawkins on tenor saxophone. Ethel Waters and Alberta Hunter, two acclaimed blues singers of the 1920s, developed even more varied repertoires, and Marion Harris, who went by the title "Queen of the Blues," recorded such songs as "Tea for Two" and George Gershwin's "The Man I Love."

Although the way local musicians in the South played the blues could vary from county to county, blues historians have identified three more or less distinct regional styles: Texas blues; Piedmont or East Coast (Georgia and the Carolinas mostly) blues; and the Delta blues, which is the most studied and admired. The Delta musicians are the most iconic, especially Robert Johnson, a second-generation bluesman. Johnson did a great favor for the Second City by composing the famous "Sweet Home Chicago," which is now something of a city blues anthem. (Listeners might be puzzled by the lines in that song that say, "Back to the land of California / To my sweet home Chicago." "California," it seems, refers not to the Golden State, but to California Avenue on Chicago's West Side.) In addition to these three regions, there is evidence that the blues was being played in New Orleans at the beginning of the twentieth century, and many of the jazz stars who came from the Crescent City, like Jelly Roll Morton and Louis Armstrong, were familiar with the blues. Where the blues ends and jazz begins is a difficult topic (see chapter 10), and in the early years many listeners believed they were more or less the same thing. By the 1930s the popularity of such jazz bands as Count Basie's, which played many blues numbers, made it nearly impossible to disentangle the two kinds of music. Nevertheless, although blues performers from all traditions played in Chicago, the sound that became identified with the city is drawn predominantly from the Mississippi Delta.

As with the term *jazz*, attempts to compose a definition of *blues* consistently run into exceptions (improvisation, for example, is often thought of as an essential jazz trait, but many jazz performances do just fine without it). Musicians, however, know what is meant when someone asks them to play or jam on a "blues"—a twelve-bar structure in 4/4 time with a chord structure of I (tonic)–IV (subdominant)–V (dominant) that employs the "blues scale," normally understood as a diatonic scale with flattened third, fifth, and seventh degrees. (Interestingly, there is also such a thing as a British blues scale. Once used by English folk singers, its preservation in Appalachia has made it difficult for folk song collectors to determine whether the bluesy character of an American tune is of British or African origin.)[3] There are also eight-bar and sixteen-bar blues, but purchasers of sheet music and records in the 1910s and 1920s weren't as much concerned about musical structure as they were about a certain sound, even a certain feeling, and not necessarily a sorrowful one. In that sense, the way to understand what the blues meant during the era of the Great War is to find out what listeners were hearing.

Early Chicago Blues and the Great Migration

The history of "Chicago blues" goes back quite a way. It's reported that the black Texas musician Henry Thomas, who was born in 1874 and who traveled widely, was in Chicago during the Columbian Exposition of 1893. Thomas made twenty-five recordings for Vocalion between 1927 and 1929, and seven of them have "blues" in the title—although the most famous, "Fishing Blues," is not a blues at all (record companies often added "blues" to a title to boost sales). Does that mean Thomas was playing the blues in Chicago in 1893? He might have been; although historians of the blues agree that the style began to take shape around 1900, when Thomas made his records he played songs that, according to blues historian Francis Davis, were "no-doubt-about-it blues" and "give us the clearest notion we have of what the blues must have sounded like in the late 1890s."[4] "Texas Worried Blues" is one such tune, a classic twelve-bar blues with the formula chord changes. Even so, Thomas was not what is thought of today as a bluesman, but rather a "songster"—a performer who played all sorts of music, whatever made his listeners happy.

And this held true for many of the early blues musicians, who were versatile. As Davis has explained, "Many of the first black performers to be marketed as 'blues' singers were, to their own way of thinking, no such thing. By their own reckoning, they were 'songsters.' In addition to blues, they sang folk ballads, work songs, hymns, ragtime numbers, minstrel and 'coon' songs, cakewalks and other dance tunes they and their audiences called 'reels' or 'breakdowns,' and their own versions of popular tunes of the day."[5] The huge cultural significance that blues music has come to assume derives in part from its position as the "root and stem of modern popular music," as Paul Oliver has put it. "This growth in importance of the blues has resulted in a distorted image, for, if the story of the blues has been told at length and in detail, as far as black music as a whole is concerned it is a half-story, though one that has become very persuasive."[6] The patrons of Chicago's blues clubs, that is, esteem blues music not only for itself but also for its having given birth to rock and roll. As the blues, as an idiom, became more and more popular, the successors of the older songsters naturally began to concentrate on the music that was most in demand. As Oliver has written, "To a considerable extent the repertoires of the singers were reflected by their generations, the oldest singers frequently recording a broad range of material, those ten or fifteen years younger combining them with blues, while the singers of a still younger generation were wholly committed to blues."[7]

Music historian Dave Oliphant has argued that Thomas's eclectic repertoire is something of a "compendium of the popular song forms of the late nineteenth and early twentieth centuries" but that most of his music derives from the 1880s "coon song, a form of white syncopated ragtime."[8] At one point Thomas was billed as "Ragtime Texas" Thomas, so in Chicago he might well have been playing not blues, but rags. Actually, it appears that it was at the Columbian Exposition that most Americans first learned about ragtime. In fact, Scott Joplin, the "King of Ragtime" himself, seems to have been in Chicago in 1893, although it's not known if he actually performed there.

But even if Thomas played a recognizable twelve-bar blues in Chicago in 1893, it did not mean Chicagoans discovered a new kind of music that would eventually come to identify the city. A few black Chicagoans who had made the trek from the South before the Great Migration brought banjos and guitars with them and played at parties, as did some piano players. However, the blues didn't become a musical phenomenon until the music was commercialized.

There was something of a blues scene in Chicago during the war years, but it was under the radar for most people.

Like jazz, the blues came to Chicago as part of the Great Migration, which was powered by the World War I labor shortage. And again like jazz, the blues began to catch on nationally at the same time as the migration. There was something of a blues scene in Chicago during the war years, but it was under the radar for most people. As Thomas A. Dorsey, a blues pianist who arrived in Chicago in 1916, said about the city, "Blues were not played or sung in high-class places, or in smart society clubs, but were heard in the black and tan joints, the smoky little places, the hole-in-the-wall joints, broken-down roadhouses, and second-rate vaudeville houses."[9] The first stars of the blues, unlike jazz musicians such as King Oliver, Jelly Roll Morton, and Louis Armstrong, did not live in Chicago. The Great Migration brought to Chicago a huge audience for the blues; the resident stars would come later.

The first sheet music to be published specifically as a blues appeared in 1912; there were three of them. The first to be copyrighted was "Dallas Blues," by a white Oklahoma bandleader named Hart Wand. The two others were "Baby Seal Blues" and W. C. Handy's "Memphis Blues." Handy's piece proved to be the most durable and was the first blues to be recorded—in 1914 by the Victor Military Band, hardly what one would think of as a blues group. In that same year, Handy's "St. Louis Blues" appeared and the blues mania was on. As Wald has explained, "The next few years brought so many blues hits that by 1917 Marion Harris, who sometimes billed herself as the 'Queen of the Blues,' was making fun of the fad."[10] Despite today's stereotype, the first blues stars were not black men with guitars, but women with big voices who let others handle the musical instruments. According to Gerard Herzhaft, writing in the *Encyclopedia of the Blues*, "A long time before the earliest bluesmen . . . first set foot in recording studios, a vast number of female blues singers were already tremendously successful among the black public. Between 1920 [more accurately, 1915] and 1930, the vocal blues was considered to be an essentially feminine art."[11]

Marion Harris was white, although, according to Handy, many listeners thought she was black, and her records were sold in black-owned stores. The *Chicago Defender* mentioned Harris admiringly in 1920, saying that she "has made a wonderful record of the St. Louis Blues."[12] Music historian Will Friedwald has written that of all the performers who made records in the acoustic era (which ended in 1925), she was the only one "who fulfills every expectation of what a jazz singer should be."[13] She began cutting discs in 1916, which makes Harris the first blues singer to be recorded.

Marion Harris, the first blues singer to be recorded, was white, but many record buyers, both black and white, thought she was an African American.
Library of Congress

Blues histories mention Harris only fleetingly, however; the breakthrough came with the first recording of a blues by a black performer. That was Mamie Smith in 1920. She had been a successful singer in Harlem since 1914; her mentor, a black composer and publisher named Perry Bradford, who was from Chicago, believed that enough black people owned phonographs to constitute a market for record companies. With some difficulty, he persuaded Okeh Records to give Mamie a try. Her first two recordings, "That Thing Called Love" and "You Can't Keep a Good Man Down," did well enough to warrant another, and "Crazy Blues," a Bradford composition, sold an amazing seventy-five thousand copies in its first month and an even more incredible million in its first year (Bradford collected a royalty check for $75,000). "Crazy Blues" marked the beginning of two crucial developments in American popular music: the rush to record black blues musicians and the beginning of what became known as "race" records. Race records were a subgenre created by record companies in order to sell records by black performers to black buyers. As it turned out, however, a lot of white consumers also bought race records.

Okeh Records was a child of World War I. The label was created by a German named Otto K. E. Heinemann ("Okeh" was formed from his initials). With two partners, Heinemann in 1902 opened in Berlin a store that sold record players; the trio then managed to buy out the Carl Lindstrom gramophone company. Heinemann became the dominant figure in the firm and by 1914 was pressing forty million records a year. In addition to classical music, his Odeon label became known for "ethnic" recordings in dozens of languages. When the war came, Heinemann decided to move his company "out of the European battle zone," as one author has expressed it, and in 1916 he formed the Otto Heinemann Phonograph Corporation in New York City and established his own recording studio and manufacturing plant; Okeh also had an office in Chicago.[14] Perhaps it was Heinemann's success in Europe with ethnic music that persuaded him to reach out to black record buyers.[15]

Mamie Smith was born in Cincinnati and made her mark in New York City, but Chicagoans knew of her even before the release of "Crazy Blues" because in July 1920 the *Defender* proudly informed its readers of her first disc: "Lovers of music everywhere, and those who desire to help in any advance of the Race should be sure to buy this record as encouragement to the manufacturers for their liberal policy and to encourage other manufacturers who may not believe that the Race will buy records sung by its own singers."[16] Inevitably, Smith was drawn to Chicago, with its large population of black music fans, and in 1921 she made her debut in the city, appearing in March in sold-out performances at the Avenue Theater. *Defender* columnist Tony Langston reported that her gowns were "wonderful" and that she wore "a flock of diamonds that has her lit up like a Polish church on Sunday night."[17]

Smith's phenomenal sales led to recordings by many other black female blues singers, some of whom became even more famous than Mamie Smith. The best known is Bessie Smith; others included Ma Rainey, Ida Cox, Lucille Bogan, Sara Martin, Sippie Wallace, Ethel Waters, Alberta Hunter, and Lucille Hegamin, who was the second black female blues singer to make a record. None of them were from Chicago (although Wallace lived in the city from 1923 to 1929), but all of them performed there during the 1920s. When Rainey first came to Chicago in April 1924, Langston wrote, "She clearly proved that she was far superior to any of her predecessors," and when Bessie Smith debuted in the city a month later, he commented, "So much has been said of Bessie that Chicagoans were looking for something far above the average in her line, and that's just what the famous artist handed them. Her routine of songs are new and well selected and she put each and every one of them over with the well-known 'Bang.'"[18] The gala benefit performance to support the musicians' union that was staged at Chicago's Coliseum on the night of June 12, 1926, must have been brilliant. Not only did Sarah Martin and Sippie Wallace perform, but so did Louis Armstrong and his Hot Five. (They were not the headliners—that honor went to Butterbeans and Susie, a black man-and-wife comedy duo.) By 1926, however, Chicago fans of the blues-belting women had known about them for over a decade. They knew them from recordings, of course, but news of their triumphs reached them during the war—well before they cut any discs. The *Defender*, for example, first publicized Ma Rainey's success in 1915 and informed its readers about the artistry of Ida Cox in 1917 and Bessie Smith in 1918.

Women blues singers carrying on the tradition of Ma Rainey, Bessie Smith, and the rest still make recordings and appearances, but the offerings at Chicago blues clubs today are overwhelmingly black male artists. They are carrying on the tradition not of Bessie Smith, but of Muddy Waters, who came to Chicago from Mississippi in 1943, and before him, Blind Lemon Jefferson, who was the first black guitar-playing solo singer to make it big on records (two black guitar players were recorded before him, Sylvester Weaver in 1923 and Ed Andrews in 1924, but their sales were marginal).

Jefferson, who was from Texas but spent most of his career on the road (he died in Chicago), began making records for Paramount in 1926. Paramount was in the unlikely location of Grafton, Wisconsin, although most of the company's records were made by Orlando Marsh, proprietor of Marsh Studios at Jackson and Wabash in Chicago.[19] Paramount came to specialize in race records, and until it closed during the Great Depression, it made many of the recordings most cherished by blues historians—sides by Charlie Patton, Son House, and others. After Jefferson's records sold so well, record companies began combing the South for what Wald has called "a varied panoply of Southern street-corner players. Many were blind men, and the more romantic historians link them to the long tradition of blind bards reaching back to Homer, but it is worth remembering that a lot of people in their home communities regarded them as essentially musical beggars, and one can only imagine how surprised these folks must have been to see them suddenly advertised as national stars."[20]

With the advent of Jefferson and his followers, the focus of the blues shifted from the female blues shouters to the male guitar pickers, where it largely remains. Davis has theorized that the hard times of the 1930s had a lot to do with this: "It wasn't as though black audiences of the 1930s suddenly outgrew their infatuation

Bessie Smith, the "Empress of the Blues," first performed in Chicago in 1924. A local reviewer said that she put her songs over with a "bang." Library of Congress

235

with female blues vaudevillians. It was just that singer/guitarists from Mississippi or Texas or the Carolinas were cheaper to record. Unlike the women, they didn't require songwriters or backup musicians. They sometimes didn't even require a recording studio."[21]

Although he might be said to have started a tradition, Jefferson was not the first black male blues performer to cut a disc or to sell a respectable number of records. That was Papa Charlie Jackson, who, despite his importance, does not figure as prominently in blues histories as Jefferson does. That oversight is probably due to two things: First, Jackson was from New Orleans, and his style owed as much to ragtime as it did to what might be called the "country blues." And second, on nearly all his recordings, he played not the guitar, but the banjo, which is hardly considered a serious blues instrument nowadays and was already going out of fashion in Jackson's time. Sometimes he played the ukulele, which is even less of a blues instrument.[22] But Jackson brought the southern songster tradition right to Chicago, for that was where he made his home. Nearly a century later Papa Charlie remains the prototype for the Chicago blues performer.

Like Jefferson, Jackson recorded for Paramount, the race records specialists. Overseeing the label's acquisition of artists was J. Mayo ("Ink") Williams, the first black executive with a major recording company.[23] Williams, who came to Chicago in 1921, became the preeminent producer of race records, bringing into his studio such performers as Ma Rainey, Tampa Red, Ida Cox, Freddie Keppard, and Jelly Roll Morton. (He got the nickname "Ink" from his ability to persuade musicians to sign contracts.) It was in August 1924 that Williams spotted Jackson singing on a Chicago street corner. He was taken by Jackson's infectious rhythm—"you could dance by nearly every song Papa Charlie made," he said. "He was a one-man band."[24] Jackson recorded sixty-six sides for Williams, and being a "one-man band," he didn't require an expensive band to back him up.

Street Music

Amateur male black musicians from the South were playing at house parties, at informal dances, and in obscure clubs years before Papa Charlie Jackson stepped into a recording studio. However, the records of Jefferson and Jackson were made in the 1920s and after, so this book will only mention the great

Chicago blues expansion that came later.[25] But one significant aspect of Jackson's career needs to be spotlighted. The corner on which "Ink" Williams first saw Papa Charlie was on Maxwell Street—a location that became central to the Chicago blues tradition and brings the story back to the 1910s. In 1925 Jackson even recorded a number titled "Maxwell Street Blues," which contains the lines "Lord, I'm talkin' about the wagons, talkin' 'bout the pushcarts too / 'Cause Maxwell Street's so crowded on a Sunday you can hardly pass through."

Crowded it certainly was. In 1891 a survey found sixteen thousand people living on just a one-mile section of the busy thoroughfare, and one analyst calculated that if all of Chicago were as densely populated as Maxwell Street, the entire population of the Western Hemisphere could fit within the city limits.[26] Every ethnic group in Chicago had its own neighborhood: the Germans in Lincoln Park, the Poles on Milwaukee Avenue, the Irish in Bridgeport, the African Americans in Bronzeville. Maxwell Street was the heart of Jewish Chicago, which explains why the Maxwell Street Market was at its busiest on Sundays (on Saturdays it was closed for the Jewish Sabbath, although in later years merchants remained open the entire weekend).

In the 1880s Jewish peddlers operating out of pushcarts had formed a market on Jefferson Street, but the trolley line made the street uncomfortably crowded, and the market spilled into nearby Maxwell Street. In 1912 the city established an official Maxwell Street Market, along with a superintendent to monitor the businesses. Four years later the city extended the market district west to Sangamon Street, and thus Maxwell Street reached its full bloom during World War I.[27] According to Irving Cutler's history of Chicago's Jews, "At its peak . . . the area contained over two thousand vendors selling from stores, stalls, pushcarts, wagons, and boxes."[28]

Histories of the Chicago blues tend to concentrate on Maxwell Street in the period after World War II. That's when street musicians plugged their electric guitars into portable amplifiers connected to stores or first-floor apartments and helped create the electrified blues heard today in Chicago clubs. Starting in the 1940s Maxwell Street blues performers included Little Walter, Pork Chop Hines, Moody Jones, Big Walter Horton, Blind Arvella Gray, Big John Wrencher, Homesick James, Shakey

Chicago's busy Maxwell Street, seen here in 1905, hardly looked like the kind of place that would figure prominently in the history of the blues, but it attracted street musicians, including some of the foremost Chicago blues players. Chicago History Museum, ICHi-19155, cropped; photographer, Barnes-Crosby

Horton, and "Maxwell Street" Jimmie Davis. Muddy Waters almost certainly played there, although after he became famous he preferred to deny it.[29] Some musicians, such as Little Walter, made records for the Ora Nelle label of the Maxwell Record Radio Company, which was owned by a Maxwell Street businessman named Bernard Abrams.[30] And more than a few returned to play the market even after they had become recording artists. Robert Nighthawk, considered one of the finest and most undeservedly little-known Chicago bluesmen, made some excellent recordings for Chicago-based Chess Records in the late 1940s. But he failed to reach the big time and in the 1960s was back on the sidewalk, where he recorded "Live on Maxwell Street 1964," a unique on-location document of the blues sound of the market during its heyday. To hear it is to realize what polished, professional music could be heard for free on the street in those days.

Although the post-1940s period has been glamorized, such a busy location seems to have attracted street musicians from the start. It's been thought that the earliest music heard at the market was Jewish klezmer music,[31] but the presence there in 1924 of Papa Charlie Jackson shows that black musicians found their way to Maxwell Street long before there were electric guitars. It was formerly thought that the earliest-born black songster to be preserved on records was Henry Thomas, who was born in 1874. But now we know that this distinction most likely belonged to Johnny Watson, who was born in Mobile, Alabama, in 1867 and became a living Chicago legend.[32] Watson, who went by the name of Daddy Stovepipe, played guitar with mariachi bands in Mexico at the dawn of the twentieth century before finding employment with the Rabbit's Foot Minstrels, a popular touring group. After going solo, he worked his way to Chicago and, according to his own testimony, began playing on Maxwell Street even before World War I.[33] In 1924 he recorded sixteen sides for Gennett Studios in Richmond, Indiana, which are some of the oldest bluesman-songster numbers on disc. After making his final records for Bluebird in 1934, he returned to the South and left the music business. However, when his wife, who had sung with him on a few records under the name of Mississippi Sarah, died in 1937, he hit the road again; some of his gigs in the 1940s were with zydeco bands in Texas and Louisiana. By 1948 he was back on Maxwell Street. Jimmie Lee Robinson, who knew Daddy Stovepipe, once recalled, "Stovepipe wore one of those top hats. He would play his guitar and rap it. He played old time harp [harmonica]. He'd be hollerin', doin' dog calls. In the 30s when I was a kid, Stovepipe would come around our house—1405 Washburn. He'd go all on down Washburn singin' and playin' the blues and stoppin' here and there on the corners."

Photos and a brief film clip of Daddy Stovepipe show a dignified old gentleman formally dressed in a top hat, black coat, white shirt, waistcoat, and tie, with a guitar on his knee and a harmonica in a holder around his neck. As a true nineteenth-century songster, he played a repertoire that included not only blues but also preblues minstrel and vaudeville numbers. On the street he even favored such tunes as "South of the Border" and "The Tennessee Waltz."[34] Daddy Stovepipe remained a fixture on Maxwell Street until he died in 1963 at age ninety-five, a true relic of a remote musical era and a living symbol of the long arc of the career of Chicago blues, which began at the time of World War I and continued into the Space Age.

12

"Coming to Stay":
The Beginning of Mexican Chicago

Mexican immigration remains one of the most debated topics in the United States. But that discussion goes back more than a hundred years. Beginning in the early twentieth century, great numbers of Mexicans started heading for a better life in the United States, and many of them came to Chicago. It was an influx almost as large as the Great Migration of black people to the city, and it had a similar result in transforming Chicago's demographic landscape. And yet, although the Great Migration is well documented, the Mexican immigration is much less so. Ray Hutchinson, a scholar of urban affairs, has said that "the Mexican community in Chicago may be one of the best-kept secrets in ethnic studies."[1] But both migrations began at the same time—during the First World War.

It might seem surprising today, but a hundred years ago U.S. public officials wanted *more* Mexicans to enter the United States. The reason was a lack of European immigrants. Next to the vote for war, one of the most significant accomplishments of Congress in early 1917 was the Immigration Act. For the first time the government placed restrictions on European immigration. The new law, which passed on February 5, was also called the Literacy Act because it banned the entry of any physically able would-be immigrant age sixteen or older who could not read thirty to forty common words "in some one of the various languages or dialects" of the immigrant's choice. The law also raised the head tax on immigrants from $4 to $8—a considerable hike for impoverished newcomers. Finally, the bill established an "Asiatic barred zone" that excluded all Asians except Japanese and Filipinos. The Chinese had been barred since 1882; now peoples from a host of other countries, ranging from Turkey to Indonesia, joined them on the unwelcome list.

Nativists who feared the dreaded "hyphenated American" (see chapter 13) and the "yellow peril" were pleased with the law, but many businessmen were not.[2] The war had already slowed the flow of immigrants, and when the United States got into the conflict, millions of young men entered the military. Where was the labor force to come from?

It turned out that there was a clause in the new immigration law that allowed the secretary of labor to set aside any of its provisions if he judged that a labor shortage was harming the country. Employers convinced Secretary of Labor William B. Wilson that there was a noncontroversial source of foreign labor right next door, and in May he exempted Mexican agricultural workers from all tests established by the law. Two months later he extended the exemption to include nonagricultural workers, thus opening up jobs for Mexicans in mining, railroad work, manufacturing, and so on. As historian Michael Innis-Jiménez has expressed it, "Bosses considered Mexicans least 'invasive,' most cooperative, and disposable."[3]

According to U.S. Census figures, in 2010 Chicago's population was 2,695,598. Of this number, 778,862, or about 29 percent, were "Hispanic or Latino," and Mexicans were by far the dominant Hispanic group, with a population of 578,100, or 22 percent (their population is surely greater, however, because an unknown number are undocumented). But one doesn't need census figures to appreciate the strong presence of Mexicans in the city. Mexican workers are everywhere, some neighborhoods look like border towns, and tacos are one of the predominant fast foods.

Early Immigration

Although the Great War brought Mexican immigrants to Chicago in significant numbers, immigration from Mexico started before that. Some historians cite the Mexican Revolution of 1910 as the key reason for this population movement. Although it's true that this upheaval created turmoil, Mexican peasants had plenty of reasons to leave home long before the revolution.

The regime of the dictator Porfirio Díaz, which lasted from 1876 to 1911, was bent on "modernizing" Mexico and did so with a free-market ideology that disdained the peasants' abilities. Díaz and his advisers sought investment from abroad and encouraged agricultural settlers from western and northern Europe, whom they thought would prove superior agents of civilization and technology. In nineteenth-century Mexico most rural *campesino* villagers lived in one of two types of farming communities: *ejidos* or haciendas. *Ejidos* were village lands held in common, a system that dated back to the pre-Columbian era. The haciendas, however, were where most peasants lived and worked. Ranging in size from forty-five thousand to one million acres, these were the estates of wealthy, politically connected landowners.[4]

Two laws—one in 1883, the second in 1894 —permitted foreign companies to settle what the regime called "public lands," which were in reality *ejidos*. Between 1883 and 1910 more than a quarter of the total area of Mexico was turned over to private companies. By the time of the revolution there were no "public lands" whatsoever in twelve states, and outside of five states not a single rural family in Mexico owned any land at all.[5] In the words of historian Lawrence A. Cardoso, "By the time of the Mexican federal census of 1910 there were so few *ejidos* left that enumerators did not bother to count them."[6] To the "modernizers" of the regime, evicting the campesinos, or Indian farmers, from their farms was an upgrade. As one hacienda owner put it, "The Indians are a burden which the Mexicans must carry; without education of any kind, they are a hindrance to progress, an obstacle to our advance."[7]

During the regime of Mexican dictator Porfirio Díaz, thousands of peasants were evicted from their lands, causing many to seek their fortunes elsewhere. Library of Congress

Some of these evicted farmers found work on the large haciendas, but this was hardly an improvement. The haciendas operated under a system of "debt peonage." The landowner would advance the farmer seed, money, food, and supplies. In practice, the farmer was never able to repay. One contemporary witness reported that at any given time, a farmer owed his patron 400 to 500 pesos, while the average annual salary was 120 pesos. In 1901 a German consul reported that at harvest time farmers in Michoacán "not only received no corn but ended up in debt to the *hacendado*."[8] As early as the 1840s outsiders were viewing the hacienda owners as the equivalent of feudal lords and the farmers as no better off than slaves. Ulysses S. Grant, who fought in the Mexican War, wrote that Mexico "has more poor and starving subjects who are willing and able to work than any country in the world. The rich keep down the poor with a hardness of heart that is incredible."[9] Adding to the woes were overpopulation (Mexico's population increased by more than 50 percent between 1875 and 1910), land shortages, rising food prices (the price of corn rose 50 percent between 1877 and 1903), stagnant wages (workers earned 15 cents a day at best), economic recession (1907–08), and poor weather (drought and frost caused crop failures in 1907–09).[10]

This misery was concentrated in the states of Mexico's central plateau, and at first those who fled headed to Mexico's northern region, where the government had stimulated growth by establishing a free zone along the U.S. border. Railroad construction was flourishing, and workers were in demand. The railroads facilitated the migration from central to northern Mexico; eventually these lines were linked to U.S. railroads, which would soon expedite immigration north of the border. As mining, agriculture, and railroad construction advanced in northern Mexico, it also did so in the southwestern United States, where the population was too small to provide enough workers and employers sought to bring in Mexicans.

The first decade of the twentieth century saw huge growth in U.S. sugar beet production, which was centered in the Rocky Mountain region and western Nebraska but also took place in California, Iowa, the Dakotas, Minnesota, Illinois, Michigan, and Ohio. Many Mexicans found work in the beet fields as *betabeleros*. The harvesting of sugar beets (and other vegetables and fruits) was labor-intensive and consisted of what was known as "stoop labor," and Mexicans, who were willing to put in long hours for low pay, became essential. Mexicans eventually constituted 75 to 90 percent of the beet workers in the Midwest.[11] One might have expected American nativists to disapprove of the inflow, but they generally did not because they

Many Mexicans who came to the United States in the early part of the twentieth century, such as this family photographed in Colorado in 1915, found work harvesting beets. From there, many of them eventually moved on to Chicago. Library of Congress

believed that Mexican laborers sought only seasonal employment and were "homing pigeons" who would eventually return to their homeland.

Soon Mexicans had become a familiar presence in the southwestern United States, and visitors to the region romanticized them as a source of local color. The "chili queens" of San Antonio had been well known to railroad passengers in the 1880s and 1890s, and residents of the United States were beginning their love affair with Mexican food, although it took some getting used to at first, and the unfamiliar spiciness of the cuisine served as a topic for humor.

And then the revolution came. Largely an agrarian rebellion, it was fueled by peasants who sought reforms that would deliver them from debt peonage. Once Díaz was overthrown in 1911, however, the rebel factions were unable to cooperate, and the internecine warfare that followed brought yet another misery—anarchy. As Cardoso has described it, "Armies and band of marauders numbering in the hundreds of thousands marched, countermarched, robbed and killed over the face of the country. In the process, the civilian government was destroyed and agriculture and other economic activities were disrupted. The resultant inflation, starvation, unemployment, and lack of personal security forced upwards of 10 percent of Mexico's population, probably in excess of 1,000,000 people, to flee to the United States. . . . As the decade closed in 1920, Mexico was a devastated land."[12]

At first the Mexican emigrants clustered in places on or just across the border. Although their numbers were large, the U.S. Immigration Service continued to think of them as temporary residents. However, overcrowding along the border compelled the Immigration Service to enlist the aid of the U.S. Employment Service in finding work for the immigrants farther north. Thanks to the exemption clause of the Immigration Act, Mexican workers now began moving north, some traveling as far as New England. And quite a few went to Chicago.

Arrival in Chicago

Although the migration of Mexicans to Chicago began during the Great War, there were small signs of a Mexican presence in the city before then.[13] The 1893 Columbian Exposition in Chicago featured the San Antonio Chili Parlor; a recipe collection titled *Favorite Dishes: A Columbia Autograph Souvenir Cookery Book* included three Mexican dishes from one Señora

The violence that accompanied the Mexican Revolution of 1910 forced as many as one million Mexicans to flee to the United States.
Library of Congress

Don Manuel Chavez: Pollo con Arroz, Pollo con Tomates, and Tamales de Chile. A Mexican artist who came to Chicago to work on his country's fair pavilion wrote a letter in which he reported finding Mexican food for sale downtown: "We ran into a man who had a tin box with a white cloth in front of it that said 'Mexican tamales,' we got closer and asked him if he was Mexican and he answered that he was, I bought 10¢ worth of tamales which he sold to me at 1¢ a piece."[14] The artist was witnessing the beginning of a tamale fad in Chicago. As historian Perry R. Duis has written, "Within months of the introduction of this item there were reportedly more than three hundred *tamaleros* cruising Chicago's streets."[15] A "tamale war" even broke out in Chicago; according to the *Chicago Tribune*, it was "hotter than the peppery food they served." The article said it was "Mexico against Texas, a regular border conflict," and the strife was so intense that the tamale vendors vanished for three years before returning in 1896.[16] By 1901 tamales had become so familiar in the United States that the *New York Times* reported that the military was purchasing 2,469 one-pound cans of chicken tamales in Chicago to be shipped to soldiers in the Philippines.[17] Chicago's meat packers had "discovered canned chili and tamales as a profitable outlet for scraps of meat off the cutting-room floor."[18]

Despite these early indications of a few Mexicans in Chicago in the 1890s, according to sociologist Wilfredo Cruz there were still "only about 1,000 Mexicans in the Chicago metropolitan area" in 1910.[19] As for the city itself, geographer Irving Cutler has reported that "in 1910 the U.S. Census listed only 102 foreign-born Mexicans in Chicago; by 1920 the number had increased to 1,224; and by 1930 it had swelled to 14,733."[20] These numbers, however, were undoubtedly low, given the Mexican immigrants' reluctance to cooperate with census officials.

Most Mexican workers found their way to Chicago gradually, and historians have collected some informative anecdotes about the process. For example, Frank Duran recalled that his father came to Texas from Guanajuato in 1911 and found railroad work that took him to jobs in different locations. "My three brothers and sisters were born in different U.S. cities," Duran said. After hearing about the opportunities in Chicago, Duran's father moved there, but that wasn't until 1929.[21] Carmen

Mendoza, another descendant of Mexican immigrants, related how her family also came by the railroad. Her grandmother's husband repaired and laid track, the family lived in converted railroad cars, and her mother took in washing and sold food to the single men. It took them five years, from 1914 to 1919, to reach metropolitan Chicago.[22] Many other workers found their way to Chicago after working in Midwestern sugar beet fields for $2 a day. When they heard about the higher wages in Chicago, they left the farms for the city.[23]

Mexican workers in Chicago took other jobs traditionally held by earlier immigrants in the steel mills, stockyards, and packinghouses, as well as on the railroads. In April 1917 a local newspaper reported that the Armour meatpacking company "had started importing Mexicans and putting them to work, but found they could not get enough of them."[24] This caused them to turn to black laborers, who clearly were the second choice.

One trait that made Mexican settlement areas different from the black neighborhoods created during the Great Migration was that the population was predominantly male. It has been estimated that in Chicago in 1924, Mexican male immigrants outnumbered females by twenty to one.[25] Known as *solos*, most of these men were unmarried, but even married men rarely brought their wives.[26] This imbalance gave a transitory quality to the Mexican population. Many of these workers did not bother to become citizens because they thought they would someday return to Mexico, a prospect that was more realistic for them than it was for most immigrants from Europe. The sense of impermanence changed as more women came north and as married couples had children who were U.S. citizens, spoke fluent English, and considered Chicago their home. By 1930 one-fourth of the Mexicans living in Chicago were women, and during the 1930s the percentage of women continued to grow.[27] One factor that helped increase the number of women was that sugar beet farms were more likely to hire entire families. Work in the beet fields was seasonal, and although many families returned to Mexico in the winter, others found temporary jobs in U.S. cities for a few months—and for many, these temporary jobs turned into permanent ones.

As early as 1910 three railroads—the Santa Fe, Burlington, and Rock Island—reported that their Chicago divisions were employing at least 1,120 Mexicans on track maintenance work.[28] By the 1920s 40 percent of the railroad maintenance workers in Chicago were Mexican.[29] In the years before the war many U.S. railroads, largely because of overexpansion, were in financial trouble, some virtually bankrupt, and in the first months of the conflict railroad competition for government business created harmful inefficiencies. By the end of 1917 "the nationwide labor shortage and increased demand on the railroads, combined with particularly bad weather and disorganized government military contracting, created a massive paralysis of railroad traffic in the Northeast."[30] As a result, on December 26 President Woodrow Wilson gave an executive order nationalizing the railroads. As in other enterprises, the wartime labor shortage opened up railroad jobs for Mexican workers, although these jobs were more irregular than those in heavy industry. Many railroad workers, or *traqueros*, grew tired of moving and chose to settle in Chicago. As Innis-Jiménez has written, "A significant number of Mexicans contracted to work on railroad maintenance-of-way crews 'jumped' their contracts for jobs with more stability. . . . Mexicans preferred the better pay, the year-around work, and the stability of employment provided by the South Chicago area steel mills, which benefited from those who left their railroad contracts. South Chicago industry provided these types of jobs, resulting in a large multi-industry influx of Mexicans throughout World War I."[31]

Many Mexican workers were drawn to Chicago by *enganchistas* or *enganchadores*, labor recruiters hired by steel mills and railroad companies to travel to the Texas border or even into Mexico's Central Plateau to offer transportation to Chicago, either free or to be repaid later. The workers would typically sign a contract that would bind them to a job for an allotted time in exchange for guaranteed work. Chicago was a long way from Mexico and therefore might have seemed mysterious, so the *enganchistas* were important in informing Mexican workers of the opportunities there and helping them make the trip.[32]

The hardships of the Díaz regime, the anarchy of the revolution, the wartime labor shortage—all of these brought Mexicans to Chicago. Then, right after the war came the Great Steel Strike of 1919, and in South Chicago and adjacent Indiana, the mill owners brought in Mexicans as strikebreakers. The strike occurred just two months after the Chicago race riot in the summer of 1919, and it's clear that the mill owners, fearing further racial unrest, preferred to employ Mexican strikebreakers instead of black ones. Some mill managers even preferred Mexicans to working-class whites; the Mexicans were perceived as more docile, while poor whites were assessed as "riff-raff."[33] One eyewitness recalled how the Mexicans were put into a boat on Lake Michigan and brought around the back of the steel mill.[34] Inland Steel in East Chicago, Indiana, became the largest single employer of Mexicans in the United States, and the company first hired them during the strike, although it fired them when the strike was settled, but then reconsidered and began employing them again.[35]

During the steel strike about forty to fifty Mexican workers, recruited mostly from Texas, arrived every few days. They were usually slipped in on trains at night and given bunk beds in barracks, while the few men with families were sheltered in nearby housing. As Innis-Jiménez has explained, "Many did not know that they had been hired as replacement workers. Others had their suspicions but were willing to enter the steel mills in search of better money and a better economic future."[36] Even after the strike was over, the mills still needed their labor, and their presence soon became a fact of life in the steel towns,

Largely because of the Great Steel Strike of 1919, Inland Steel in East Chicago, Indiana, became the largest single employer of Mexicans in the United States. Author's collection

although for many years Mexicans were relegated to the most menial jobs and rarely rose to the rank of foreman.[37] By 1925 Mexican workers made up 11.7 percent of the steel industry workforce in the Chicago area.[38] At Inland Steel nearly one-third of the workers were Mexicans.[39]

Settlement in the City

Chicagoans might have expected that the Mexicans would follow the paths of the older immigrants, gradually mixing into the culture after initial inhospitality, adopting English, and intermarrying. It didn't quite work out that way. The case of a Mexican immigrant named José Blanco was an indication that they might have special problems.

The Chicago race riot of 1919 was a clash between white and black Chicagoans, but it had a Mexican component. Amid the turmoil, a white mob attacked Blanco and another Mexican, Elizondo González. González was wounded, but Blanco managed to stab a member of the mob named Joseph Schoff, who later died of blood poisoning. Blanco was enraged that the white mob had mistaken him and his companion for black people, but in Schoff's mindset there were only two races—white and black—and Blanco, in his view, wasn't white.[40] Blanco's trial resulted in a hung jury, and he was then freed by actions of the Mexican vice consul, but the racial confusion signaled that the Mexican immigrants might face a prejudice deeper than their European predecessors had.

In the early days of Mexican immigration to Chicago, "there existed no predominantly Mexican neighborhood. Mexican settlement was always interwoven with residents of other ethnic and racial groups. Nevertheless, there were certainly areas of Mexican concentration where signs of their daily lives were clearly visible."[41] By the 1920s there were three identifiable places of Mexican settlement: in the Hull-House area on the West Side, in the "Back of the Yards" area near the packinghouses, and in South Chicago and Irondale, where the steel mills were. There were also two Mexican colonies in nearby Indiana: in Indiana Harbor (East Chicago) and Gary, both home to enormous steelworks.

Although the Mexican immigrants were not confined to a ghetto, the areas in which they lived tended to be among the poorest in Chicago. They usually lived near where they worked—the steel mills on the South Side and the packing-houses near Back of the Yards. The West Side Mexicans tended to have jobs on the railroads, in downtown hotels, and in candy and radio factories and other small industries, many of which were located on Roosevelt Road. Some landlords would not rent to Mexicans at all; others charged them rents higher than they did other tenants. A Chicago real estate agent noted that Mexicans were paying $52 a month for an apartment in Back of the Yards that had previously rented for $38. "Since the Mexicans have come in the real estate values have declined to almost nothing," he explained. "But the rental value of the buildings has gone up."[42] Landlords justified the higher rents by arguing that Mexicans crowded into apartments, with two or more families inhabiting a space meant for one. It's difficult to say, however, which came first—the higher rents or the crowded conditions. The evidence indicates that Mexicans commonly doubled up in apartments in order to share the cost of the rent.

Even in poor neighborhoods, Mexicans often lived in the worst apartments or in shanties. It was reported, for example, that the Quintero family, consisting of two adults and eleven children, lived in two dark rooms, only one of which had a window.[43] As a contemporary observer put it, Mexicans lived in "the old tenement districts [that had] long been experiencing a steady encroachment by industry and commerce" and were "destined for extinction."[44] Some Mexican families had no apartments or shacks at all. Colonies existed in several Chicago locations where Mexican families lived in empty boxcars, which were often infested with bedbugs. A union organizer testified that Mexican laborers "live in adobe huts and boxcars along the right of way and are so underfed they cannot do a proper day's work."[45]

Some landlords would not rent to Mexicans at all; others charged them rents higher than they did other tenants.

As the Blanco case illustrates, previous immigrants tended to view Mexicans as nonwhite, and there were many ethnic clashes, especially between Mexicans and Poles but also between Mexicans and Italians. Some white ethnics disparaged the newcomers as job competition. It was said that "the Lithuanians and Poles thought the Mexicans came in to lower wages. . . . They beat up Mexicans coming home at night."[46] White ethnics gradually began to view Mexicans as a different type of immigrant—ones who resisted learning English and whose loyalty remained with the homeland. In 1919 the *Chicago Daily Herald* reported that earlier Italian immigrants were beginning to be replaced by Mexicans "and they are some 'rough stuff.'"[47] The Mexicans inhabited an ambiguous area between white and black, being neither one nor the other but, in many people's view, closer to black. A theater owner said, "White people don't like to sit next to the colored or Mexican . . . many of them are not clean and we can't separate them on the basis of dress, so we separate them on the basis of nationality."[48] This color prejudice was compounded by some public officials' belief that Mexicans presented a menace to health. Addressing members of the Public Health Institute in Chicago's Stevens Hotel, Dr. Benjamin Goldberg warned that the immigrants were a danger:

> The industrialist and agriculturalist of the west and southwest, in importing Mexican laborers, is also importing a race sizzling with susceptibilities. His gain in cheap wages is more than counterbalanced by the loss to the taxpayers in the increased charity expenditures that will continue to grow in proportion to the growth of the Mexican population. . . . We seem, all through the United States, to be asleep to the menace of the immigrant Mexican. . . . They live in densely populated urban centers, in contact with grades of the white race whose food, housing, etc., make them most prone to tuberculosis, among other diseases.[49]

Throughout the 1920s Chicagoans began to realize that, as the *Tribune* put it in 1924, Mexicans "are coming to stay."[50] Four years later the *Tribune* ran an article titled "Immigrant Tide from Mexico Still Vexes U.S."[51] During the Depression of the 1930s efforts were made to return many of the immigrants to Mexico. Some left voluntarily; others did not. It has been estimated that as many as four hundred thousand Mexicans were repatriated between 1929 and 1935 and that as many as half of these returnees were involuntary. Between 1930 and 1940 the Mexican population of Chicago dropped from 19,632 to 16,000.[52] In 1930 a geneticist from Vanderbilt University told a House committee that the minds of Mexicans "run to nothing higher than animal functions—eat, sleep, and sexual debauchery. . . . Yet there are Americans clamoring for more of this human swine to be brought over from Mexico."[53]

Not everyone viewed the Mexican newcomers unfavorably. Gertrude Britton of Hull-House thought that they had "an unusual native intelligence as well as a pleasing courtesy and the faculty to adjust" and believed them to be "a very desirable addition to our American mixture."[54] Britton, however, was speaking from the view of the dedicated social worker; such tolerance was rare among the white ethnic groups who competed with the newer immigrants for housing and jobs and among the government officials who worried about the size of the Mexican influx.

A Community and an Identity

As their numbers grew, the Mexicans began to build their own community and create their own identity. The first specifically Mexican Catholic church was Our Lady of Guadalupe, which began life in an old army barracks transported from Michigan in 1923. The church was staffed by members of the Claretian Missionaries, and a school was established in 1928. Besides the church, Mexican community life centered on social organizations, mutual aid societies (*mutualistas*), labor unions, and political clubs. According to Innis-Jiménez, "Between 1917 and 1928, Mexicans in Chicago started a total of thirty-nine organizations."[55] Pool halls were especially popular with young single men; they became social centers where men could find a bed or a meal and an address to which mail could be sent. By the late 1920s there were twenty-nine such pool halls in the city.[56] Settlement houses, such as Hull-House on the West Side and the University of Chicago Settlement House in Back of the Yards, provided meeting rooms, athletic facilities, and English language instruction. Many Mexican ceramic artisans honed their skills in the Hull-House kilns. Spanish-language newspapers, such as *México* (founded in 1924 and renamed *El Nacional* in 1930) and *La Raza*, kept newcomers informed.

One of Chicago's unique institutions is the National Museum of Mexican Art. Founded in 1982, it moved to its present location in Chicago's Pilsen neighborhood in 1987. The aim of the museum is to promote and showcase Mexican art and culture, and its mission statement defines Mexican culture as "*sin fronteras*" (without borders).[57] The slogan is significant. After the revolution, Mexico was fragmented, and the national government struggled to unify the population. One strategy was the construction of rural schools in which would be taught a national curriculum stressing the common elements of Mexican identity, or what was known as *Mexicanidad*, or "Mexican-ness." Another was the idealization of a mythical pre-Columbian past. The idea of a Mexico without borders had a powerful restorative appeal.

The veneration of pre-Columbian culture resonated in Chicago, where Mexicans used it as a way to maintain ethnic pride in the face of prejudice. In the early period of immigration, many Mexicans were not especially eager to become U.S. citizens, and this indifference has been partly explained as the result of a feeling that citizenship did not deter discrimination. A Mexican immigrant living in Packingtown said, "Even if we do become citizens here, we always remain Mexicans." And a researcher from the U.S. Department of Labor reported that a Mexican immigrant complained, "If you carry naturalization papers in your pocket . . . you may hold your head up and say to yourself, 'Now I am as good as anybody.' But that won't prevent an American from kicking you and saying, 'Get out of here, you damned Mexican!'"[58] Many Mexicans viewed racism from whites not only as an assault on their skin color but also as an indictment of their culture. This perception lay behind their efforts to establish institutions that celebrated Mexican civilization and to celebrate Mexican holidays.[59]

Racial prejudice had both a divisive and a unifying influence among Mexicans in Chicago. Some Mexicans, because of their lighter complexion, superior education, higher economic status, and fluency in English, were able to disappear into the white culture. Some brought with them the class prejudices of their native land, looking down on peons and Indians as uncivilized and fearing that the lower-class elements of the Mexicans in Chicago would reflect badly on them. The unifying element came from a feeling that it was necessary for Mexican immigrants to band together to combat prejudice. If outsiders saw all Mexicans as alike, then the Mexican community was, almost by definition, unified—"Mexicans in effect became interchangeable."[60] As Marcia Farr has noted, as larger and larger numbers of immigrants came to Chicago after World War II, Mexican nationality became so potent that the term "Mexican American" fell out of favor: "Mexican Americans . . . formed ethnic organizations, although there were tensions between immigrants and Mexican Americans as the latter tried to represent the entire community. . . . Ultimately outnumbered, Mexican Americans no longer dominated the ethnic scene. . . . The term 'Mexican American' dropped out of local rhetoric, and people identified simply as Mexican, in contrast to Polish, Irish, and so forth, as an affirmation of the continuing connection with Mexico."[61]

The fostering of cultural pride, as it developed in Chicago, combined respect for the achievements of the pre-Columbian Mexicans with acclaim for the leaders of the nineteenth-century independence movement and a celebration of folkloric customs, along with fiestas, parades, and outdoor murals, a distinctive feature of Mexican culture. The National Museum of Mexican Art is a landmark of this encouragement of Mexican identity.

It's been commonly observed that when people come to a big city, they often find themselves. That's what happened to the Mexican immigrants. More than they had ever discovered it in their homeland, they found their Mexican identity, their *Mexicanidad*, in Chicago.

13

The End of *Kultur*:
The Plight of Chicago's Germans

Tall, dignified, and inspirational, the statue of Friedrich Schiller in Lincoln Park is one of Chicago's finest public sculptures. A copy of the Schiller statue in Marbach, Germany, the poet's birthplace, it was unveiled in May 1886. Thirty-two years later, however, it was wantonly and angrily defaced. A coat of yellow paint—the color of cowards—was slathered onto the noble monument.

Why would anyone want to vandalize a memorial to the poet who wrote *William Tell*, that enduring denunciation of tyranny? The poet who wrote the "Ode to Joy," that paean to universal brotherhood that concludes Beethoven's Ninth Symphony? Unfortunately, Schiller happened to be German. In Chicago in 1918 that was reason enough.

In February 2014 the Chicago public radio station WBEZ reported that 204,510 people in Chicago identified themselves as being of German ethnic origin. This was a greater number than those who reported being Irish (199,294) or Polish (182,064).[1] And yet it's evident that the Irish and Polish have a higher profile in the city. They have their gathering places, shops, drinking establishments, museums, and heritage societies. In Catholic churches Mass is still commonly said in Polish, but a German Mass is rare. Politicians reach out to ethnic Irish and Polish voters in a way that they do not to Germans. A few German restaurants still exist, the Steuben Day parade continues, and the DANK Haus German American Cultural Center (1959) continues to promote German language and culture, but Chicago's Germania is a faint shadow of what it once was.

In 1900 Germans constituted by far the largest ethnic group in Chicago; visitors to the heart of the German district at Halsted and North Avenues might think they were in Frankfurt.

The city's German population numbered some 470,000—one out of every four Chicagoans either had been born in Germany or had a parent who had. The German community made its presence known with its beer gardens, concerts, parades, and an array of other public activities, such as excursions, picnics, gymnastic presentations, carnivals, and Christmas bazaars. Masquerade balls were especially popular. Any savvy politician had to woo the German vote. In the mayoral race of 1911, for example, both candidates, Carter Harrison II and Charles Merriam, addressed German audiences in their native tongue, and they even had a friendly competition about whose German was better.

The Schmidt Metzgerei (Butcher Shop) is in the Old Town neighborhood of Chicago, which was settled by German Catholics in the 1850s. Now a law office, it's a striking reminder of how German Chicago once was.
Photograph by the author

One of the most significant effects that the First World War had on Chicago was that it smothered the city's German culture. The German community did not go away; it went underground.

The War in Europe

When war broke out in Europe in August 1914, many Americans viewed Germany favorably as a vibrant nation on the rise. For example, Max Annenberg, circulation editor of the *Chicago Tribune*, called France "a corrupt and immoral nation," hailed Germany as being "in the full bloom of health and power," and predicted that Germany, a "peaceful nation" that had been "forced to mobilize for self-protection," would conquer Belgium and France "inside of a week."[2]

Only five days before the assassination of the Austrian archduke Franz Ferdinand, twenty thousand Chicagoans braved the rain to gather in Lincoln Park for the dedication of a monument to Germany's greatest writer, Johann Wolfgang von Goethe. The German ambassador, Count Johann Heinrich von Bernstorff, who unveiled the statue, said, "Today we are assembled here to unveil a monument which is to serve as a new bond of intellectual and cultural relations between Germany and the United States and a token of our desire to bind together our two nations ever more closely." Governor Edward F. Dunne praised the contributions of Germans to the development of the nation, and Mayor Harrison said that "none of the many peoples which have contributed their quota to the making of the twentieth century Americanism in this representative city has given more bountifully than the Germans."[3]

Chicago's Germans were not exempt from the xenophobia that arose among nativists with the massive immigration in the nineteenth century. Today many Americans are proud to claim a hyphen in their heritage, such as Italian-American or Chinese-American, but the term "hyphenated American" was used differently at the time of World War I. In 1916, in fact, one author assessed the term as a "malodorous title."[4] Someone who would willingly add a hyphen to his or her heritage was seen as a doubtful citizen and patriot, perhaps one whose true allegiance lay abroad. In a widely circulated address delivered in October 1915, Theodore Roosevelt stated, "There is no room in this country for hyphenated Americanism. When I refer to hyphenated Americans, I do not refer to naturalized Americans. Some of the very best Americans I have ever known were naturalized Americans, Americans born abroad. But a hyphenated American is not an American at all."[5]

As early as the 1870s the Germans' eagerness to keep the customs of their homeland raised doubts about their willingness to assimilate. In addition, there was a strong German presence in the anarchist movement; five of the eight "anarchists" accused of murder and conspiracy in the 1886 Haymarket Affair in Chicago, during which a bomb blast during a labor rally killed eight policemen, were German immigrants. On the whole, however, Germans had earned a reputation as an industrious, thrifty people (if, perhaps, too fond of lager—a sore spot with the temperance forces). A survey taken in 1908 found that German immigrants were rated number one of all the ethnic groups in the United States.[6] But with the coming of the First World War, the Germans' hyphen became the thickest of all.[7] And Chicago, being one of the most German cities in the United States, was again a microcosm of a national trend.

On December 10, 1914, more than five thousand Germans and Austrians attended a rally at Chicago's Medinah Temple. The featured speaker, Dr. Bernhard Dernberg, formerly the German colonial minister, stood before an array of flags from various Chicago German and Austrian societies and explained that Britain was to blame for the war and democratic Germany was forced to violate the treaty guaranteeing Belgian neutrality because "no nation is morally bound to the terms of an agreement involving either a sacrifice of its own existence or an abdication of its sovereign function."[8]

Back in Berlin, German authorities agreed that supporting pro-German sentiment in the United States might help the Wilson administration retain its neutrality. A group of experts was sent to the United States, the Germany treasury supported the propaganda effort to the tune of an estimated $35 million, and no fewer than eight million copies of pro-German pamphlets and books were circulated. One of the most eloquent appeals was the 1914 book *The War and America*, by the eminent German-American psychologist Hugo Münsterberg, who had been one of the celebrities at the unveiling of Chicago's Goethe statue. He explained that the war was "central Europe's desperate defense against the mighty neighbors of east and west who have prepared and prepared for the crushing blow to the Germanic nations. The war had to come sooner or later. Russia spent billions to be ready to push the steamroller of its gigantic population over the German frontier. France armed as no civilized nation ever armed before."[9] The volume was dedicated "to all lovers of fair play."

Fair play was one of the qualities believed to define Americanism, but one of the characteristics that got German-Americans into trouble was their inclination to proclaim the superiority of German *Kultur*, even above that of the United States. Some also saw crude, raw America as a blank slate on which civilization could, and should, be written by the Teutonic race. This was why some Chicago Germans advocated that German be taught in all public schools and be placed, as the German-language newspaper *Abendpost* put it, "on equal footing with English." As the *Abendpost* explained, "The German language surely is bound to become the second language of the land and the world language in the near future."[10]

It was one thing for outsiders to view Germany as a militaristic nation, but it was another when the Germans themselves did.

This hubris was aggravated by the linking of German culture with German militarism. It was one thing for outsiders to view Germany as a militaristic nation, but it was another when the Germans themselves did. In a follow-up book by Münsterberg, *The Peace and America* (1915), he stated, "The German army is the strongest expression of the moral national will to fulfill the ethical mission of Germany, and in this sense it is indeed an embodiment of German Kultur."[11] Sentiments like these heralded an epochal shift in how outsiders have assessed Germany ever since. Whereas once, in the nineteenth century, it was hailed as a land of poets, musicians, and philosophers, it was now acquiring a reputation that still haunts it, as a land of rigidly efficient soldiers. Many Americans justified World War I as protection against German militarism, and this explanation was later repeated in World War II.

The attempts by Berlin to influence American opinion largely backfired because of their heavy-handedness. One notorious incident was a statement by Arthur Zimmermann, Germany's foreign minister, in which he warned the American ambassador, James Gerard, that 500,000 German-American men "will rise in arms against your government if your government should dare to take any action against Germany." Gerard retorted that there were 501,000 lampposts in the United States from which to hang them.[12] In October 1917 the *Tribune* reported that the German government had given more than $100,000 to a pro-German Chicago-based organization called the American Embargo Conference; the funds were to be used to influence the 1916 congressional and presidential elections in a way favorable to Germany.[13] Germany's image was made even more unfavorable by its clumsy attempts at sabotage and to provoke strikes in American munitions factories and among longshoremen. These efforts did not amount to much, but they were wildly exaggerated in the American press, leading to an atmosphere in which all Germans were liable to be suspected of treachery, and nervous citizens were imagining German spies around every corner.

Chicago's Germans did find friends of a sort among Irish-Americans, who were hostile toward Ireland's British colonial masters. As early as December 1, 1914, the bonds between the Irish and the Germans were solidified at a meeting organized by a German-Irish committee and held at North Side Turner Hall. The overflow crowd of five thousand, spilling out onto Chicago Avenue, cheered when Patrick H. O'Donnell, an Irish-American lawyer, exclaimed, "With German victory will also come Irish liberty."[14] Most nationalists in Ireland agreed to back the British war effort in the hope that it would expedite Irish independence, and over two hundred thousand Irish soldiers served in the British forces during World War I, but in 1916 exasperated Irish patriots, who feared the war would go on a very long time, launched the Easter Rebellion. Chicago's sometimes fractious Irish bonded in solidarity with the rebels and reaffirmed their links with the city's Germans.

Although the Irish were not adversaries of the Germans in Chicago, other ethnic groups took on that role, most notably the Slavs. Some Germans considered the war a battle of cultures. The president of Chicago's Germania Club called it "a war of the Teutonic race against the Slavic," and a German newspaper called it "a battle to the bitter end between German civilization and the pan-Slavic, half-Asiatic, and thinly veneered barbarism of Russia." The *Abendpost* opined, "A Slav victory means the obliteration of four centuries of European culture."[15] Chicago's Slavs let it be known what they thought of such sentiments. In early August three young Serbs wrecked a tavern belonging to an Austrian, and later in the month five Russians pummeled a former German officer with bottles. The Bohemians, who longed to be free of Hapsburg rule, were solidly on the side of the Entente Allies. They also avowed that they, unlike the Germans, were not hyphenated. A Bohemian publication declared, "Bang! Goes the Hyphen" and said, "There are no Bohemian-Americans," but only "Americans of Bohemian extraction."[16] Chicago's Poles could possibly have gone either way—the Russians had joined with the Germans and Austrians to annihilate and divide up their country in 1795—but the anti-Slav racism expressed in so many German publications turned their ire against the Teutons. Most of Chicago's Poles supported the Allied side, and many young Chicago Poles eagerly volunteered for the U.S. Army (see chapter 2). Chicago's Polish daily newspaper, *Dziennik Zwiazkowy*, urged a "holy war" against the Hun and the "Prussophiles."[17]

Anti-German Hysteria

It might not have been a "holy war," but after the United States declared war, a campaign broke out against the "Hun"—not only in France, but also at home. Xenophobia, never far from the surface in many parts of America, now had free rein, its fires enkindled by patriotism and fanned by hysteria. In her Chicago novel *On Dearborn Street*, writer Miles Franklin noted how the "suspension of internationalism" was a "great social loss": "people had to remember whether their fellow citizens were British or German, Russian or Scandinavian, Latin or Oriental before they went into a friendly discussion on anything more fundamental than the weather."[18] Looking back at the atmosphere of those frenzied times, a German-American socialist named Oscar Ameringer recalled, "Those were the sweetless, wheatless, meatless, heatless, and perfectly brainless days when your fathers broke Beethoven's records, boycotted Wagner's music, burned German books, painted German Lutheran churches and Goethe's monument in Chicago the color of Shell filling stations today; strung up a Mennonite preacher in Collinsville,

Oklahoma, by the neck until he fainted, repeated the process until he fainted again, and graciously relented; hanged another to the limb of a tree in Collinsville, Illinois, until he was dead."[19] The Collinsville event was the most appalling of the anti-German incidents of the war years. A German-American named Robert Prager was accused of making disloyal statements, and a mob of more than three hundred men and boys seized him from jail and hanged him from a tree outside of town on the morning of April 5, 1918. The leaders of the mob were brought to trial but acquitted; their lawyer's ingenious defense of "patriotic murder" convinced the jury.

This appears to have been the only anti-German occurrence that ended in murder, but many other Germans were taunted, beaten, tarred, and forced to kiss the flag. Local governments passed ordinances forbidding German to be spoken in public and ordered loyalty investigations. German language instruction was discontinued in schools, Lutheran churches were warned to stop using German, Congress passed restrictions on the German-language press, and employers of Germans were harassed. Many German-Americans lost their jobs. In Chicago the president of the Illinois Athletic Club saw to it that all the German employees were fired, and two weeks later the Chicago Athletic Association did the same. Signs went up reading, "No Germans Need Apply Here," and the German Aid Society of Chicago reported that a great many unemployed Germans had to be supported by charity because work could not be found for them.[20]

Americans could hardly deny the greatness of German music, but audiences decided they could live without it. The American Defense Society warned that German music was "one of the most dangerous forms of German propaganda, because it appeals to the emotions and has the power to sway an audience as nothing else can."[21] As of November 10, 1917, the Philadelphia Orchestra eliminated German music from its performances, and New York's Metropolitan Opera, long a Wagner bastion, followed suit. Karl Muck, the conductor of the Boston Symphony, was sent to jail as an "alien enemy." Although he was a Swiss citizen, he had been born in Bavaria and had been the conductor of the kaiser's Royal Orchestra. Most damning, it had been charged that he once refused to play "The Star-Spangled Banner" before a concert. (Actually, the orchestra's executive director had neglected to tell Muck that the song had been requested.)[22] Muck spent nearly a year and a half incarcerated in Georgia before being deported; the camp to which he had been sent contained so many German musicians that they held concerts.

Chicago's own symphony conductor, Frederick Stock, also German born, inevitably came under suspicion. At first he seemed cooperative: he warned the German members of the orchestra to be on their most patriotic behavior, and in September 1917 he announced that every future concert given by the Chicago Symphony Orchestra would contain at least one composition by an American, which meant that audiences could now enjoy the music of Henry K. Hadley, Leo Sowerby, and Felix Borowski, three of the composers who were named.[23] Interestingly, with a few exceptions, the music of Beethoven rarely came under censure, even in Great Britain and France, and his music tended to be regarded as universal. In fact, Beethoven's Sixth Symphony was on the program of the Chicago Symphony's opening night in October 1917. According to one historian, "Beethoven's music was performed more frequently than the music of any other composer, regardless of nationality," and at the time, music critics understandably began to stress Beethoven's Flemish ancestry.[24] Stock's gesture of including American music was appreciated, but he had not taken out U.S. citizenship papers, so in early October 1918 he resigned in order not to stain his orchestra's reputation, a move that the *Tribune* lauded as an expression of a "very fine spirited sense of responsibility and unselfish devotion."[25] The following May the newspaper was happy to report that Stock had appeared before a judge, renounced the former kaiser and the present German government, and was now a bona fide American citizen.[26]

A frightening example of the way xenophobia could damage an individual was the case of a Chicagoan named August Weissensel, a naturalized American citizen who had the temerity to visit a Polish-owned barbershop for a shave and utter pro-German remarks, such as that the kaiser was the "greatest man alive." Two outraged Polish women promptly denounced him, and three months later Weissensel found himself on trial before Judge Kenesaw Mountain Landis. A jury found Weissensel guilty of sedition, and Landis sentenced him to ten years in the

Children in
Chicago's Edison
Park neighborhood
get the message
that pro-Germans
are unacceptable.
Chicago History
Museum, DN-0069264,
cropped; *Chicago Daily
News* photograph

federal penitentiary in Leavenworth, Kansas. Landis explained
that this was actually a light sentence; he could have given him
twenty years but chose the shorter term because Weissensel had
a son in the U.S. Army.[27]

One of the best-known manifestations of anti-German hysteria was the renaming craze. German shepherds were now "police dogs" or "Alsatians," dachshunds became "liberty hounds,"
hamburger became "Salisbury steak," German measles were
renamed "liberty measles," and sauerkraut became "liberty
cabbage," a term that the *Tribune* began using in its recipes.[28]
Renaming also affected place names. In Chicago the name
of the Germania Club was changed to the Lincoln Club, the
Bismarck Hotel became the Randolph Hotel, the German
Hospital became Grant Hospital, and the Kaiser Friedrich
Mutual Aid Society was renamed the George Washington
Benevolent Aid Society.[29] Chicago streets that underwent
name changes were Berlin, Hamburg, Coblentz, Lubeck,
and Rhine.[30] What is now Eleanor Street was then Cologne

Street, Bismarck Place became Ancona Street, and Frankfort Street became Charleston Street. The debate over street renaming continued after the armistice, when it was thought that Teutonic-sounding thoroughfares should be renamed after war heroes. In 1919 an effort was made to change Goethe Street to Boxwood Place, but there was pushback. The chairman of the City Club committee on street names wrote, "I do not approve of changing the names of such streets as Mozart, Schiller, Beethoven, Goethe. As far as I know they did nothing offensive to America."[31] Goethe Street kept its name, although the *Tribune* pointed out that everyone would pronounce it "Goat Street."

Many Germans decided it was safer to have an English-sounding name, and thus Schmidt became Smith, Guttmann became Goodman, Mayer became Mayor, and Griescheimer became Gresham. In August 1918 Harry H. Feilchenfeld, general manager of the Chicago Piggly Wiggly stores, petitioned a circuit court judge to have his name changed to Harry H. Field. Renaming also applied to pets; a Chicagoan changed the name of his dog from Kaiser to Fido.

A protracted instance of name changing in Chicago involved the Bismarck School. In the spring of 1917 a group of Poles and Bohemians led by school board member Anthony Czarnecki proposed renaming the school, but some other board members, dubbed the "solid six," resisted. One of them, Lulu Snodgrass, argued, "Let us attack the living, rather than one who has gone to his reward," whereupon Czarnecki fired back, "What difference does it make if he is dead? Nero and Attila are dead, too, but we don't seem to revere their names."[32] The vice president of the Board of Education then proposed that the name of the Kosciuszko School be changed too, causing Czarnecki to threaten "the wrath of a great body of citizens of Polish birth or descent."[33] Finally, in May 1918 the "solid six" were defeated and the school was renamed after General Frederick Funston, who had won the Medal of Honor in the Philippines and had died in 1917. A disgruntled Snodgrass huffed that Czarnecki "can talk to me about patriotism when he has proved that he was born in this country. . . . When he can prove to me that his ancestors fought for independence in 1776 then he can take me to task for my Americanism and my patriotism."[34]

Schoolchildren salute the flag at Chicago's Bismarck School. The name of the school triggered a bitter controversy that was resolved only when its name was changed to something suitably patriotic. Chicago History Museum, DN-0067757, cropped and cleaned; *Chicago Daily News* photograph

One of the liveliest kerfuffles in Chicago education during World War I had to do with the "kaiser page" in the eighth-grade section of the standard spelling book. The text relied on essays in which words to be learned were italicized, and one of those essays was "The Kaiser in the Making," an admiring look at Wilhelm's school days that praised his "fine *character*" and "*chivalrous* sense of fair play." Unsurprisingly, many wanted the page removed. The school board agreed that a new speller would be prepared, but the anti-German faction wanted the page torn out, which the school board refused to condone. Once again Lulu Snodgrass and Anthony Czarnecki were at odds, with Snodgrass arguing, "If we were to take the action that would cause the children to tear out the page we would have a lot of anarchists in the making" and Czarnecki demanding "the elimination of praise of the worst despot the world has ever known."[35] The *Tribune* helpfully printed a facsimile of the page with the title "How to Tear It Out" and urged schoolchildren to send it the excised pages, which they did. One eleven-year-girl attached a letter in which she said she was glad to "have done my bit in a little way with 'down with the kaiser.'"[36] A few days later John Shoop, superintendent of the board of education, sent workers to the board's storeroom, where a cache of spellers were located; after about a month the board's assistant business manager reported that the "kaiser page" had been removed from 10,411 spellers. Other ripping crews were dispatched to city schools to deal with the 60,000 other spellers owned by the board. Many of the spellers, however, were owned by the students, and when the new school year began in September, Shoop finally agreed that the students should remove the offending page themselves, adding, "I suggest that it be replaced with a picture of the American flag or with a portrait of Washington or Lincoln."[37]

About ten days later Shoop began looking into the text of the books used by students studying the German language. He was fairly certain that the elementary texts contained mostly legends and fairy tales, but he wasn't sure about those used in the upper grades. However, this wasn't a long-term project—the board was no longer buying German textbooks because no new students were being taught German. In September 1917 the board had discontinued elementary-level German classes, largely because so few students were choosing to take them. The board allowed high schools to continue to teach German, but many of these schools also dropped it because of a lack of students.[38] The number of students studying German at Englewood High, for example, went from 150 to 0.[39]

At the beginning of 1918 it came to the attention of the authorities that Chicago's pro-Germans tended to repeat the same arguments. These arguments were traced to certain books in the city's libraries, the chief culprit being *Whose Sin Is the World-War?* by Jules Andrassy, Austria-Hungary's foreign minister. An embarrassed librarian explained that such books were common before the declaration of war and were "considered harmless," but now all copies would be withdrawn forthwith: "We are making systematic efforts to weed out all books of this class."[40]

Chicago also possessed the only German-language theater in the United States. There had been at least two others—one in Milwaukee, one in New York—but they closed down in 1917, leaving Chicago with the Bush Temple Theater on Clark Street and Chicago Avenue, which in January 1918 was presenting a popular Viennese operetta titled *Das Dreimaedlerhaus*.[41] This was an affront to a loyalist named Earl A. Stevenson, who on New Year's Day used a long pole to knock down the sign bearing the show's title. Although cheered by onlookers, this act of patriotism earned him a trip to jail. The *Tribune* reported that Stevenson's neighbors said "they thought it was a darned shame that the police hadn't allowed him to finish up the job properly, and that it was a gol darned shame to permit a German comedy to be produced in an American city."[42] The State Council of Defense summoned the theater manager, Conrad Seiteman, who argued that "art has no language," he was a "good American," and he couldn't see any reason not to stage plays in German. The theater managed to survive the inquiry, but it did not thrive. In 1917 some wealthy Chicago Germans kept the theater going by subsidizing it, but they ceased to do so the following year, attendance dropped off, and Seiteman admitted that German theater would soon die.[43]

The Bush Temple of Music in Chicago once housed the last remaining German-language theater in the United States, a situation that troubled self-proclaimed patriots in the anti-German atmosphere of World War I.
Author's collection

In the summer of 1918 a group of fourteen Chicago women formed the Use Nothing German (UNG) society. They were attending a breakfast at the South Shore Country Club when they developed the idea to boycott all things Teutonic. As the *Tribune* put it, "No 98 cent knocked down from a dollar bargain will tempt these hardy souls, who believe that one way to beat the kaiser is to encourage home industry and to banish forever all 'made in Germany' marks from dishes, gloves, tin soldiers, dolls, and everything that comes into their households."[44] The day after launching their association, the UNG members assembled for a "smashing party" in which they sang, "One, two, three / Down with Germany," while shattering a hand-painted pretzel dish, a beer stein, and a doll. The women's activities inspired a letter to the *Tribune* by Edward L. Burchard, a prominent museum director, in which he sarcastically proposed that the destruction should not stop with pretzel dishes but should extend to the works of Albrecht Dürer and other artists hanging in the Art Institute. Then the protestors could see to the elimination of the "several thousand volumes by German savants" from the scientific and medical holdings of the Crerar Library. For that matter, since practically every home in Chicago contained fabrics that used German dyes, they would have to go too.

Whereas 191,000 Chicagoans had identified as German in 1914, the 1920 census reported only 112,000 doing the same.[45] This wasn't due to a mass outflow of Germans from the city; it was because thousands of people had grown ashamed of their ethnic heritage and chose to identify themselves differently. As historian Melvin G. Holli has expressed it, "The war damaged German ethnic, linguistic, and cultural institutions beyond repair."[46] And historian Frederick C. Luebke has written that by the mid-twentieth century "the Germans as a group had disappeared, completely assimilated into mainstream America."[47]

World War I and Prohibition

Narratives describing the anti-German hysteria of the First World War tend to overlook one profound result: the acceleration of the drive toward national prohibition. Without the war, a constitutional amendment banning alcoholic beverages probably would never have been passed.

Efforts to abolish, or at least limit, the sale and consumption of alcohol began in the colonial era, but they became organized, powerful, and national in scope in the later nineteenth century. By the time of the First World War, the Anti-Saloon League (ASL) had become the dominant group agitating for a constitutional amendment prohibiting the manufacture and sale of alcoholic beverages in the United States.

Prohibition was most popular in rural and small-town America, where its backers often displayed a nativist, anti-immigrant outlook. The movement did not have much support in the big cities, where immigrant populations were fond of their saloons, beer gardens, and homemade wine. The German brewers were horrified by the possibility of a ban on alcohol. The great American breweries were headed by wealthy and powerful "beer barons." Most prominent among them was Adolphus Busch of St. Louis, who had established his brewery in partnership with his father-in-law, Eberhard Anheuser; others included Valentin Blatz, Bernhard Stroh, Frederick Pabst, Joseph Schlitz, Frederick Miller (originally Friedrich Eduard Johannes Müller), and the brothers Frederick and Maximilian Schaefer. All had been born in Germany. The United States Brewers' Association, which they founded, formed a partnership with the National German-American Alliance, which had been created in 1901 to preserve German culture in the United States. The brewers funded the alliance and turned it into a major antiprohibition lobby with over two million members. Chicago's own resident suspect brewer was Charles H. Wacker. He had, however, been born in Chicago, although he went to school in Stuttgart, and despite having donated to the German Red Cross in the early days of the war, he worked overtime to prove his patriotism by serving with various organizations aiding the war effort, including the Illinois State Council of Defense. He was also esteemed as the chairman of the Chicago Plan Commission, and Wacker Drive was named after him.

One of the key factors working against the adoption of a federal ban on alcohol was the federal government's reliance on excise taxes, most of which came from the duties on alcohol. In 1910 the government was collecting over $200 million a year in excise taxes on beer and liquor, which amounted to 71 percent of all internal revenue and more than 30 percent of all federal revenue.[48] The brewers and distillers supported the excise tax because they believed that the government's dependence on their products made national prohibition impossible. But the prohibitionists made an end run around the excise tax by winning the passage of the Sixteenth Amendment, which established a national income tax. The amendment was ratified in early 1913; a prohibition amendment was introduced in Congress at the end of that same year.

Nevertheless, a prohibition amendment was still a hard sell because most inhabitants of the expanding cities opposed it. The prohibitionists knew that they had to get the amendment passed before 1920 because the new census would surely show a large growth in the urban population. That would raise the number of urban representatives in the House, thus depriving the drys of the two-thirds majority required to pass a constitutional amendment.[49] Consequently, the declaration of war on Germany must have seemed heaven sent because the demonization of the Germans was the ultimate weapon. Now beer could be painted as un-American. The ASL equated beer with treason and singled out the brewers as enemies of America. It didn't help that Adolphus Busch had been personally presented the Order of the Red Eagle by Kaiser Wilhelm II and owned a castle on the Rhine. As historian Richard F. Hamm has explained, "The war made it easy for drys to portray the predominantly German American brewers as subversives, if not traitors."[50]

In October 1918 Senator Wesley Jones of Washington filed a memorandum with a Senate committee charging that the brewers' association had secretly financed newspapers, bribed national and state legislators, and contributed to the National German-American Alliance, "even after the sinking of the Lusitania and other similar German atrocities." He concluded that "the brewery trade and liquor traffic is pro-German in its sympathy."[51] The previous year E. J. Davis of the Chicago district of the ASL had made a similar charge that the brewers were helping finance the alliance in promoting "the interests in this country of the pro-German, or war element in control of the German nation, against the interests of the United States government." Prohibition could now be portrayed as patriotic. Anna Gordon, president of the Women's Christian Temperance Union (WCTU), spoke of "the Un-American liquor traffic . . . of alien

IF THIS
TOWN GOES
DRY
US GERMANS
VILL HANG
TOGEDER
(NICHT WAHR)

As this macabre cartoon illustrates, many Americans would not have been upset at the demise of the country's German-born brewers. During the war prohibitionists shrewdly exploited anti-German hatred to help secure the passage of the Eighteenth Amendment, which outlawed "intoxicating liquors." Author's collection

and autocratic origin," and the WCTU praised the "Prohibition Patriot."[52] Congress revoked the charter of the National German-American Alliance in 1918, and it went out of business.

In addition to demonizing the Germans, World War I brought three other developments that favored prohibition: it centralized authority in Washington; it made citizens aware of the need to save food; and it raised awareness that if soldiers were going to be fit to fight, they needed to be protected from "demon rum." Arguing the need for national conservation, the Wilson administration received authority to regulate fuel and food. It seemed wasteful to dedicate agricultural land to the production of spirits, and many asked, "Shall the many have food, or the few have drink?"[53] Consequently, Congress in August 1917 passed a law that banned the use of food products in the manufacture of distilled liquor; this was followed in November 1918 by the Wartime Prohibition Act, which banned the manufacture of wine and beer. Meanwhile, Congress "mandated liquor-free zones around military camps."[54] With so many states and counties already having passed prohibition laws such that more than half the U.S. population lived under some form of alcohol ban—combined with the wartime distilling, winemaking, and brewing restrictions—the United States was practically dry even before the passage of the Eighteenth Amendment, which made prohibition the law of the land.

The English writer G. K. Chesterton, who visited the United States in 1921, astutely recognized that the war spirit that had seized the country encouraged a willingness to sacrifice that was made to order for the prohibition forces. "Prohibition," he said, "was largely passed in a sort of fervor or fever of self-sacrifice, which was part of the passionate patriotism of America in the war. . . . Prohibition was partly a sort of patriotic renunciation." Chesterton could understand why prohibition would be accepted as a necessary wartime measure; what irked him was that the policy would be continued in peacetime.[55]

The Eighteenth Amendment was ratified on January 16, 1919, just two months after the armistice. National prohibition would most likely not have been enacted without the war and the anti-German hysteria because the prohibitionists would otherwise not have succeeded in getting the needed votes before the 1920 census. And what prohibition meant to Chicago is one of the most often told tales in American history. Because of the First World War, Chicago lost the Bismarck School and Berlin Street, and it got bootleggers and bathtub gin. It lost *Kultur*, and it got Capone.

Thomas Dorsey. Author's collection

Thomas A. Dorsey
The Father of Gospel Music

In addition to jazz and the blues, in the first half of the twentieth century African Americans in Chicago forged a third type of music with global appeal: hand-clapping, roof-raising gospel music. Thousands come to the Chicago Gospel Music Festival every year, the Chicago Gospel Music Awards have become an annual event, and a visitor can even book passage on a Chicago gospel lunch cruise. Although the modern development of this jubilant sound did not take place until the 1930s, the "father of gospel music" was a bluesman who came to Chicago during the Great Migration.

Thomas Andrew Dorsey was born in Villa Rica, Georgia, on July 1, 1899. His father, a graduate of Atlanta Baptist College, was an itinerant preacher who also did some sharecropping. Dorsey's mother played the organ, one uncle was a blues guitarist, and another uncle wrote hymns and taught the disciplined art of choral "shape-note" singing. With one parent a preacher and the other a musician, from his earliest years Dorsey viewed religion and music as the two poles of his life, although he wavered between them a long time before reconciling them as a church musician.

After his family moved to Atlanta around 1908, the musically curious young Dorsey began hanging around the theaters, watching the pianists and then going home to try to duplicate what he'd heard. "I'd ring those blues on that organ," he said.[1] He was a quick study: by age sixteen he was an accomplished blues pianist. He took a few lessons and began learning how to write music down.[2]

Like so many others, Dorsey read the *Chicago Defender* and heard its call to come north. As he put it, "I wanted to go where the lights were brighter and you didn't have to run to get the last street car at midnight."[3] He arrived in Chicago, where he had several relatives, in the summer of 1916. When the war came, he was able to avoid being drafted by taking a job in a steel mill. He began playing at unlicensed after-hours clubs known as "buffet flats" and became known as the "whispering piano player" for his unusually soft touch on the keyboard.[4]

In 1921 Dorsey heard a performance by a singing preacher named W. M. Nix, who was an expert in musical improvisation. Dorsey vowed to take religion seriously and found a job as music director at a South Side Baptist church. The conversion didn't last, however, and lured by the prospect of $40 a week, he took a job in a band, although he did write a couple of sacred songs, including "We Will Meet Him in the Sweet By and By." He also began writing blues numbers; one of them, "Riverside Blues" of 1923, was recorded by the great King Oliver. Eventually, Dorsey became accompanist, bandleader, and arranger for the blues singer Ma Rainey, and it seemed that the "gutbucket, lowdown" blues had become his ticket to success. He made recordings under the name "Georgia Tom" and earned a good amount from sheet music sales of his songs. Dorsey's most popular tune was the naughty double-entendre "It's Tight like That," which he recorded with the guitarist Hudson Whitaker, who went by the name Tampa Red.

And yet God kept tapping Dorsey on the shoulder. In 1928 he had a kind of nervous breakdown that plunged him into such despair that he contemplated suicide. However, a minister told him, "Brother Dorsey, there is no reason for you to be looking so poorly and feeling so badly. The Lord has too much work for you to do to let you die."[5] Soon after, the death of a good friend inspired Dorsey to write his third gospel song, "If You See My Savior."

In 1931 Dorsey was invited to form a gospel choir at Ebenezer Baptist Church. The following year he became the choirmaster at Chicago's Pilgrim Baptist Church, a post he retained for more than four decades. From his boyhood days in Atlanta, Dorsey had been a blues musician, and when he turned to sacred song, he remained one. Applying the blues idiom to church music appealed to the rural immigrants from the South, but traditionalist black ministers in Chicago were horrified. "Degrading" and "desecration" were some of the words used. To them, riling up the congregation and bringing them to their feet with hand-clapping were "rural practices" and distasteful reminders of the days of black oppression and ignorance. Dorsey himself acknowledged that his gospel sound, with its moans, shouts, declamations, and amens, was not new but a throwback to a more animated form of black worship. "I embellished gospel," he said, "made it beautiful, more noticeable, more susceptible with runs and trills and moans in it." In a sense, Dorsey *restored* blues to black church services. The way a Dorsey song is notated in sheet music is only a framework; Dorsey expected the performer to add improvisation and embellishment.

Dorsey wrote an estimated eight hundred songs. Artists who have performed his music run the gamut from Guy Lombardo to Aretha Franklin to Elvis Presley to Beyoncé.[6] Dorsey's most famous song was born from deep tragedy. In August 1932 his wife, Nettie, died in childbirth; the newborn boy died the next day. Dorsey thereupon composed "Take My Hand, Precious Lord," which has been sung around the world. When it was first performed, Dorsey once recalled, "The folk went wild. . . . They broke up the church. Folk were shouting everywhere."[7] It became a favorite of Dr. Martin Luther King Jr., who requested to hear the song just moments before he was murdered.[8]

When, in the 1950s and 1960s, singers like Ray Charles and Aretha Franklin began using gospel techniques such as melisma (singing many notes on one syllable of text) in love songs, Dorsey's sound had become so identified with African American religion that its use in secular music was ironically now considered a desecration. Today pop divas use gospel techniques so heavily that their melismatic flights invite parody.

By the time Dorsey died in Chicago on January 23, 1993, at age ninety-three, he knew well what he had wrought. In an interview conducted late in his life, he said, "There's something in gospel music. You know there must be something, else it wouldn't have the coverage it's made throughout the world."[9]

Emil G. Hirsch
The Mistrusted Rabbi

Rabbi Emil Hirsch of Sinai Temple in Chicago could speak seventeen languages, but only one of them got him into trouble during World War I—German.

Emil Gustav Hirsch was born on May 22, 1851, in Luxembourg, where his father was chief rabbi of the Grand Duchy. The family was German by inclination and by culture, however, and when the United States entered the Great War, that was enough to place Rabbi Hirsch under suspicion. But he had already done plenty to raise doubts.

Hirsch came to the United States at the age of fifteen when his father accepted a rabbinical position in Philadelphia. After graduating from the University of Philadelphia, where he had played on the football team, Hirsch did his postgraduate work at the universities of Berlin and Leipzig, and then became a rabbi in Baltimore. This was followed by a brief stint in Louisville, and in 1880 Rabbi Hirsch came to Chicago.[1]

As chief rabbi of Sinai Temple, Hirsch soon became one of Chicago's most distinguished churchmen (and, it was believed, the highest paid) and a leading figure in the formation of Reform Judaism.[2] He was a progressive who championed workers' rights, unemployment compensation, the abolition of child labor, slum clearance, prison reform, and improved public education. In 1892 he became a professor of Semitic languages at the University of Chicago, and he also was president of the board of the Chicago Public Library. He was a featured speaker at the World's Parliament of Religions, part of the 1893 Columbian Exposition, and he delivered a moving oration in which he said that when Gentiles learned what Judaism really was, they would exclaim, "Why, you Jews are not different from us; you are men as we are; your hopes are our hopes; your beliefs are our beliefs. And why should the world not say this? Have we not all one Father? Has not one God created us all?"[3]

The talented, intelligent, and altruistic rabbi was certainly eloquent, but eloquence can be a double-edged sword—if it's used to praise unpopular views. When the war began in Europe, Chicagoans took sides, usually based on their ethnic heritage, so it's no surprise that Hirsch favored Germany. But he probably didn't need to do it with such outspokenness. On December 10, 1914, he gave a speech in which he said, "Our hopes are with those German and Austro-Hungarian soldiers in the trenches over there. . . . If you win, the best there is in the human race will have also won, and with you, the German element of America." He accused Russian soldiers of raping Jewish girls and announced that the "German Army is the incarnation of loyal fulfillment of duty, and therefore upholds Kant's philosophy."[4] This equating of German culture with

Emil Hirsch. Chicago History Museum, ICHi-35875, cleaned; photographer, Varney

militarism was especially troubling to those who considered German belligerence a frightening new development.

And as for the Jews? Hirsch went on to say that "the Jews all over the world, with the exception of the Spanish Jews, are with Germany in this war."[5] Later, he proudly noted that in the German Army, "4,000 Jewish soldiers were awarded the Iron Cross of the second class and nineteen Jews earned the Iron Cross of the first class."[6] Hirsch was also vice president of the Illinois Branch of the East Prussia Relief Society, which raised funds to rebuild towns destroyed by the Russians.[7]

Once the doughboys were on their way to France, such sentiments could seem unpatriotic, if not treasonous. And it didn't help that no fewer than nine of Hirsch's relatives were serving in the German forces, although he pointed out that some were with the British and French military. Apparently fearing that their own Americanism— along with that of Jews in general—might come under suspicion, some of his congregants called for his ouster.[8]

Hirsch moved quickly to undo the damage. In November 1917 it was announced that, at Hirsch's urging, Sinai Temple would soon be flying a "service flag" with more than a hundred stars on it, representing the members of the congregation who were in the service.[9] The gesture was not enough to silence the rabbi's critics, and on April 14, 1918, an overflow crowd jammed into Sinai Temple to hear Hirsch as he, "in a burst of patriotic fervor . . . affirmed his undivided, single-hearted allegiance to the nation's cause," as the *Chicago Tribune* put it. He also prayed that "the error of the rulers of Germany may be overthrown, that these rulers themselves may be overthrown." Following the sermon, hundreds of congregants announced that "they would stand by him."[10]

Hirsch's efforts kept him at the head of Sinai Temple, but four months later it was reported that he was ill, his doctors had ordered "complete rest," and he would be absent for several weeks. He went to California to recuperate and was actually gone for months—he had suffered a stroke. Hirsch believed that his loyalty was still questioned and that the stress had sickened him, and when he returned to the pulpit in April 1919, he challenged those who had doubted him. At the end of his sermon, he stepped back and called out, "Does anyone in this congregation accuse me of disloyalty?" No one spoke, and the rabbi went on to say:

> Under the false and malicious accusations made against me, I spent many nights without a wink of sleep. I walked the streets of Chicago, looking back often, wondering whether I would see a mob which would put a rope around my neck and string me up to a lamp post. . . . One of my boys went into the army and another one volunteered and was rejected on account of his eyes. I offered my services to the government and received an answer saying I had passed the age when such service could be accepted. . . . Unfortunately I was not born in this country, but it was not my fault. This is my country, and that is my flag, and I will have no other.[11]

Hirsch was never quite the same and might be considered a war casualty of a sort, although he remained at the head of Sinai Temple until his death on January 7, 1923. Two years before, on the occasion of his seventieth birthday, the *Reform Advocate*, a Jewish weekly that Hirsch had founded, published a special issue crammed with glowing tributes from all corners, Christian and Jew. When he saw the publication, Hirsch turned with tear-filled eyes to his son David and said, "Ich kenn mich nicht" (I do not recognize myself). The old rabbi was still speaking German.

PART SIX

After the War

14

"Taking New Heart": Organized Labor and the Postwar Strikes

The year 1919 saw what was probably the greatest episode of strikes in U.S. history, as more than one in five American workers of all sorts, including policemen, steelworkers, textile workers, stockyards laborers, and coal miners, took to the picket lines. In Chicago the industries most affected were the city's largest—the packinghouses and steel mills.

The war set the stage. Although labor unrest exploded afterward, it began during the war. As historian Robert H. Zieger has put it, "In the years of the Great War, confrontations between workers and employers in the United States peaked. Between 1914 and 1920, an average of more than 3,000 significant strikes erupted annually. In the years 1916–1918 more than four million workers conducted work stoppages, and in 1919 alone, the figure reached 4,160,000. Violence marked many of these contests."[1] For organized labor in Chicago, the war unlocked doors that seemed to open onto a bright future. Workers were in demand, corporate profits were high, and organized labor had a friend in the White House.

As in so many other facets of American life, on labor issues Chicago was a microcosm of the United States, and its labor movement was probably the most sophisticated in the country. Chicago, according to a contemporary observer, was "the place where labor is most riotous, most expressive, where the working man abounds in his own sense and has formed an atmosphere of democracy extending far beyond his own class."[2]

The CFL: Chicago's Own

At the time of the war the most prominent labor leader in the country was Samuel Gompers, who had been president of the American Federation of Labor (AFL) for three decades. The AFL, founded in 1886, was the largest union organization in the

Chicago's preeminent position in the American labor movement was unmistakable when delegates from labor unions across the country assembled in the city in 1919, a year in which some four million American workers walked off the job. Library of Congress

United States. Gompers had close ties to President Woodrow Wilson, who described Gompers as a man who knew how "to pull in harness." Counting on support from the Wilson administration, Gompers adopted a "corporatist" view of business-labor relations that deemphasized the strike and favored a system in which outside mediators would objectively settle labor disputes. In early 1918 the National War Labor Board was established to prevent strikes by acting as a kind of referee between management and labor.

But back in Chicago, that quintessential labor town, labor leaders did not exactly agree with Gompers's prowar, corporatist stance. The most prominent labor organization in the city was the Chicago Federation of Labor (CFL), which represented 350 local unions and had 350,000 members.[3] The AFL had created the CFL in 1896, but under its local leaders the CFL tended to set its own policies, sometimes at odds with the AFL. Once war broke out in Europe, the CFL became one of the most prominent antiwar organizations, casting a skeptical eye on American calls for preparedness, which the AFL supported. In November 1915 a CFL committee concluded that preparedness was not the way to prevent war; the best way to do that would be to pass progressive legislation that would benefit working people. The CFL staged counterdemonstrations at preparedness events, opposed military training in schools, argued that companies that sold munitions and other items to belligerents were engaging in treasonous activities, and attacked newspapers that supported the preparedness campaign. For the CFL, war was

a capitalist conspiracy that enabled the "exploiters of labor" to oppress workers.

After the U.S. declaration of war, however, the CFL's leaders realized that an antiwar stance might taint the labor movement with disloyalty, and after much debate, the majority of members came to support Gompers's argument that it would be wrong to strike during wartime. But the CFL never wholeheartedly accepted Gompers's corporatist vision, suspecting that the outside moderators would consistently make rulings favorable to business owners, and the head of the CFL, the Irish-born John Fitzpatrick, reserved the right to strike if he thought that business owners were exploiting workers during wartime.

Another issue on which the CFL split with the AFL was immigration policy. Gompers and the AFL backed a literacy test for immigrants because it would "protect the workers from unfair competition resulting from indiscriminate immigration."[4] Gompers was rewarded by the Immigration Act of 1917, which included a literacy requirement for immigrants (see chapter 12). But in Chicago immigrants from southern and eastern Europe were the core of the working force and the heart of organized labor. As recent arrivals, they were mostly nonunionized and therefore prized by the CFL. In addition, they had formed their own ethnic organizations, giving them a solidarity that translated into political power. Accordingly, the CFL opposed immigration restrictions.

Unionization of the Stockyards

Seizing the opportunities provided by the war, Chicago union organizers set their sights on nothing less than the industry that practically defined the city: the stockyards. Packinghouse workers were represented by the Amalgamated Meat Cutters and Butcher Workmen of North America (AMC), founded in 1897 and affiliated with the AFL. The local units were well organized and included a women's organization, and the union had some success in surmounting the ethnic differences that had previously divided older German and Irish workers from eastern European newcomers.[5]

The war enhanced the prospects of the packinghouse workers in several ways. First, the military draft and enlistment, along with the near halt in immigration, had created a labor shortage. Second, there was a huge increase in demand for meat and meat products, and the output of the packing industry soared. In the three years before the war average monthly beef exports were just over one million pounds; by June 1918 they were ninety-two million. And as union leaders knew, the packers were experiencing record profits. In 1912–14 the four largest packing companies showed an aggregate profit of $19 million; in 1916 profits were $46 million, and in 1917 they were $68 million.[6] Third, Chicago packinghouse workers had a new organization to represent them: the Stockyards Labor Council (SLC). The SLC had been organized under the aegis of the CFL, not the AFL, and in effect, the SLC replaced the AMC as the voice

William Z. Foster (*right*) was the organizer of the Stockyards Labor Council, which came to represent Chicago's packinghouse workers. He also played a major role in organizing steelworkers. Library of Congress

of the packinghouse worker. The SLC was the invention of a well-known radical named William Z. Foster, who was able to unite his union, the Brotherhood of Railway Carmen, with other craft unions operating in the stockyards.

By November 1917, six months into the war, Foster's SLC had unionized between one-fourth and one-half of all the stockyard employees, and Foster threatened to call out the workers, who had already overwhelmingly voted to endorse a strike.[7] The union bosses even argued that the government should take control of the packinghouses similarly to the way Wilson had nationalized the railroads at the end of 1917.[8] As head of the CFL, Fitzpatrick approved Foster's actions, and the prospect of a strike caused alarm in Washington, where the Wilson administration set up a mediation board. Union leaders had reason to expect favorable treatment, because William B. Wilson, the secretary of labor, was one of their own. He had been a secretary-treasurer of the United Mine Workers before entering Congress, where he secured the passage of laws championed by union leaders, and once he became labor secretary, he forged what has been called "a virtual alliance of the Wilson White House and the AF of L."[9] Throughout the war, the Wilson administration stood for the eight-hour day, equal pay for women, and the right of workers to bargain collectively.

To arbitrate the stockyards conflict, the secretary of labor appointed Judge Samuel Alschuler of the U.S. Circuit Court. As the *Chicago Tribune* put it, the issues before the judge were the "eight-hour day, overtime, three work shifts, a wage increase, equal pay for men and women, and a guaranteed forty-hour work."[10] For the SLC the issue of equal pay for women was not a side issue. Women had been working in packinghouses before the war, but most of them were single. With the coming of the war, however, more married women sought jobs in the stockyards, and many of them had dependents to support. A week after his appointment, Alschuler visited four of the major Chicago packinghouses. He was especially interested, it was reported, in the "luncheons served to employees by the packers at a nominal cost, in the work of the 'killing gangs,' and in the departments where women are employed."[11]

At the time, the packers were operating two ten-hour shifts, and the general superintendent of Armour & Co. explained in court that the "tremendous pressure of war orders" necessitated this schedule. He blamed overregulation for part of the problem: because of government cleanliness mandates, it took at least four hours to clean the killing departments, reducing daily production by 30 percent. He also said that Armour's policy was to give men and women equal pay, but he knew of "no department in the plant where both were doing the same work." Finally, he said that the wage scale "compared favorably with the pay in other industries."[12] Gompers countered that the eight-hour day would actually *increase* production. It had already been proven, he said, that the eight-hour day improved the "physical welfare and the morale of the working people" and that an overworked employee was less effective. "Depend upon it," he declared, "when [the packers] see their men rejuvenated by the eight hour day, when they see the increased efficiency, they won't want to go back to the old conditions."[13]

The mediation sessions were open to the public, and "large groups of packinghouse laborers, social workers, and other interested observers thronged to the Federal Building each day."[14] Workers and their wives testified about their shabby houses and ailing children, while the packers' lawyers told about the workers' growing savings accounts and the large numbers of neighborhood saloons. The packers' case was greatly damaged when an executive of United Charities explained that the minimum yearly budget for a "pauper family" of five was $1,106.82, and the average annual income for a packinghouse worker was about $800.

The judge handed down his decision on March 31, 1918, and the union got almost everything it wanted: an eight-hour day and seven paid holidays, double time for Sundays and holidays and time and a quarter for other overtime, twenty minutes for lunch with pay, a guaranteed forty-eight-hour workweek, and equal pay for men and women. Labor's only complaint was about the wage hike, which ranged from 5¼ cents an hour for the lowest-paid workers to 3½ cents for the highest-paid. Fitzpatrick commented, "We had hoped for a larger increase in wages than was allowed." He added, however, "[We] consider we have won a great victory for labor."[15]

At the time, a story circulated that when Gompers heard that the armistice had been signed, he was disappointed. The labor movement, he believed, hadn't had time to consolidate all of its wartime successes.[16] By the end of the war the CFL had come to view the National War Labor Board as a group of "labor baiters and labor crushers."[17] The no-strike policy needed another look. The CFL also believed that the time was ripe to create a new political party, the Farmer-Labor Party; use it to take control of the federal government; and enact prolabor legislation.

As the cost of living rose after the war, wages failed to keep pace. In November 1919 Judge Alschuler reviewed labor's complaints, but the wage raise he granted was small; he also ruled against the union's demands for a forty-four-hour workweek and double pay for overtime.[18] The CFL's wartime agreement that disputes would be settled by an arbitrator was fine as long as the judge ruled in the union's favor, but now labor leaders were learning that judges could rule the other way.

In the spring of 1919 the SLC began a strong effort to put pressure on the packers and to increase union membership. The organization held open-air meetings, sent out trucks with loudspeakers, and formed organizing committees. Union leaders tried hard to bring in black members, who had traditionally been skeptical of unions as being mostly for the benefit of white workers. Black workers, however, were so reluctant to unionize that at one point white workers staged a walkout to protest black resistance. The eagerness to admit black workers was due more to the union bosses' realization that a strike would fail without them than to a sense of equality. Some leaders of the Chicago Urban League (CUL) thought that the unions might promote racial harmony, but for the most part the CUL's "involvement with organized labor was characterized largely by circumspection and even antagonism."[19] As one historian has said of Chicago's black workers, "the effort at unionization was doomed to failure."[20] Complicating things further was the race riot that broke out in Chicago in July 1919. Much of the violence was in the Packingtown area, and any hope of racial harmony was dead for years. Thus black-white antagonism was added to the already prevalent ethnic discord among immigrant white workers, who often couldn't speak English and couldn't communicate with workers from other countries.

In June 1919 a series of small strikes flared up, and policemen were sent to the stockyards. Their presence only angered the workers more, and on July 18 ten thousand walked off the job.

A union organizer explained, "The men do not want to work under police protection and they are not going back until the policemen are out."[21] The policemen were speedily withdrawn and the strike ended, but the workers were still restive, seeking wage increases that would keep pace with inflation.

Meat prices continued to rise, but demand then began to drop, and by 1921 prices were what they were before the war. The packers had tolerated unions during the war but never really accepted them, and as demand for their products declined, they began to lay off workers in large numbers. The number of packinghouse workers in Chicago declined 40 percent between 1919 and 1921.[22] The packers, who were now losing money, announced the reestablishment of the ten-hour day and an 8 percent wage cut. Under arbitration, the AMC, which had regained its status among the stockyard workers, agreed to the wage cut to save the eight-hour day.[23]

The packers also sought to pacify the workers by establishing welfare measures, such as an expanded health and safety program, better working conditions, an employee representation plan, sports teams, day-care facilities, Americanization classes, and a stock-sharing plan, recognizing that a worker was less likely to strike a factory if he was part owner of it.[24] The packers also formed worker representation systems, which were in effect company unions that competed with the labor unions. The packers also engineered a propaganda campaign that issued pamphlets, factory newspapers, and other materials extolling their good works and explaining that wage cuts were necessary to save jobs. In November 1921 the packers announced that the lowest-paid workers would have their hourly pay reduced from 45 to 37½ cents. The pay of semiskilled workers went down 5 cents. The higher-paid workers came off relatively well; their pay dropped from 50 to 47 cents.

The wage cuts provoked a large stockyard strike at the end of 1921. Walking out during a time of high unemployment is not usually effective, and the packers easily found strikebreakers, especially among Chicago's black population. Many immigrant stockyard workers were permanently replaced by black ones. A judge ruled that picketing was illegal, and a small army of policemen overran the area to compel compliance with his order. Sporadic rioting, which involved thousands, was met with police gunfire, and many strikers, men and women, were arrested. The strikers tried to hold out, but the strike was called off on February 1, 1922. Chicago's stockyard workers would not return to union building until the Great Depression, when unions nationwide returned in force to the streets, and the SLC rose from the ashes.

Unrest in the Steel Mills

The situation in the steel mills was similar to that in the packinghouses: restlessness before the war, optimism during it, militancy afterward, defeat and disillusion in the 1920s, and a labor renaissance during the Great Depression and World War II. Although the stockyards were the most celebrated symbol of Chicago's industrial strength, it was also a major steel town. When most of the area's mills joined together to create the Illinois Steel Company in 1889, Chicago possessed what at the time was the largest steel company in the world, employing ten thousand workers. In 1901 banker J. P. Morgan oversaw the creation of U.S. Steel, which became the world's largest corporation; it operated huge mills in South Chicago and nearby Gary, Indiana. Other companies that operated steel mills in Chicagoland included Acme Steel, Republic Steel, Union Steel, Wisconsin Steel, Inland Steel, and Youngstown Sheet & Tube.

Steel mills were treacherous workplaces, and a twelve-hour day was standard, as was "shift work," which obligated the workers to switch from day to night every few weeks and to work a twenty-four-hour shift while doing so. About one-fourth of the mill hands worked a seven-day week. As early as the 1860s Chicago-area steelworkers had begun forming unions to press for better pay, safer working conditions, and shorter hours, and in 1901 the AFL began an effort to create a federal union of iron and steel workers.

As with the packing industry, the steel business boomed during the Great War, and the CFL's success in organizing the stockyard workers made the possibilities in the mills seem bright. As a contemporary observer put it, "If an industry so completely non-union . . . may become organized under the new conception of human rights as formulated at Washington, what may not be possible"?[25] After the war began in Europe, orders started to pour in from the Allied powers, and once the

United States entered the war, the Federal Trade Commission reported that the steel industry was making huge profits. At one point a steel executive candidly admitted, "We are all making more money out of this war than the average human being ought to."[26]

After a bitter strike began in Youngstown, Ohio, at the end of 1915, the steel mill owners temporarily bought labor peace by modestly raising wages. The steelworkers were gratified, but they understood that the belligerent countries depended on American steel, and "the steelmaking function assumed in the working man's mind a value much in excess of its monetary return." Although by June 1916 wages had increased 21 percent, steel prices had doubled or even tripled. The workers also had to contend with inflation; although during the war steelworkers' wages rose 45 percent, the cost of living rose 70 percent.[27] And there were two other problems. First, although workers had succeeded in reducing work hours before the war, when the demand for steel rose the mill owners gradually began reintroducing the seven-day workweek and twelve-hour day. And second, the owners refused even to consider recognizing the workers' right to organize.

In the spring of 1918 Foster of the SLC began taking up the cause of the steelworkers. He and Fitzpatrick, head of the CFL, began making plans to vastly increase union membership among the mill hands. The time was ripe. As Foster later wrote:

> As the war wore on . . . , the situation changed rapidly in favor of the unions. The demand for soldiers and munitions had made labor scarce; the Federal administration was friendly; the right to organize was freely conceded by the government and even insisted upon; the steel industry was the masterclock of the whole war program and had to be kept in operation at all costs; the workers were taking new heart and making demands. . . . The gods were indeed fighting on the side of Labor. It was an opportunity to organize the industry such as might never again occur.[28]

In August, under the auspices of Gompers and the AFL, a conference of steelworkers union leaders from across the country met at the New Morrison Hotel in Chicago and formed the National Committee for the Organization of Iron and

Steel Workers, an alliance of twenty-four trade unions that included not only mill hands but also workers in enterprises that served the steel industry— machinists, electrical workers, mine workers, and so on. Foster called it "the largest body of workers ever engaged in a joint movement in any country."[29] Fitzpatrick was named acting chairman of the National Committee, and Foster was made secretary-treasurer. Gompers spent most of the following months in Europe, so the two Chicagoans were the main drivers of the national organizing effort, with Fitzpatrick being the decision maker and Foster the tactician. Their list of demands included twelve items, the most important being the right of collective bargaining, the eight-hour day, "one day's rest in seven," and a wage raise "sufficient to guarantee an American standard of living."[30]

John Fitzpatrick, head of the Chicago Federation of Labor, was instrumental in organizing strikes in the stockyards and steel mills. Library of Congress

The steel tycoons were passionately antiunion, refusing even to recognize labor organizations. After Carnegie Steel had crushed a strike organized by the Amalgamated Association of Iron and Steel Workers in 1892, it had declared that it would "never again recognize the Amalgamated Association or any other labor organization."[31] This was the unbending policy of the entire steel industry for the next quarter century. In 1909 an ultimatum from Carnegie that the workers must give up their union and accept a wage reduction was followed by a fourteen-month strike. The union lost again, and in 1919 Elbert Gary, CEO of U.S. Steel, reaffirmed, "It has been my policy, and the policy of our corporation, not to deal with union labor leaders . . . we do not believe in contracting with unions."[32] Unsurprisingly, union recognition was demand number one for the strikers of 1919.

The workers in the mills were enthusiastic about the new organizing efforts of the National Committee for the Organization of Iron and Steel Workers. In September 1918 a union official in Gary reported, "Overflow meetings were held in the streets—the same in South Chicago, Joliet, and Indiana Harbor." By the end of 1918 Foster observed, "Beyond all question the steel industry is being organized."[33] And as a vivid example of how events that began in Chicago could ripple across the country, it was the success of the organizing efforts in Chicago that inspired the national committee to widen its efforts.[34] In this case Chicago was more than just a microcosm of America; it was a catalyst. However, it was not until August 20, 1919, that a national vote was held, and 98 percent of the steelworkers approved a strike.

Although the Great Steel Strike of 1919, which began on September 22, was nationwide, the biggest group of workers to walk out was in Chicago and the surrounding area, where 90,000 workers out of a national total of 350,000 went on strike. The strike had enormous support in Chicago, where, Foster reported, "practically all the men struck, hamstringing the big plants in the various steel towns of that section."[35] Replicating that success elsewhere, however, proved problematic, as local unions tended to go their own way, and ethnic rivalry and racial antagonism divided the steelworkers as they had the packinghouse employees. The employers were aware of the ethnic strife; a detective hired by the mill owners, for example, was instructed, "Stir up as much bad feeling as you possibly can between the Serbians and the Italians."[36] Foster attributed much of the failure to achieve solidarity to the American-born workers who refused to cooperate with immigrants.

The steel bosses decided to institute an eight-hour day on their own, thus removing one of the workingmen's major grievances. In addition, Elbert Gary persuaded other steel bosses not to quickly reduce wages, arguing, "Let us retain their confidence and loyal support by our action."[37] This practice of mollifying workers through appeasement was known as welfare capitalism, and its use by business leaders during the 1920s was a large reason for the weakness of the unions in that decade.

By waiting until the war was over to press their demands, union organizers were operating in a time of decreased demand

A union spokesman stirs up a crowd of workers in Gary, Indiana, during the Great Steel Strike of 1919. Library of Congress

for steel. Gradually, the fear of layoffs, not unionizing, began to take precedence in workers' minds. The National War Labor Board, which had aided the stockyard workers during the war, was no longer operating, and no help would be coming from the government. Neither was it coming from President Wilson, who remained aloof and indifferent. Even before the strike, the employers had begun firing workers who had joined the union, and intimidation only increased during the walkout. The bosses threatened to oust workers from company-owned housing and bar strikers from future employment. The steel bosses also waged a red-baiting propaganda campaign that stoked fears of Bolshevism. With Europe being seen as the source of revolution, anarchy, communism, and other un-American doctrines, this argument found traction with the public because of the European backgrounds of so many strikers. According to a contemporary *New York Times* article, the Slavic steel-workers were "steeped in the doctrines of the class struggle and social overthrow." Foster's radical background was also brought up. It was charged that he was an un-American revolutionary, and the public was reminded that he had once been a member of the extremist Industrial Workers of the World (IWW) and back in 1911 had affirmed that capitalism was "the most brazen gigantic robbery ever perpetrated since the world began."[38]

Threats and propaganda were one thing, but violence was another. In many areas police, militia, citizen committees, and armed "deputies" hired by the steel companies broke up meetings and scattered pickets. Army troops were sent into Gary, where pickets were arrested and martial law was declared, and western Pennsylvania was, as one writer has put it, turned "into an armed camp."[39] "It is as though preparations were made for actual war," commented the *New York World*.[40] At a time of rising unemployment, strikebreakers were easy to find, and many anxious steelworkers, worried about making a living, decided to cross the picket lines. Labor leaders in Chicago confessed that it hurt "the morale of the white men to see blacks crowding into the mills to take their jobs," and the importation of Mexican strikebreakers was likewise disheartening.[41] The strike was called off on January 8, 1920.

The Labor Movement after World War I

By the end of the 1920s the labor movement had been nearly routed, and the decade marked a period of dormancy for unionization in Chicago and elsewhere. As historian Lizabeth Cohen has explained, "In each of the major industries, except the garment trade, workers' drive to sustain wartime gains and establish collective bargaining had failed."[42] Perhaps Chicago's labor leaders didn't realize that world wars, which mobilize an entire nation, create an artificial environment in which normal

Enthusiastic women supporters rally to the cause of the striking steelworkers. Library of Congress

economic realities are suspended or superseded. When peace came, the conditions that had presented the unions with opportunities were gone.

Yet the impetus that World War I gave to organized labor did not entirely fade. According to labor historian Elizabeth McKillen, "In many ways the CFL remained an independent and visionary force in the labor movement."[43] For example, under the energetic direction of its secretary, Edward Nockels, in 1926 the CFL established a radio station, WCFL. Called "the Voice of Labor," it mixed entertainment with labor news and remained on the air until 1978. And for his part, John Fitzpatrick remained a leading union figure until his death in 1946.

However, before union organizers could renew their endeavors with anything like the same success as during World War I, another historical upheaval would have to occur. And it did soon enough. But this time it was a financial calamity—the Great Depression. With the election of Franklin D. Roosevelt in 1932, labor once again had a friend in the White House. Many prolabor laws were enacted, especially the National Industrial Recovery Act of 1933 and the Fair Labor Standards Act of 1938. During the Great Depression, workers went out on strike in large numbers, with over eighteen hundred work stoppages in 1934 alone, and this time they had greater success in winning concessions from management. Also, union membership markedly increased, with union members constituting 7.4 percent of the national labor force in 1930 and 16.6 percent in 1935. In Chicago two new organizations had success with unionization: the Packinghouse Workers Organizing Committee and the Steel Workers Organizing Committee. In addition, the Farm Equipment Workers unionized Chicago's massive International Harvester Company, the nation's leading manufacturer of farm equipment.

Then another war came and with it a golden age for labor. The number of union workers in the United States increased from 3.5 million in 1930 to 15 million in 1945.[44] It was the second time in the century that a global conflagration had uplifted the nation's workers. "War," as General William Tecumseh Sherman famously said, "is hell," but some people do benefit from it.

15

"Eyes to the Future": Chicago in 1919

On the eve of 1919 Chicagoans turned out to cheer the coming of the New Year, just as they had done in 1913. Happily, a threatened strike by waiters and cooks had been called off, and even though the police had been ordered to enforce the 1 A.M. closing time, patrons already indoors were allowed to continue carousing until much later. Although the streets were slushy and just after midnight a cold wave turned the slush to ice, a large group of soldiers and sailors tramped through the Loop, "shouting and hammering and singing, gathering girls and women into the revel as it moved." Merrymakers strutted through the streets until nearly dawn.[1] Jazz poured out of the cafés, but at midnight the song most heard was "The Star-Spangled Banner." Peace was being celebrated just as much as the New Year. The crowds also knew this was kind of a final fling—when 1920 rolled around, prohibition would be in effect and New Year's Eve would be "bone dry."

Also as in 1913 politicians contemplated what lay ahead. The *Chicago Tribune* solicited remarks from Midwestern governors, and as a sign that the automobile age was imminent, most called for a system of "hard-surfaced" roads. The governor of Indiana sounded another common theme, noting the need to convert to a peacetime economy and to ensure jobs for returning servicemen. Wisconsin's E. L. Philipp said that women would need to give up their wartime jobs to "return to such occupations as women are fitted for." He also warned that an economic slowdown might develop and hoped that labor and management would then "be reasonable with each other." Governor Frank Lowden of Illinois expressed confidence that his state's abundant natural resources would ensure prosperity, and as for Chicago, even though it had already experienced tremendous growth and success, "her commercial career is only at its beginning."[2] For his part, Mayor Big Bill Thompson urged, "Now that the war seems to be at an end, let us turn our eyes to the future with a determination to solve every question of reconstruction and to meet all problems of future progress of our beloved city." He noted that Chicago's finances were in the red and that the city would need state aid, but he was proud that the police department had reduced crime by nearly two-thirds, even though no new officers had been added.[3] Chicagoans were also relieved that they had seen the end of the influenza epidemic of 1918, which had sped around the world and killed some fifty million people, much more than the sixteen million that had died in the war. In Chicago, the epidemic had lasted from September to November; at least eighty-five hundred people had died, and thousands more had suffered through the illness.

When many Chicagoans, like their mayor, turned their "eyes to the future," they were thinking that now that the war was over, they could get back to that great roadmap for the city's development, the *Plan of Chicago*. The principal author of this book-length document, published in 1909, was Chicago's world-renowned architect and city planner Daniel Burnham. He had envisioned a sweeping transformation of the city involving an extensive park system, harbor improvements, a regional highway network, improved passenger and freight rail systems, and a massive new civic center at the junction of Halsted and Congress Streets, with wide boulevards radiating out from it across the city. At the beginning of 1919 the *Tribune*, a fervent backer of the plan, hailed the work that had been done so far to meet its goals and urged vigorous action to complete it, despite the great expense. "The expenditures of today are the economies of tomorrow," the newspaper said. It predicted that Chicago, which was already "strong and big," would now become "truly fine and great."[4] When the city council passed the Chicago Plan ordinances on July 21, 1919, Charles Wacker, president of the Chicago Plan Commission, called it "the greatest day, barring none, in Chicago's history."[5] (Parts of the Chicago Plan were completed over the succeeding years; others were not.)

The year was hardly a month old when it became evident that unexpected events were thwarting the rosy predictions. The industrial activity spurred by the war quickly diminished, and unemployment rocketed. Many returning soldiers found that their old jobs were not waiting for them after all, in some cases having been taken by black workers. And yet black workers suffered even more—when industries cut back, they were the first to be let go. As one historian has put it, "The temporary wartime welcome mat that had been extended was withdrawn."[6] In January 1919 a black official of the U.S. Employment Service said, "There has not been a single vacant job in Chicago for a colored man."[7]

Given the cutback in employment, the bosses' hostility to unions, and the confidence that labor leaders had felt during the boom war years, it was understandable that 1919 saw the greatest number of labor strikes in U.S. history (see chapter 14). Yet these efforts by organized labor nearly all ended in defeat; the movement faded in the 1920s, not to be revived until the Great Depression of the 1930s. But taking a longer view, the labor movement merely became dormant in the 1920s; the gains of the war years and the strikes of 1919 were not forgotten, and many of the labor leaders continued on through the 1930s. The labor movement rebounded and flourished throughout World War II and into the 1950s.

Other distressing events followed in 1919.[8] By far the worst was the race riot that erupted in the summer.[9] Although black incursions into formerly white neighborhoods had been causing friction and even violence for months, the immediate cause was something of a turf battle between black and white Chicagoans over who had access to the South Side beaches. The igniting spark was an incident on July 27 in which a raft carrying five black teenage boys drifted into the area considered whites-only. A white bather began throwing rocks; one of them struck sixteen-year-old Eugene Williams and he drowned. Before long a crowd of one thousand, both black and white, had gathered. Shots were fired, the police arrived, the conflict spread inland, and the streets erupted in violence and flame, fed mostly by wandering gangs, while the police acted noticeably favorably to the white mobs. Even as the death toll rose, it took three days for Mayor Thompson to accede to widespread pleas and accept the governor's offer to send in the state militia. By the time the riot was over, thirty-eight people—twenty-three black and fifteen white—were dead, and hundreds had been burned out of their homes. More important, however, was that bitter feelings arising from the episode lasted for years, and as white residents, feeling threatened in their neighborhoods by the incursion of black homebuyers, dug in their heels, enmity between the races in Chicago would endure through the civil rights era and beyond; indeed, it became a defining feature of life in the city in the twentieth century.

Just six days before the race riot broke out, Chicago witnessed one of the most bizarre calamities in its history when a dirigible crashed into a downtown building. The airship, called the Wingfoot Air Express, was returning from the Grant Park aerodrome to its base at the White City Amusement Park when, twelve hundred feet above the Loop, it burst into flame. Below it was the Illinois Trust and Savings Bank building, which was crowned by a skylight that sheltered some 150 employees. The fuselage of the dirigible, along with its engines and fuel tanks, smashed through the glass, and burning gasoline poured down. Thirteen people were killed (ten in the bank, two blimp passengers, and one crew member), and twenty-six were injured. It has been called "the first major aviation disaster in the nation's history."[10]

Policemen gaze on the smoldering ruins of houses destroyed by fire during the massive Chicago race riot of 1919. From Chicago Commission on Race Relations, *The Negro in Chicago: A Study of Race Relations and a Race Riot* (Chicago: University of Chicago Press, 1922)

As an example of Chicago optimism gone sour, the story of the 1919 White Sox ranks high. This superb team, which featured such stars as "Shoeless Joe" Jackson, Buck Weaver, Eddie Collins, and Ray Schalk, was rated a 7–5 favorite to defeat the Cincinnati Reds in the 1919 World Series. But the Sox lost the first game 9–1 and then the series, five games to three, while playing uncharacteristically sloppy ball. In 1920 eight Sox players were accused of throwing the series. Even to this day it's not clear how many gamblers were involved in corrupting the players, how many games the players deliberately lost, and just which players were involved. During the series, for example, the great Shoeless Joe batted .375, knocked in six runs, hit the only home run, and was errorless in the field, yet he was one of the eight players accused. The trial lasted two weeks, and although all eight were acquitted of criminal charges, the commissioner of baseball, Kenesaw Mountain Landis (the same man who had presided over the Chicago trial of the Wobblies in 1918), banned them from professional baseball for life, Shoeless Joe among them. Chicago already had a reputation for venality, and now the city became known as the home of the "Black Sox."

It was during World War I that black sharpies on the South Side perfected what became known as the "policy" racket.[11] Plenty of black-owned gambling joints had been operating in Chicago's Black Belt at least since the turn of the century, and prohibition had brought countless speakeasies, but policy was a uniquely home-grown vice. It was a game in which participants would bet usually small amounts of money in hopes of matching the daily winning three numbers. It was pioneered in the 1890s by a black Chicago gambling boss named John "Mushmouth" Johnson, and by 1901 the city had more than four thousand policy shops, but the game just about disappeared when a 1905 state law came down hard on it. It was revived in Chicago in 1915 by a former railroad porter named Sam Young, who became known as "Policy Sam."

During World War I several black nightclub owners got into the racket, and it became big business. The game operated without police interference and employed hundreds of bet takers, or "walking writers." By the mid-1920s it was "estimated that one million dollars a month was being wagered with the policy barons, with less than one percent of the sum being returned to players in the form of winnings."[12] Historians have been divided on the effects of the policy racket. Christopher Robert Reed has written that policy "drained the financial lifeblood of the residents of the Black Belt."[13] According to Davarian L. Baldwin, however, policy "stabilized the black economy and social world" by underwriting "a vibrant urban culture of theaters, dance halls, and athletic and traditional business enterprises." Although Baldwin acknowledges that policy was exploitative, he argues that it circulated money back into the black community and says that "many migrants also saw direct parallels between their bets and the investments whites placed in the stock market, except that policy didn't discriminate. Moreover, policy provided a relatively higher rate of return while becoming another avenue toward race advancement."[14] In any case, Italian organized crime eventually muscled in on the racket and took it over.

Seven years in the life of a city—even one as young as Chicago—is not an especially long time. But in Chicago the years from 1913 through 1919 were momentous. If, for example, we were to look at the years from 1907 through 1913, we would find interesting events—the opening of Essanay Studios; the notorious First Ward Ball, in which aldermen "Hinky Dink" Kenna and "Bathhouse John" Coughlin broke all records for flamboyant display of corruption; the publication of the *Plan of Chicago*; the installation of Edgar Cameron's *Spirit of Chicago* murals; and the Cubs' back-to-back World Series victories—but nothing as transformative as what happened between 1913 and 1919.

This book has attempted to make two major points: first, that Chicago was profoundly changed by, and during, World War I; and second, that Chicago was in many ways a microcosm of America. Following is a summary of the ways in which the Great War transformed Chicago:

- Chicago's ethnic composition began to undergo major change. In what is now known as the Great Migration, thousands of black southerners came to the city. In just two years (1916–18) the black population of Chicago doubled, from 58,056 to 109,594. At the same time, Mexican workers began to arrive in Chicago to take advantage of the labor shortage caused by the war. This influx was more gradual than that of the African Americans, but by the time of the steel strike of 1919, Chicagoans were beginning to notice their presence, and not always with approval.

- Two types of music that became particularly identified with Chicago took root in the city during the war: jazz and blues. Jazz, which was nearly unknown before the war, quickly became the dominant popular music of the era. With such musicians as Freddie Keppard, King Oliver, Louis Armstrong, the Original Dixieland Jazz Band, and later Bix Beiderbecke, Chicago lit the fire, which then spread across the country. The Chicago influence culminated with the popularity of the "King of Swing," Benny Goodman. Regarding the blues, an excellent example of how events of World War I still vividly resonate in Chicago today is the continuing popularity of the city's blues clubs, which still draw large crowds, many of them tourists.

- The other major ethnic change was one of diminution. Chicago was the most German of American cities, and it was there that the wartime anti-German sentiment was at its most dramatic. In 1914, 191,000 Chicagoans identified as German; in 1920 only 112,000 did.

- It is arguable that prohibition would not have become a national law without the impetus given to it by the anti-German mania and the patriotic spirit of self-sacrifice during World War I, especially because the results of the 1920 census would have been unfavorable for the prohibitionists. And what prohibition meant to Chicago has now practically become a feature of American folklore.

- The job opportunities that Chicago offered drew thousands of young women, who came not only to find work but also to find social and sexual freedom, and Chicago, the home of the *Flapper* magazine, became a focal point of America's first sexual revolution. By the time the war was over, the "new woman" had appeared in Chicago, bringing an upheaval in fashion, morals, and dating practices.

In his important 1991 book, *Nature's Metropolis: Chicago and the Great West*, William Cronon has described how in the last half of the nineteenth century, Chicago became not just the main city of the Midwest but the dominant capital of a huge inland empire whose influence streamed out across the nation. In arguing that Chicago was a microcosm of the United States, this present book has stressed that Chicago encapsulated national trends, sometimes by originating or dominating them and other times by reflecting them most brightly. For example, fear of German spies and saboteurs was national, but it was only in Chicago that a loyal citizen created the American Protective League. And it was only in Chicago that another patriot created the Four Minute Men, a national entity that bordered on the inescapable. There are other examples. The pacifist and isolationist movements were national, but they were especially prominent in Chicago, which was home to both the indefatigable reformer Jane Addams and, at the far end of the political spectrum, the radical Industrial Workers of the World (IWW), or Wobblies. Finally, as the industrial center of the nation, Chicago experienced most strongly the forces that were bringing women into unprecedented workplaces, and it became the focal point of a rejuvenated labor movement. It was only when union organizers in the steel industry had success in Chicago that they decided to go national.

One of the most significant events of 1919 went unnoticed at the time, but it had a profound effect on Chicago—and its global image. At the time, the most powerful gangster in the city was "Big Jim" Colosimo, who was aided by his top lieutenant, Johnny Torrio, his wife's nephew. Big Jim had been in the rackets for a long time, and his underlings interpreted his aspirations to gentility as a sign that he was getting soft.[15] The ambitious Torrio had already been put in charge of nearly all Big Jim's operations and aimed to replace him one way or another, so he felt the need to add some muscle to his staff. Thus it was that late in 1919 he recruited from New York a young tough named Al Capone, who had to lam out of his hometown because he had thrashed an Irish gangster and was a marked man. The following year Colosimo was gunned down and Torrio took over. In 1925 Torrio himself was riddled with bullets. He miraculously survived, but he was persuaded to retire at age forty-four, saying, "Al, it's all yours."[16]

In late 1919 a young New Yorker named Al Capone moved to Chicago. The gangster's activities and the reputation he earned would forever change the image of the city. U.S. Department of Justice

Chicago now had a new face— "Scarface." The figure of racketeer Al Capone would rise to prominence as one of the most notorious of all Chicagoans and a symbol of the city that many would like to see vanish. By the time the 1920s dawned, the speakeasies and the sexual revolution were in full swing. The war had brought the city's women new opportunities, and they were not turning back. Chicago was no longer a city with a German identity but was becoming one in which African-Americans were an unmistakable presence—and the Mexican influx was not far behind. Chicago's gangster legend had begun, and jazz was the soundtrack.

Notes

Index

Notes

Part One. Before the War

1. "Throw the Dictionary at It": Chicago in 1913

1. "New Year's Orgy in Crowded Loop Wildest of Years," *Chicago Tribune*, Jan. 1, 1913, 1.

2. "Mayor Points to City's 1913 Hopes," *Chicago Tribune*, Dec. 31, 1912, 4.

3. "Gain in Chicago Realty Values Called Wonder of World," *Chicago Tribune*, Apr. 13, 1913, I2.

4. *Richardson's Chicago Guide* (Chicago: Monarch Book Co., 1905), 17.

5. Julian Street, *Abroad at Home* (1913), in Bessie Louise Pierce, ed., *As Others See Chicago: Impressions of Visitors, 1673–1933* (Chicago: Univ. of Chicago Press, 2004), 442.

6. "Picnic Recalls Bygone City Days," *Chicago Tribune*, Aug. 5, 1913, 13.

7. A few visitors arrived by boat. *Richardson's Chicago Guide* lists 12 "principal steamship passenger lines," although they chiefly served only Great Lakes ports, most on Lake Michigan.

8. Chicago Association of Commerce and Industry, *A Guide to the City of Chicago* (Chicago: Chicago Association of Commerce, 1909), 9.

9. Edward Hungerford, *The Personality of American Cities* (1913), in Pierce, *As Others See Chicago*, 435.

10. Chicago Association of Commerce and Industry, *Guide to the City of Chicago*, 26.

11. "Chicago's Future Depends on Care for Immigrants," *Chicago Tribune*, June 24, 1913, 1.

12. Quoted in Harold M. Mayer and Richard C. Wade, *Chicago: Growth of a Metropolis* (Chicago: Univ. of Chicago Press, 1969), 226.

13. James R. Grossman, Ann Durkin Keating, and Janice L. Reiff, eds., *The Encyclopedia of Chicago* (Chicago: Univ. of Chicago Press, 2004), 515, s.v. "meatpacking."

14. Irving Cutler, *Chicago: Metropolis of the Mid-Continent* (Carbondale: Southern Illinois Univ. Press, 2006), 228.

15. Mayer and Wade, *Chicago*, 230.

16. Grossman et al., *Encyclopedia of Chicago*, 309–10, s.v. "football."

17. Raymond Schmidt, "Golf and the Chicago Girl," *Chicago History* 38, no. 2 (Fall 2012): 40.

18. Chicago Association of Commerce and Industry, *Guide to the City of Chicago*. For an excellent history of sports in the city, see Elliott J. Gorn, ed., *Sports in Chicago* (Champaign: Univ. of Illinois Press, 2008).

19. Elizabeth McNulty, *Chicago Then and Now* (San Diego: Thunder Bay Press, 2000), 68.

20. "New Lake Sport Thrills Beaches," *Chicago Tribune*, Aug. 4, 1913, 4.

21. Grossman et al., *Encyclopedia of Chicago*, 470, s.v. "leisure." See chapter 10 for more on the city's cabarets and nightclubs.

22. Glenn Dillard Gunn, "Grand Opera Season Ends; the Best in Its History," *Chicago Tribune*, Feb. 1, 1914, G1.

23. Craig W. Campbell, *Reel America and World War I: A Comprehensive Filmography and History of Motion Pictures in the United States, 1914–1920* (Jefferson, NC: McFarland, 1985), 6.

24. J. A. Lindstrom, "Film," in Grossman et al., *Encyclopedia of Chicago*, 293.

25. Michael Corcoran and Arnie Bernstein, *Hollywood on Lake Michigan: 100+ Years of Chicago and the Movies* (Chicago: Chicago Review Press, 2013), 24.

26. Davarian L. Baldwin, *Chicago's New Negroes: Modernity, the Great Migration, and Black Urban Life* (Chapel Hill: Univ. of North Carolina Press, 2007), 92.

27. Michael Glover Smith and Adam Selzer, *Flickering Empire: How Chicago Invented the U.S. Film Industry* (New York: Wallflower Press, 2015), 2. See also Corcoran and Bernstein, *Hollywood on Lake Michigan*.

28. Before 1907, the term of a Chicago mayor was two years. The first four-year mayor was Fred A. Busse, who was in office from 1907 to 1911.

29. See Richard C. Lindberg, *The Gambler King of Clark Street: Michael C. McDonald and the Rise of Chicago's Democratic Machine* (Carbondale: Southern Illinois Univ. Press, 2009).

30. Quoted in James L. Merriner, *Grafters and Goo Goos: Corruption and Reform in Chicago, 1833–2003* (Carbondale: Southern Illinois Univ. Press, 2004), 70.

31. Dominic A. Pacyga, *Chicago: A Biography* (Chicago: Univ. of Chicago Press, 2009), 161.

32. See Carolyn O. Poplett, *The Woman Who Never Fails: Grace Wilbur Trout and Illinois Suffrage* (Oak Park, IL: Historical Society of Oak Park and River Forest, 2000).

33. Marion Walters, "Jeering Mobs Are Silenced by Illinois Women in Parade," *Chicago Tribune*, Mar. 9, 1913, H2.

34. Suellen Hoy, "Sideline Suffragists," *Chicago History* 29, no. 1 (Summer 2013): 4.

35. Harriet Monroe, "Art Show Open to Freaks," *Chicago Tribune*, Feb. 17, 1913, 5. The title of the article so clashes with Monroe's admiring tone that one suspects it was added by an editor.

36. "The Cubist Costume: Milady in Crazyquilt," *Chicago Tribune*, Apr. 6, 1913, 53.

37. Milton W. Brown, *The Story of the Armory Show* (New York: Abbeville Press, 1988), 210–13; Monroe, "Art Show Open to Freaks," 5.

38. I. F. Clarke, *Voices Prophesying War: Future Wars, 1763–3749* (New York: Oxford Univ. Press, 1992), 37.

39. "O'Connor Tells Big War Scare Felt in Europe," *Chicago Tribune*, Mar. 16, 1913, A1.

40. Quoted in Alan Valentine, *1913: America between Two Worlds* (New York: Macmillan, 1962), 214.

41. "Great Choirs Due at City Yule Tree," Dec. 24, 1913, 5.

2. Preparedness and Public Opinion: Why Chicago Went to War

1. "May Foreshadow Revolt of Slavs," *Chicago Tribune*, June 29, 1914, 3; Paul M. Angle, "Chicago and the First World War," *Chicago History* 7, no. 5 (Fall 1964): 129.

2. "Hyde Tells How One Week Threw Powers into War," *Chicago Tribune*, Aug. 9, 1914, 6.

3. "Brokers Survive Pit's Wildest Day," *Chicago Tribune*, July 29, 1914, 1; Angle, "Chicago and the First World War," 135–36.

4. "Sees U.S. Boom as War Result," *Chicago Tribune*, Oct. 21, 1914, 3.

5. Francis G. Walett, *An Economic History of the United States* (Abingdon, UK: Routledge, 2006), 193.

6. James A. Martin, "Chicago's Bid for Empire: World War One and the Regional Myth," 14, Illinois Manufacturers Association Papers, Chicago Historical Society, ca. 1979.

7. Ibid., 21; "$25,000,000 for New Bank; Seek Trade of the World," *Chicago Tribune*, Apr. 24, 1919, 1.

8. Martin, "Chicago's Bid for Empire," 20, 22.

9. David M. Kennedy, *Over Here: The First World War and American Society* (New York: Oxford Univ. Press, 2004), 337.

10. Gerd Hardach, *The First World War, 1914–1918* (Berkeley: Univ. of California Press, 1977), 255, 137.

11. Walett, *Economic History*, 194.

12. "Thousands Back at Work," *New York Times*, Nov. 24, 1914.

13. Hardach, *First World War*, 256.

14. "Packers Gains Big in Spite of Curbs," *New York Times*, Sep. 25, 1919.

15. "Opera Singers Victims of War?" *Chicago Tribune*, Sep. 17, 1914, 1; "Chicago Opera Despite War," *Chicago Tribune*, Sep. 30, 1914, 13.

16. Barry D. Karl, *Charles E. Merriam and the Study of Politics* (Chicago: Univ. of Chicago Press, 1974), 88.

17. Robert J. Thompson, "Thompson Says Most of Stories of Atrocities by German Soldiers Were Manufactured by Press and Special Writers in Allies' Lands," *Chicago Tribune*, Feb. 18, 1915.

18. Angle, "Chicago and the First World War," 136. At the time, the standard spelling of the Balkan nation was Servia, which was how it appeared in the newspapers.

19. Pacyga, *Chicago*, 190. See also Frank S. Magallon, *Chicago's Little Village: Lawndale-Crawford* (Charleston, SC: Arcadia Publishing, 2010), 53–55.

20. Alex Gottfried, *Boss Cermak of Chicago: A Study of Political Leadership* (Seattle: Univ. of Washington Press, 1962), 92.

21. Nancy Gentile Ford, *Americans All! Foreign-Born Soldiers in World War I* (College Station: Texas A&M Univ. Press, 2001), 34.

22. Pacyga, *Chicago*, 190.

23. Malynne Sternstein, *Czechs of Chicagoland* (Charleston, SC: Arcadia Publishing, 2008), 59.

24. Edward R. Kantowicz, *Polish-American Politics in Chicago, 1888–1940* (Chicago: Univ. of Chicago Press, 1975), 110–11.

25. Pacyga, *Chicago*, 201.

26. Kantowicz, *Polish-American Politics*, 112.

27. Dominic A. Pacyga, *Polish Immigrants and Industrial Chicago: Workers on the South Side, 1880–1922* (Columbus: Ohio State Univ. Press, 1991), 196.

28. "Germans Here Rush to Arms," *Chicago Tribune*, Aug. 4, 1914, 5.

29. "Gay Fete Opens to Aid German War Sufferers," *Chicago Tribune*, Mar. 29, 1916, 17.

30. Melvin G. Holli, "The Great War Sinks Chicago's German *Kultur*," in *Ethnic Chicago*, ed. Melvin G. Holli and Peter d'A. Jones (Grand Rapids: Eerdmans Publishing Co., 1981), 467.

31. "Ignore Warning Not to Embark," *Chicago Tribune*, May 8, 1915, 3.

32. Burton Rascoe, "If Germany Should Fight the United States," *Chicago Tribune*, June 27, 1915, D1.

33. "Chi. Federation of Labor Unanimously Opposed to Preparedness Parade," *(Chicago) Day Book*, May 22, 1916, 3.

34. "Detail Story of Greatest Parade in Chicago's History," *Chicago Tribune*, June 4, 1916, 3.

35. "Way Out on Chicago's Municipal Pier," *Chicago Tribune*, July 5, 1916, 13.

36. Douglas Bukowski, *Navy Pier: A Chicago Landmark* (Chicago: Metropolitan Pier and Exposition Authority, 1996), 16–20.

37. "Press Views German Note in Grave Tone," *Chicago Tribune*, Feb. 1, 1917, 1; Robert H. Zieger, *America's Great War: World War I and the American Experience* (Lanham, MD: Rowman & Littlefield, 2000), 46–51.

38. Thomas Fleming, *The Illusion of Victory: America in World War I* (New York: Basic Books, 2003), 2.

39. Ibid., 38.

40. June Skinner Sawyers, *Chicago Portraits: Biographies of 250 Famous Chicagoans* (Chicago: Loyola Univ. Press, 1991), 142.

41. Kennedy, *Over Here*, 49.

42. "Why America Is Fighting," *International Socialist Review* 18, no. 1 (July 1917): 6.

43. "Two Sorts of Pacifists," *Chicago Tribune*, June 4, 1916, A5.

44. Glenn Watkins, *Proof through the Night: Music and the Great War* (Berkeley: Univ. of California Press, 2003), 249.

45. Stevenson Swanson, ed., *Chicago Days: 150 Defining Moments in the Life of a Great City* (Wheaton, IL: Cantigny First Division Foundation, 1997), 109.

46. Louisa Thomas, "Give Pacifism a Chance," *New York Times*, Aug. 28, 2011.

47. "Comment by Mme X," *Chicago Tribune*, Apr. 8, 1917, C6.

48. "The Twilight of the Kings," *Chicago Tribune*, Apr. 1, 1917, D6.

49. "Chicago in the World's War," *Chicago Tribune*, Apr. 7, 1917, 10.

50. "Chicago Sailors to War," *Chicago Tribune*, Apr. 9, 1917, 1.

51. "Chicagoans Rush to Follow Flag," *Chicago Tribune*, Apr. 21. 1917, 7.

One Chicagoan's War
Jane Addams:
The "Impertinent Old Maid"

1. Valentine, *1913*, 185.
2. Louise W. Knight, *Jane Addams: Spirit in Action* (New York: W. W. Norton, 2010), 198. On the subject of pacifism during the war, see Frances H. Early, *A World without War: How U.S. Feminists and Pacifists Resisted World War I* (Syracuse, NY: Syracuse Univ. Press, 1997), which describes the activities of a civil rights organization called the Bureau of Legal Advice.
3. Jane Addams, *Peace and Bread in Time of War* (New York: Macmillan, 1922), 12.
4. Ibid., 13.
5. Knight, *Jane Addams*, 200, 199.
6. James Weber Linn, *Jane Addams: A Biography* (New York: D. Appleton-Century, 1936), 306.
7. Addams, *Peace and Bread*, 18.
8. Knight, *Jane Addams*, 204.
9. Edward Goldbeck, "Dangerous Attitudes," *Chicago Tribune*, July 18, 1915, A5; "French Poet Chides Jane Addams," *New York Times*, July 30, 1918; Christopher Capozzola, *Uncle Sam Wants You: World War I and the Making of the Modern American Citizen* (New York: Oxford Univ. Press, 2008), 149.
10. Knight, *Jane Addams*, 216.

William Hale Thompson: "Kaiser Bill"
1. Curt Johnson, *The Wicked City: Chicago from Kenna to Capone* (Boston: Da Capo Press, 1998), 141; Douglas Bukowski, *Big Bill Thompson, Chicago, and the Politics of Image* (Champaign: Univ. of Illinois Press, 1997), 63.
2. "Thompsonism," *Chicago Tribune*, Sep. 9, 1918, 8.
3. Lloyd Wendt and Herman Kogan, *Big Bill of Chicago* (Evanston, IL: Northwestern Univ. Press, 1953), 122.
4. Ibid., 151.
5. Ibid., 155.

Part Two. Chicago's Soldiers
3. "Kia-Kiak": The Black Hawk Division
1. "Standing Army (1) Arrives Bit Early in Camp," *Chicago Tribune*, Sept. 2, 1917, 1. Smollen was originally from Racine, Wisconsin.

2. John G. Little, *The Official History of the Eighty-Sixth Division* (Chicago: States Publication Society, 1921), 10–11.
3. Zieger, *America's Great War*, 58.
4. Anne Cipriano Venzon, *The United States in the First World War: An Encyclopedia* (New York: Garland, 1995), 540, s.v. "Selective Service"; Fleming, *Illusion of Victory*, 87.
5. Capozzola, *Uncle Sam Wants You*, 22.
6. Ibid., 18.
7. "Few Political Lights on Draft Boards in City," *Chicago Tribune*, June 27, 1917, 6.
8. Jennifer D. Keene, *Doughboys, the Great War, and the Remaking of America* (Baltimore: Johns Hopkins Univ. Press, 2001), 18.
9. "Draft Brings Forth Chicago Health Secrets," *Chicago Tribune*, Aug. 12, 1917, 7.
10. Little, *Official History of the Eighty-Sixth Division*, 2.
11. "Maj. Gen. Barry Takes Command at Rockford," *Chicago Tribune*, Aug. 26, 1917.
12. Walter L. Haight, *Racine County in the World War* (Racine, WI: Western Printing and Lithographing Co., 1920), 412.
13. "Barry Unites 'His Boys' under a Vow of Victory," *Chicago Tribune*, Sept. 11, 1917, 5.
14. See Mark Ethan Grotelueschen, *The AEF Way of War: The American Army and Combat in World War I* (New York: Cambridge Univ. Press, 2006).
15. Edward G. Lengel, *To Conquer Hell: The Meuse-Argonne, 1918, The Epic Battle That Ended the First World War* (New York: Henry Holt, 2008), 34.
16. Keene, *Doughboys*, 13.
17. "Old Time Scout Gives Dusty 86th Redskin War Cry," *Chicago Tribune*, June 29, 1918, 12. An essay by Dr. Woodcock can be found in a contemporary outdoorsmen's magazine, *Hunter-Trader-Trapper* 14, no. 2 (May 1907): 101–2.
18. "Private at Camp Grant Gives Red Cross $15,000," *Chicago Tribune*, June 23, 1918, 14.
19. Little, *Official History of the Eighty-Sixth Division*, 41.
20. Keene, *Doughboys*, 30, 47.
21. Charles V. Julian, "Split Up Units of the 86th Reach Gotham," *Chicago Tribune*, Jan. 4, 1919, 5.

22. Donald F. Biggs, ed., *Illinois in the World War: An Illustrated History of the Thirty-Third Division* (Chicago: States Publications Society, 1921), 1:6–7.

23. Little, *Official History of the Eighty-Sixth Division*, 65.

24. C. V. Julian, "Blackhawks on Hilarious Way to Home and 'Her,'" *Chicago Tribune*, Jan. 12, 1919, 6.

25. Biggs, *Illinois in the World War*, 3–4.

26. Ibid., 107.

27. Ibid., 118.

28. For an excellent firsthand description of this kind of warfare, see the World War I memoir *Toward the Flame* (1926) by novelist Hervey Allen.

29. Biggs, *Illinois in the World War*, 5.

30. Keene, *Doughboys*, 50–51.

31. David Laskin, *The Long Way Home: An American Journey from Ellis Island to the Great War* (NY: HarperCollins, 2010), xviii, 124, 134–35. Laskin's book recounts the stories of twelve immigrants who served in the U.S. military in World War I. See also Keene, *Doughboys*, 20.

32. "His Morning's Mail Is 8,000 Letters," *Stars and Stripes* 1, no. 1 (Feb. 8, 1918).

33. "Allex, Jake," *Congressional Medal of Honor Society*, accessed April 8, 2014. http://www.cmohs.org/recipient-detail/2495/allex-jake.php.

34. Yolanda Weisensel, director of the Camp Grant Museum, Rockford, IL, personal communication with the author, July 21, 2014.

35. Little, *Official History of the Eighty-Sixth Division*, 68.

36. "Artillery Unit of Blackhawks Back in America," *Chicago Tribune*, Feb. 16, 1919, 6.

37. "Men Who Were in Blackhawk Division Unite," *Chicago Tribune*, July 28, 1919, 15.

38. The team had been going by the two-word name Black Hawks, but in the late 1980s someone looked at its original National Hockey League contract and saw that the name was one word, Blackhawks. Since then the team has been using the one-word version, even though the original tribal leader's name was given as two words. During World War I both versions seem to have been used interchangeably; the *Tribune* favored "Blackhawks," but John G. Little's official history of the division uses "Black Hawks." Interestingly, the original Black Hawk logo, a stylized black-and-white profile of the Indian leader, was created in 1927 by McLaughlin's wife. She happened to be the former Irene Castle, who, along with her husband, Vernon, was greatly responsible for the social dancing craze of the early twentieth century (see chapter 10). Vernon, who was also an aviator, was killed in a plane crash in 1918, and Irene married Major McLaughlin in 1923. Although a machine gunner could conceivably have served as a team logo, Irene wisely went back to the nickname's original source.

4. Black Devils and Partridges: The 370th Infantry Regiment

1. J. Clay Smith Jr., *Emancipation: The Making of the Black Lawyer, 1844–1944* (Philadelphia: University of Pennsylvania Press, 1999), 376.

2. Frank E. Roberts, *The American Foreign Legion: Black Soldiers of the 93d in World War I* (Annapolis, MD: U.S. Naval Institute Press, 2004), 21; Christopher Robert Reed, *Knock at the Door of Opportunity: Black Migration to Chicago, 1900–1919* (Carbondale: Southern Illinois Univ. Press, 2014), 215.

3. "Some Chicagoans of Note," *Crisis* 10, no. 5 (Sept. 1915): 238.

4. For a short biography of Denison, see Catherine Reef, *African Americans in the Military* (New York: Facts on File, 2010), 89–90.

5. For information on other period films documenting the experience of black U.S. soldiers in World War I, see Jacqueline Stewart, *Migrating to the Movies: Cinema and Black Urban Modernity* (Oakland: Univ. of California Press, 2005).

6. Capozzola, *Uncle Sam Wants You*, 33.

7. Kennedy, *Over Here*, 156. Foreign-born white men were also overdrafted.

8. Chad L. Williams, *Torchbearers of Democracy: African American Soldiers in the World War I Era* (Chapel Hill, NC: Univ. of North Carolina Press, 2010), 6.

9. Keene, *Doughboys*, 22–23.

10. Williams, *Torchbearers*, 14.

11. Kennedy, *Over Here*, 279; Fleming, *Illusion of Victory*, 108.

12. Reed, *Knock at the Door of Opportunity*, 281.

13. Ibid., 214.

14. Miles Vandahurst Lynk, *The Negro Pictorial Review of the Great World War* (Memphis: Twentieth Century Art Company, 1919), 13.

15. W. T. B. Williams, "The World War and the Race," *Chicago Defender*, Jan. 5, 1918, 10.

16. Williams, *Torchbearers*, 56.

17. Reed, *Knock at the Door of Opportunity*, 281.

18. Roberts, *American Foreign Legion*, 23.

19. Arthur E. Barbeau and Florette Henri, *The Unknown Soldiers: African-American Troops in World War I* (New York: Da Capo Press, 1996), 76.

20. Emmett J. Scott, *Scott's Official History of the American Negro in the World War* (Chicago: Homewood Press, 1919), 76.

21. William S. Braddan, *Under Fire with the 370th Infantry* (printed by author, 1923), 19.

22. Ibid., 29.

23. "Camp Logan," *Chicago Defender*, Jan. 18, 1919, 5.

24. Scott, *Scott's Official History*, 37.

25. Kennedy, *Over Here*, 162.

26. Alfred E. Cornebise, *War as Advertised* (Philadelphia: American Philosophical Society, 1984), 23.

27. Edward M. Coffman, *The War to End All Wars: The American Military Experience in World War I* (Lexington: Univ. Press of Kentucky, 1986), 320.

28. Williams, *Torchbearers*, 164.

29. Keene, *Doughboys*, 128.

30. Williams, *Torchbearers*, 199, 267.

31. "Our Negro Troops Training in France," *New York Times*, June 18, 1918.

32. It is possible that Gibbons misidentified this song and that the soldiers were playing "I Ain't Got Nobody," which was composed by the black songwriter Spencer Williams in 1915 and was very popular.

33. "Negro Troops Winning Popularity in France," *Chicago Tribune*, Nov. 15, 1918, 8.

34. Addie W. Hunton and Kathryn M. Johnson, *Two Colored Women with the American Expeditionary Forces* (Brooklyn, NY: Brooklyn Eagle Press, 1920), 217.

35. William Howland Kenney, *Chicago Jazz: A Cultural History, 1904–1930* (New York: Oxford Univ. Press, 1993), 52. On the activities of other black military jazz bands in France, see Williams, *Torchbearers*, 165–66.

36. Gilbert Elliot Jr., "The Doughboy Carries His Music with Him," *Music Review*, Aug. 1919, in *Jazz in Print: An Anthology of Selected Early Readings in Jazz History*, ed. Karl Koenig (Hillsdale, NY: Pendragon Press, 2002), 136–38.

37. Barbeau and Henri, *Unknown Soldiers*, 112.

38. Scott, *Scott's Official History*, 217.

39. Braddan, *Under Fire with the 370th Infantry*, 51, 58.

40. Barbeau and Henri, *Unknown Soldiers*, 120. Williams, *Torchbearers*, 130.

41. Barbeau and Henri, *Unknown Soldiers*, 122–23.

42. Braddan, *Under Fire with the 370th Infantry*, 70–71.

43. "Col. Franklin A. Denison, 370th Infantry, in Chicago for a Few Hours," *Chicago Defender*, Sep. 28, 1918, 11. Four sons was a lot, but a black clergyman named R. H. Windsor sent twelve sons into the army. President Wilson sent him a letter expressing his admiration and congratulations. Lynk, *Negro Pictorial Review*, 39.

44. Braddan, *Under Fire with the 370th Infantry*, 67, 71.

45. Barbeau and Henri, *Unknown Soldiers*, 124.

46. W. Allison Sweeney, *History of the American Negro in the Great World War* (Chicago: G. G. Sapp, 1919), 155.

47. "Allies Class Negroes Best with Bayonet," *Chicago Tribune*, Oct. 10, 1918, 6.

48. Monroe N. Work, ed., *Negro Year Book: An Annual Encyclopedia of the Negro, 1918–1919* (Tuskegee, AL: Negro Year Book Publishing Co., 1919), 219.

49. Reed, *Knock at the Door of Opportunity*, 284.

50. "Camera's Story of How Chicago Showered Affection on Her Famous 'Black Devils,'" *Chicago Tribune*, Feb. 18, 1919, 3.

One Chicagoan's War
John T. McCutcheon:
The Candid Cartoonist

1. Douglas Gilbert, *Floyd Gibbons: Knight of the Air* (New York: Robert M. McBride, 1930), 18–19.

2. John T. McCutcheon, *Drawn from Memory* (Indianapolis: Bobbs-Merrill, 1950), 269.

3. Ibid., 270.

4. Ibid.

5. Ibid., 271.

6. The episode is related in an article by McCutcheon's colleague James O'Donnell Bennett, "Deceiving the Whole World," in *War Echoes; or, Germany and Austria in the Crisis,* ed. George William Hau (Chicago: Open Court Publishing Co., 1915).

7. John T. McCutcheon, "Press Agents Color the News of the Great War," *Chicago Tribune,* Dec. 20, 1914, A3.

8. McCutcheon, *Drawn from Memory,* 454.

Samuel J. "Nails" Morton:
The Mobster as War Hero

1. Michael Berkowitz, "Crime and Redemption? American Jewish Gangsters, Violence, and the Fight against Nazism," in *Jews and Violence: Images, Ideologies, Realities,* ed. Peter Y. Medding (New York: Oxford Univ. Press, 202), 100.

2. Walter Roth, *Looking Backward: True Stories from Chicago's Jewish Past* (Chicago: Academy Chicago Publishers, 2002), 236.

3. Ibid., 237.

4. "Former Boxer Wins Decoration," *Chicago Sentinel,* September 17, 1918.

5. Jay Robert Nash, "Samuel J. 'Nails' Morton: From War Hero to Gangster," *Annals of Crime,* accessed May 10, 2012, http://www.annalsofcrime.com. Morton's great-niece, Lisa Safron, wrote an account of her relative for the website *Oy!Chicago* (http://www.oychicago.com). It contains a photo of Nails in the army. Morton was just one of many gangsters who served in the military during World War I. Others were Legs Diamond, Monk Eastman, and Wild Bill Lovett, who was awarded a Distinguished Service Cross. See Lengel, *To Conquer Hell,* 35.

6. Hal Andrews, *X Marks the Spot: Chicago's Gang Wars in Pictures* (Rockford, IL: Spot Publishing Company, 1970), 14.

7. "'Nails' Morton Killed by Horse," *Chicago Tribune,* May 14, 1923, 1.

8. Johnson, *Wicked City,* 164.

Robert R. McCormick: The Colonel

1. Richard Norton Smith, *The Colonel: The Life and Legend of Robert R. McCormick, 1880–1955* (Boston: Houghton Mifflin, 1997), 195.

2. Ibid., 199.

3. For a description of the Battle of Cantigny, see Allan R. Millett, *Well Planned, Splendidly Executed: The Battle of Cantigny, May 28–31, 1918* (Wheaton, IL: Cantigny Military History Series, 2010). Also see Grotelueschen, *AEF Way of War,* 72–83.

Floyd Gibbons:
The Reporter Who Lost an Eye

1. "Fired First Shot of War," *New York Times,* Sept. 8, 1918. A corporal named Osborne de Varila claimed to have fired the first shot and wrote a best-selling book about his deed titled *The First Shot for Liberty.* Gibbons, however, averred that although de Varila was a member of the battery and "witnessed the shot," it was actually Sergeant Arch who fired it.

2. "Floyd Gibbons, Famous War Writer, Is Dead," *Chicago Tribune,* Sept. 25, 1939, 1.

3. "How Laconia Sank," *Chicago Tribune,* Feb. 28, 1917, 1. An abridged version of the story can be found in Jon L. Lewis, ed., *The Mammoth Book of Eyewitness World War I* (New York: Carroll & Graf, 2003), 268–71.

4. "Floyd Gibbons, 'Tribune' Man, Shot on Duty," *Chicago Tribune,* June 8, 1918, 1; "Gibbons Not Surprised by Bullet Wound," *Chicago Tribune,* June 9, 1918, 3; Douglas Gilbert, *Floyd Gibbons: Knight of the Air* (New York: Robert M. McBride, 1930), 51–55.

5. "Back with the Home Folks," *Chicago Tribune,* Sept. 28, 1918, 5.

6. Even as late as the early 1960s, Gibbons's legend was still familiar enough to be the basis of a television drama. In December 1962 the crime series *The Untouchables* broadcast an

episode that featured Gibbons as the main character, with the globe-trotting reporter stopping in Chicago in 1932 to investigate the murder of an old reporter pal.

Part Three. Life on the Home Front

5. Wheatless, Meatless, and Coalless: Patriotic Chicago

1. Perry R. Duis, *Challenging Chicago: Coping with Everyday Life, 1837–1920* (Champaign: Univ. of Illinois Press, 1998), 141.

2. Rae Katherine Eighmey, *Food Will Win the War: Minnesota Crops, Cooks, and Conservation During World War I* (St. Paul: Minnesota Historical Society Press, 2010), 8.

3. Ruth Tenzer Feldman, *World War I: Chronicle of America's Wars* (Minneapolis: Lerner Publications, 2004), 34.

4. "Sow and Till If You'd Eat to Your Fill," *Chicago Tribune*, Feb. 28, 1918, 7.

5. Duis, *Challenging Chicago*, 141.

6. "One Billion Capital Idle in City Today," *Chicago Tribune*, Jan. 18, 1918, 1.

7. "Cubs to Hold Opener with Army Setting," *Chicago Tribune*, Apr. 11, 1917, 18.

8. The Cubs played their 1918 World Series home games in Comiskey Park, home of the White Sox, because it had a larger capacity than the Cubs' Weeghman Park (later renamed Wrigley Field). The Red Sox won the game 1–0 behind the pitching of Babe Ruth.

9. "The Star Spangled Banner" was not officially the national anthem and would not be until 1931. However, it gained steadily in popularity during the First World War, and in 1916 President Wilson issued an executive order designating it the "national air" for military use. See Watkins, *Proof through the Night*, 288–91.

10. "All Primed to Yell, but Precise Hurling Gives Fans No Chance," *Chicago Tribune*, Sep. 6, 1918, 9.

11. "One Run Gives Red Sox First Game of Series," *New York Times*, Sep. 8, 1918.

12. David Fischer, *Smithsonian Q & A: Baseball: The Ultimate Question & Answer Book* (New York: Harper Perennial, 2007), 129.

13. "Chicago Swarms War Exposition Despite Rains," *Chicago Tribune*, Sep. 3, 1918, 7.

14. "Chicago Breaks All Records for War Exposition," *Chicago Tribune*, Sep. 16, 1918, 13.

15. Campbell, *Reel America and World War I*, 62.

16. "Hero in Reel War Is Forced into Real War," *Chicago Tribune*, Aug. 22, 1917, 1.

17. "Doubt Why We're at War? Then See This Gerard Film," *Chicago Tribune*, May 3, 1918, 14.

18. "The Beast of Berlin," *Chicago Tribune*, Mar. 25, 1918, 14.

19. "Anti-German Film Rejected by Funkhouser," *Chicago Tribune*, June 30, 1917, 17.

20. Melvyn Stokes, *American History through Hollywood Film: From the Revolution to the 1960s* (New York: Bloomsbury Academic, 2014), 12.

21. "Police Guard Orchestra Hall: Bar '76 Film," *Chicago Tribune*, May 15, 1917, 17.

6. Chicago's Bright Ideas: The Four Minute Men and the American Protective League

1. George Creel, *How We Advertised America* (New York: Harper and Brothers, 1920), 4.

2. For a book-length study of Creel and the CPI, see Alan Axelrod, *Selling the Great War: The Making of American Propaganda* (New York: Palgrave Macmillan, 2009).

3. Creel, *How We Advertised America*, 5.

4. Kennedy, *Over Here*, 72.

5. Ibid., 63.

6. Laurence Stallings, *The Doughboys: The Story of the AEF, 1917–1918* (New York: Harper & Row, 1963), 16.

7. A contemporary survey of the company is "Ryerson Historical Review," *American Contractor*, Nov. 3, 1917, 76.

8. History Committee, *The Four Minute Men of Chicago* (Chicago: History Committee of the Four Minute Men of Chicago, 1919), 10–11.

9. Alfred E. Cornebise, *War as Advertised: The Four Minute Men and America's Crusade, 1917–1918* (Philadelphia: American Philosophical Society, 1984), 1.

10. Ibid., 3.

11. Creel, *How We Advertised America*, 84.

12. Blair's wife, the former Helen Haddock Bowen, whom he had married in 1912, was the daughter of Louise deKoven Bowen, Jane Addams's partner in the founding of Hull-House in Chicago.

13. Cornebise, *War as Advertised*, 22.

14. Ibid., 53–54.

15. History Committee, *Four Minute Men of Chicago*, 7.

16. A complete list can be found in ibid., 17.

17. Cornebise, *War as Advertised*, 129, 134.

18. "Bar 'Hymns of Hate,'" *New York Times*, Feb. 4, 1918.

19. "Four Minute Men Engaged in Vast Win-War Work," *Chicago Tribune*, May 17, 1918, 17.

20. "William McCormick Blair," *Chicago Tribune*, Mar. 31, 1982, 10.

21. "1,137 Men Held out of 10,000 in Draft Raid," *Chicago Tribune*, July 13, 1918, 1; "Slackers' Net Draws Again; 1,135 Detained," *Chicago Tribune*, July 14, 1918, 3; "Slacker Drive Ends; Check Up to Start Today," *Chicago Tribune*, July 15, 1918, 15.

22. Emerson Hough, *The Web: A Revelation of Patriotism* (Chicago: Reilly & Lee, 1919), 49.

23. Capozzola, *Uncle Sam Wants You*, 44.

24. Fleming, *Illusion of Victory*, 96.

25. Venzon, *United States in the First World War*, 540–42, s.v. "Selective Service."

26. Capozzola, *Uncle Sam Wants You*, 10.

27. Athan G. Theoharis, ed., with Tony Poveda, Susan Rosenfeld, and Richard Gid Powers. *The FBI: A Comprehensive Reference Guide* (Westport, CN: Greenwood, 1998), 106; *The World Almanac and Encyclopedia, 1916* (New York: Press Publishing Co., 1915), 19.

28. Joan M. Jensen, *The Price of Vigilance* (Chicago: Rand McNally, 1968), 15. By war's end, the bureau would have fifteen hundred agents.

29. Clabaugh's reminiscences of the formation of the American Protective League can be found as an appendix in Hough, *Web*.

30. Hough, *Web*, 486.

31. Ibid., 43.

32. Ibid., 30.

33. "200,000 U.S. Agents Cover Nation," *Chicago Tribune*, August 25, 1917.

34. Jensen, *Price of Vigilance*, 144.

35. Hough, *Web*, 187, 190.

36. Jensen, *Price of Vigilance*, 158.

37. Venzon, *United States in the First World War*, 219, s.v. "Espionage Act of 1917."

38. The bulk of this speech can be found in Michael P. Johnson, *Reading the American Past*, vol. 2, *From 1865: Selected Historical Documents* (New York: Bedford/St. Martin's, 2008), 127–30.

39. Zieger, *America's Great War*, 198.

40. Jensen, *Price of Vigilance*, 161.

41. Zieger, *America's Great War*, 198.

42. Margaret A. Blanchard, *Revolutionary Sparks: Freedom of Expression in Modern America* (New York: Oxford Univ. Press, 1992), 96; Brian Farmer, *American Conservatism: History, Theory and Practice* (Newcastle upon Tyne: Cambridge Scholars Publishing, 2005), 199.

43. Hough, *Web*, 133.

44. Ibid., 136.

45. "Haywood Given 20 Year Term; 93 Sentenced," *Chicago Tribune*, Aug. 31, 1918, 1. A complete list of the convicted and their sentences was printed in the *New York Times* on August 31, 1918. Other mass trials of Wobblies were also held in Oklahoma and California.

46. Hough, *Web*, 180.

47. "200,000 U.S. Agents Cover Nation," *Chicago Tribune*, August 25, 1917.

48. Hough, *Web*, 183.

49. Jensen, *Price of Vigilance*, 154.

50. "Lightless Rule Violators Face A.P.L. Vengeance," *Chicago Tribune*, July 30, 1918, 13; "Lightless Rule Obeyed Better Second Night," *Chicago Tribune*, July 31, 1918, 8.

51. Hough, *Web*, 184–85.

52. Ibid., 186.

53. Kennedy, *Over Here*, 82.

54. When Wilson first heard of the proposal to institute the APL, he was concerned that it might be dangerous and asked, "I wonder if there is any way in which we could stop it?" But he ultimately decided not to buck Gregory on the issue. Ibid., 83.

55. Hough, *Web*, 14.

56. Arthur M. Evans, "Find All Shades of Reds among 60,000 Studied," *Chicago Tribune*, Jan. 4, 1920, 2.

57. Jensen, *Price of Vigilance*, 242.

58. Ibid., 240.

One Chicagoan's War
Charles E. Merriam:
The Professor in Italy

1. Louis John Nigro Jr., *The New Diplomacy in Italy: America Propaganda and U.S.-Italian Relations, 1917–1919* (New York: Peter Lang Publishing, 1999), 28.

2. An essay by Merriam, "American Publicity in Italy" appeared in *American Political Science Review* 13, no. 4 (Nov. 1919): 541–55. In it, Merriam commends several Italians who helped him but understandably does not mention Contessina Loschi.

3. Anne Lewis Pierce, "What Italy Needs Most," *Red Cross Bulletin* 2 (1918): 6.

4. Barry D. Karl, *Charles E. Merriam and the Study of Politics* (Chicago: Univ. of Chicago Press, 1974), 84, 87.

Ernest Hemingway:
The Adventurous Writer

1. Michael Reynolds, *The Young Hemingway* (New York: Basil Blackwell, 1986), 41.

2. Karsten H. Piep, *Embattled Home Fronts: Domestic Politics and the American War Novel of World War I* (New York: Rodopi, 2009), 84.

3. Kenneth Lynn, *Hemingway* (Cambridge, MA: Harvard Univ. Press, 1995), 107.

4. Hemingway's grandson Sean edited a collection of his grandfather's war writings: Sean Hemingway, *Hemingway on War* (New York: Scribner, 2004).

5. Ernest Hemingway, "Notes on the Next War: A Serious Topical Letter," *Esquire*, Sept. 1935, in *By-Line: Ernest Hemingway: Selected Articles and Dispatches of Four Decades*, ed. William White (New York: Charles Scribner's, 1967), 209–11.

6. Ernest Hemingway, *A Farewell to Arms* (New York: Macmillan, 1986), 184–85.

Clarence Darrow:
Defender of the War—and Its Opponents

1. Andrew E. Kersten, *Clarence Darrow: American Iconoclast* (New York: Hill and Wang, 2011), 99.

2. Clarence Darrow, *The Story of My Life* (Cutchogue, NY: Buccaneer Books, 1932), 210–11.

3. John A. Farrell, *Clarence Darrow: Attorney for the Damned* (New York: Doubleday, 2011), 327.

4. Ibid., 326.

5. Darrow, *Story of My Life*, 212.

6. Kersten, *Clarence Darrow*, 184.

7. Darrow, *Story of My Life*, 218.

8. Kersten, *Clarence Darrow*, 190.

Part Four. Chicago Women and the Sexual Revolution

7. "The Work Is There to Do": Chicago Women in Wartime

1. Harriot Stanton Blatch, *Mobilizing Woman-Power* (New York: Womans Press, 1918), 34.

2. Belle Squire, "Supremacy of Man Threatened in World of Brains and Action," *Chicago Tribune*, October 1, 1911, F9; Belle Squire, *The Woman Movement in America: A Short Account of the Struggle for Equal Rights* (Chicago: A. C. McClurg, 1911).

3. Maurine Weiner Greenwald, *Women, War, and Work: The Impact of World War I on Women Workers in the United States* (Ithaca, NY: Cornell Univ. Press, 1980), 5.

4. "College Girls Ready to Take Places of Men," *Chicago Tribune*, Apr. 8, 1917, 3.

5. Henry M. Hyde, "Illinois Women Organize for Service in War," *Chicago Tribune*, May 10, 1917.

6. Capozzola, *Uncle Sam Wants You*, 8.

7. "Woman Conservation Chief Outlines Work," *Chicago Tribune*, Apr. 25, 1917, 8.

8. "Women in Wartime," *Chicago Tribune*, July 8, 1918, 14.

9. "Women of Illinois Enlist for Service behind Uncle Sam," *Chicago Tribune*, July 1, 1917, C5.

10. A reproduction of the form can be found in Ida Clyde Clarke, *American Women and the World War* (New York: Appleton, 1918), 50–51.

11. "Rounding Up Feminine Slackers," *Chicago Tribune*, Aug. 25, 1918, B2.

12. Clarke, *American Women and the World War*, 36, 261.

13. Lucy Calhoun, "Women Must Be on the Job as Men Go to War," *Chicago Tribune*, June 9, 1918, 14.

14. Florence Schee, "Need of Trained Women Workers for Many Jobs," *Chicago Tribune*, July 28, 1918, C5.

15. "Hire Women, Let Men Go to War, Employers Told," *Chicago Tribune*, Sep. 27, 1918, 7.

16. Mary King, "Doing Work of Men," *Chicago Tribune*, Oct. 13, 1918, B4.

17. See Carrie Brown, "The Great Migration: Chicago, 1917," in *Rosie's Mom: Forgotten Women Workers of the First World War* (Boston: Northeastern Univ. Press, 2002), 69–94.

18. Ibid., 86.

19. Ibid., 83.

20. Doris Weatherford, *American Women during World War II: An Encyclopedia* (New York: Routledge, 2009), 304, s.v. "munitions."

21. "Women in Wartime," *Chicago Tribune*, May 21, 1918, 14.

22. "Munition Plant Service Blights Women Workers," *Chicago Tribune*, Apr. 11, 1917, 15.

23. Unsurprisingly, the employment of women in European nations was even greater than in the United States: "by the end of the war women would fill more than a third of all industrial jobs in Britain and France, and more than half of such jobs in Germany." G. J. Meyer, *A World Undone: The Story of the Great War, 1914 to 1918* (New York: Delacorte Press, 2006), 275.

24. "Women Entering War Factories to Do Their Bit," *Chicago Tribune*, June 7, 1918, 7.

25. Greenwald, *Women, War, and Work*, 58.

26. "The Limits of Opportunity: Working for the Railroads," in Greenwald, *Women, War, and Work*, 86–138.

27. "Women Making Good in Track Repair Labor," *Chicago Tribune*, Nov. 10, 1917.

28. Brown, "Great Migration," 161.

29. Mary Anderson, *Woman at Work* (Minneapolis: Univ. of Minnesota Press, 1951), 90.

30. Ibid., 104, 106.

31. Francine J. D'Amico and Laurie L. Weinstein, eds., *Gender Camouflage: Women and the U.S. Military* (New York: NYU Press, 1999), 39.

32. Lettie Gavin, *American Women in World War I: They Also Served* (Boulder: University Press of Colorado, 1997), 1.

33. "Yeomanette Is First Woman to Ride Navy Plane," *Chicago Tribune*, Apr. 8, 1919, 4.

34. The U.S. Marines also admitted women into their ranks, but much later and in much fewer numbers than did the navy. The call did not go out until August 1918, only three months before the armistice, and by war's end just 305 women had enlisted in the Marine Corps. Gavin, *American Women in World War I*, 25–26. The Coast Guard also enrolled a few women.

35. "Fate," *Chicago Tribune*, May 23, 1917, 7.

36. See Dorothy and Carl J. Schneider, *Into the Breach: American Women Overseas in World War I* (New York: Viking, 1991).

37. Gavin, *American Women in World War I*, 44.

38. "Field Hospitals of Mrs. Turner Get Bazaar Aid," *Chicago Tribune*, Jan. 8, 1917, 5.

39. In 1929, Mary Borden Turner published *The Forbidden Zone*, a group of sketches and stories about the war. An excerpt can be found in Yvonne M. Klein, ed., *Beyond the Home Front: Women's Autobiographical Writing of the Two World Wars* (New York: New York Univ. Press, 1997), 65–75.

40. Ellen N. La Motte, *The Backwash of War* (New York: G. P. Putnam's Sons, 1916), 154–55.

41. "Maude Radford Warren a Major in Record Time," *Chicago Tribune*, Feb. 3, 1919, 10.

42. Hunton and Johnson, *Two Colored Women*, 135.

43. Ibid., 33.

44. Gavin, *American Women in World War I*, 77–78.

45. "'Hello Girls' Being Trained for Pershing," *Chicago Tribune*, Mar. 26, 1918, 5.

46. "Chicago Girls 'Hello' in France," *Chicago Tribune*, May 16, 1918, 5.

47. Lucy Calhoun, "Girls in Navy to Join the Nation's Job Hunters Soon," *Chicago Tribune*, Apr. 11, 1919, 21.

48. "Girl Workers Find Hardships of War in Peace," *Chicago Tribune*, Nov. 22, 1918, 10.

49. Lucy Calhoun, "Girls in Navy to Join the Nation's Job Hunters Soon," *Chicago Tribune*, Apr. 11, 1919, 21.

50. Brown, "Great Migration," 176.

51. "Girl Workers to Get Peace Jobs Back after War," *Chicago Tribune*, Nov. 24, 1918, 9.

52. Greenwald, *Women, War, and Work*, 235.

53. Brown, "Great Migration," 187.

54. Joanne J. Meyerowitz, *Women Adrift: Independent Wage Earners in Chicago, 1880–1930* (Chicago: Univ. of Chicago Press, 1988), xvii.

55. Ibid., 5.

56. Zieger, *America's Great War*, 144.

57. "Women Retain Grip on Business Won during War," *Chicago Tribune*, Dec. 15, 1919, 10.

58. Greenwald, *Women, War, and Work*, 45.

59. Gavin, *American Women in World War I*, ix.

60. Frances Donovan, *The Woman Who Waits* (Boston: Richard G. Badger, 1920), 14.

61. Karen Zeinert, *Those Extraordinary Women of World War I* (Brookfield, CT: Millbrook Press, 2001), 79.

8. "Sex O'Clock in America": Chicago and the First Sexual Revolution

1. Louise James, "Fetching Indeed Are Fashions for the Flapper," *Chicago Tribune*, Dec. 5, 1915, H3.

2. A reprint of the article can be found in Jeffrey Escoffier, ed., *Sexual Revolution* (New York: Thunder's Mouth Press, 2003), 4–19.

3. Fleming, *Illusion of Victory*, 200.

4. Joshua Zeitz, *Flapper: A Madcap Story of Sex, Style, Celebrity, and the Women Who Made American Modern* (New York: Broadway, 2007), 23.

5. John Alfred Heitmann, *The Automobile and American Life* (Jefferson, NC: McFarland, 2009), 91.

6. John D'Emilio and Estelle B. Freedman, *Intimate Matters: A History of Sexuality in America* (Chicago: Univ. of Chicago Press, 1997), 233.

7. "Good Music Is Needed—Jazz Is Evil Spirit," *Englewood (IL) Economist*, May 11, 1921, 1.

8. For an early example, see "Blames 'Rags' for Dance Evil," *Chicago Tribune*, Jan. 19, 1912, 12, which quotes the manager of the dancing pavilion at Sans Souci Park as charging that "ragtime and its offshoots" were "more demoralizing than alcohol." In 1913 the Chicago City Council banned dancing in restaurants. The owners of the Blackstone Hotel challenged the law in court, and it was overturned.

9. "We Must Toddle in 1917," *New York Times*, Dec. 29, 1916, 7.

10. "Can You Toddle?—Better Learn—It's All the Rage," *(Chicago) Day Book*, Dec. 29, 1916, 28.

11. "Shimmy? Toddle? No Such Doin's in Our Schools," *Chicago Tribune*, Jan. 18. 1921, 3. Another new dance much disliked by moralists was the tango, which became a craze around 1913.

12. Donovan, *Woman Who Waits*, 32.

13. Charles P. Neill, *Report on Condition of Women and Child Wage Earners in the United States*, vol. 5, *Wage-Earning Women in Stores and Factories* (Washington: Government Printing Office, 1910), 157. This survey reported that 20.3 percent of women in Chicago working in department and other retail stores were "women adrift." For factories, mills, and the like, the figure was 16.4 percent.

14. Meyerowitz, *Women Adrift*, 102.

15. Ibid., 106.

16. D'Emilio and Freedman, *Intimate Matters*, 194.

17. Beth L. Bailey, *From Front Porch to Back Seat: Courtship in Twentieth-Century America* (Baltimore: Johns Hopkins Univ. Press, 1988), 17. See also Kevin White, *The First Sexual Revolution in America: The Emergence of Male Heterosexuality in Modern America* (New York: New York Univ. Press, 1993), 14. On George Ade, see Joseph Gustaitis, "The Birth of Urban Literature," in *Chicago's Greatest Year, 1893: The White City and the Birth of a Modern Metropolis* (Carbondale: Southern Illinois Univ. Press, 2013), 151–80.

18. Lauren Rabinovitz, *For the Love of Pleasure: Women, Movies, and Culture in Turn-of-the-Century Chicago* (New Brunswick, NJ: Rutgers Univ. Press, 1998), 122–135.

19. Quoted in D'Emilio and Freedman, *Intimate Matters*, 197.

20. "Women Chosen to Make Survey of Movie Houses," *Chicago Tribune*, Feb. 27, 1916, A7. For a provocative contemporary report on the sexual dangers in Chicago, see Louise de Koven Bowen, *The Road to Destruction Made Easy in Chicago* (Chicago: Hale-Crossley, 1916).

21. Donovan, *Woman Who Waits*, 9, 20, 81, 145.

22. Ibid., 219–20.

23. Daniel Scott Smith, "The Dating of the American Sexual Revolution: Evidence and Interpretation," in *The American Family in Social-Historical Perspective*, ed. Michael Gordon (New York: St. Martin's Press, 1973), 321–35.

24. Ibid., 332.

25. Meyerowitz, *Women Adrift*, xxiii.

26. "Women Start War on Sex Novel," *Chicago Tribune*, June 14, 1914, 2.

27. Valentine, *1913*, 79.

28. "Hobble Skirt Invades Park," *Chicago Tribune*, May 19, 1911, 9.

29. "Woman Bathing in Bloomers Held," *Chicago Tribune*, July 28, 1913, 1; "Women May Swim in Bloomer Suits," *Chicago Tribune*, July 29, 1913, 1.

30. D'Emilio and Freedman, *Intimate Matters*, 230. See also Henry F. May, *The End of American Innocence: A Study of the First Years of Our Time, 1912–1917* (Chicago: Quadrangle Books, 1964), 307–10.

31. Floyd Dell, *Women as World Builders: Studies in Modern Feminism* (Chicago: Forbes and Co., 1913), 13–14.

32. A good brief biography of Ella Flagg Young can be found in Sawyers, *Chicago Portraits*, 279–80.

33. "Will Teach Sex Hygiene in Chicago High Schools," *Chicago Tribune*, June 20, 1913, 10. See also Jeffrey P. Moran, "'Modernism Gone Mad': Sex Education Comes to Chicago, 1913," *Journal of American History* 83, no. 2 (Sep. 1996): 481–513.

34. Moran, "'Modernism Gone Mad,'" 502.

35. Ibid., 506; "Loeb Fights Opposition to Sex Hygiene Course," *Chicago Tribune*, June 27, 1913, 10.

36. Moran, "'Modernism Gone Mad,'" 510.

37. D'Emilio and Freedman, *Intimate Matters*, 213.

38. Kennedy, *Over Here*, 187.

39. "Immorality in War Time Work," *Chicago Tribune*, Aug. 15, 1917, 7.

40. Elmer T. Clark, *Social Studies of the War* (New York: George H. Doran, 1919), 33–34.

41. Alyse Gregory, "The Changing Morality of Women," *Current History* 19 (1923): 298–99, reproduced in William Bruce Wheeler, Susan Becker, and Lorri Glover, *Discovering the American Past: A Look at the Evidence*, vol. 2, *Since 1865* (Stamford, CT: Wadsworth Publishing, 2011), 176.

42. Meyerowitz, *Women Adrift*, 126–29.

One Chicagoan's War
Eunice Tietjens: The Disillusioned Poet

1. Eunice Tietjens, *The World at My Shoulder* (New York: Macmillan, 1938), 174.

2. Ibid., 101.

3. Ibid., 135.

4. Ibid., 142.

5. Ibid., 145.

6. Ibid., 162.

7. Sergeant described the incident in *Shadow Shapes: The Journal of a Wounded Woman* (1920). An excerpt can be found in Yvonne M. Klein, ed., *Beyond the Home Front: Women's Autobiographical Writing of the Two World Wars* (New York: New York Univ. Press, 1997), 76–81.

8. Tietjens, 176.

9. Ibid., 332.

Part Five. Chicago's Changing Ethnic Landscape
9. "The Biggest Town in the World": The Great Migration

1. An interview with Davis can be found in Timuel D. Black Jr., *Bridges of Memory: Chicago's First Wave of Black Migration* (Evanston, IL: Northwestern University Press, 2003), 46–54. A much longer interview, conducted by Horace Q. Waggoner in 1979 and 1982, was collected as part of the Illinois General Assembly Oral History Program and is available online at http://www.uis.edu/archives/memoirs/DAVISCORNEALvI.pdf.

2. Isabel Wilkerson, *The Warmth of Other Suns: The Epic Story of America's Great Migration* (New York: Vintage Books, 2010), 9.

3. James R. Grossman, *Land of Hope: Chicago, Black Southerners, and the Great Migration* (Chicago: University of Chicago Press, 1989), 4. Chicago was a magnet not only for blacks but also for whites, most notably small-town or rural Midwesterners who also listened to the whistle of the locomotive during the night and fantasized about making it big in Chicago. In fact, a book has been written about that subject. See Timothy B. Spears, *Chicago Dreaming: Midwesterners and the City, 1871–1919* (Chicago: Univ. of Chicago Press, 2005).

4. Emmett J. Scott, *Negro Migration during the War* (New York: Oxford Univ. Press, 1920), 102.

5. Allan H. Spear, *Black Chicago: The Making of a Negro Ghetto, 1890–1920* (Chicago: Univ. of Chicago Press, 1967), 141.

6. Reed, *Knock at the Door of Opportunity*, 220.

7. Touré F. Reed, *Not Alms but Opportunity: The Urban League & the Politics of Racial Uplift, 1910–1950* (Chapel Hill: Univ. of North Carolina Press, 2008), 28; Wilkerson, *Warmth of Other Suns*, 11.

8. The map from this study is reproduced in Grossman, *Land of Hope*, 148–49.

9. Spear, *Black Chicago*, 131,

10. Henry M. Hyde, "Immigration Flood Shrinks to Mere Trickle," *Chicago Tribune*, Sept. 20, 1917, 15; Henry M. Hyde, "Negroes Lead as Immigrants; Population Cut," *Chicago Tribune*, Feb. 20, 1918, 3.

11. James R. Barrett, *Work and Community in the Jungle: Chicago's Packinghouse Workers, 1894–1922* (Urbana: Univ. of Illinois Press, 1990), 189.

12. "South Howls!," *Chicago Defender*, Sep. 23, 1916, 6.

13. Grossman, *Land of Hope*, 13–14.

14. "Reasons Why Our People Come North," *Chicago Defender*, May 31, 1924, A1.

15. Grossman, *Land of Hope*, 16.

16. A lengthy list of survey questions and answers can be found in Chicago Commission on Race Relations, *The Negro in Chicago: A Study*

of Race Relations and a Race Riot* (Chicago: University of Chicago Press, 1922), 100–103.

17. "In Jackson, Mississippi, classes in the two black schools ranged from 75 to 125." Grossman, *Land of Hope*, 247.

18. Ibid., 247.

19. Wilkerson, *Warmth of Other Suns*, 39.

20. Grossman, *Land of Hope*, 130.

21. Ibid., 185.

22. Scott, *Negro Migration during the War*, 102.

23. Grossman, *Land of Hope*, 185–86; Scott, *Negro Migration during the War*, 103.

24. Grossman, *Land of Hope*, 184.

25. Quoted in Spear, *Black Chicago*, 134.

26. Reed, *Not Alms but Opportunity*, 63–65.

27. Richard Sudhalter, *Lost Chords: White Musicians and Their Contribution to Jazz, 1915–1945* (New York: Oxford University Press, 1999), 86.

28. Grossman, *Land of Hope*, 167.

29. Chicago Commission on Race Relations, *Negro in Chicago*, 245.

30. Grossman, *Land of Hope*, 248.

31. Chicago Commission on Race Relations, *Negro in Chicago*, 252.

32. Wilkerson, *Warmth of Other Suns*, 190.

33. Quoted in Grossman, *Land of Hope*, 110.

34. Ibid., 111.

35. Roi Ottley, *The Lonely Warrior: The Life and Times of Robert S. Abbott* (Chicago: H. Regnery, 1955), 70–71.

36. Ibid., 74.

37. Ibid., 86.

38. Biography of Robert S. Abbott in Sawyers, *Chicago Portraits*, 2.

39. Scott, *Negro Migration during the War*, 30.

40. Reed, Knock at the Door of Opportunity, 224.

41. Ethan Michaeli, *The Defender: How the Legendary Black Newspaper Changed America from the Age of the Pullman Porters to the Age of Obama* (New York: Houghton Mifflin Harcourt, 2016), 62–63.

42. Ibid., 64.

43. Quoted in Scott, *Negro Migration during the War*, 31.

44. Kennedy, *Over Here*, 280.

45. Scott, *Negro Migration during the War*, 78.

46. "Emigration Worries South," *Chicago Defender*, Mar. 24, 1917, 1.

47. "Some Neighborhood Comment," *Atlanta Georgian*, Mar. 31, 1917.

48. "Tale of Two Cities," *Chicago Defender*, June 7, 1919, 15.

49. Arvarh E. Strickland, *History of the Chicago Urban League* (Columbia: Univ. of Missouri Press, 2001), 63–64.

50. Spear, *Black Chicago*, 135.

51. Thomas Dyja, *The Third Coast: When Chicago Built the American Dream* (New York: Penguin, 2013), 315.

52. "What the Defender Has Done," *Chicago Defender*, Feb. 2, 1918, 11.

53. "How Negroes Are Helping to Win the War," *New York Times*, July 7, 1918.

54. Ottley, *Lonely Warrior*, 156.

55. Reed, *Knock at the Door of Opportunity*, 16.

56. Ibid., 228.

57. Grossman, *Land of Hope*, 156.

58. Wilkerson, *Warmth of Other Suns*, 288.

59. Between 1915 and 1919 Urban League branches were founded in Chicago, Pittsburgh, Detroit, Cleveland, Newark, Milwaukee, and Columbus. On the Chicago branch, see Strickland, *History of the Chicago Urban League*.

60. Grossman, *Land of Hope*, 142–43, 102.

61. Reed, *Knock at the Door of Opportunity*, 5.

62. Baldwin, *Chicago's New Negroes*, 27; Strickland, *History of the Chicago Urban League*, 44.

63. Reed, *Not Alms but Opportunity*, 29, 35.

64. Strickland, *History of the Chicago Urban League*, 49.

65. Baldwin, *Chicago's New Negroes*, 34.

66. Reed, *Knock at the Door of Opportunity*, 248.

67. Spear, *Black Chicago*, 201.

68. Thomas Lee Philpott, *The Slum and the Ghetto: Immigrants, Blacks, and Reformers in Chicago, 1880–1930* (Belmont, CA: Wadsworth Publishing Co., 1991), 170.

69. Baldwin, *Chicago's New Negroes*, 25.

70. See "Holding the Line: Restriction" in Philpott, *Slum and the Ghetto*, 183–202.

71. Philpott, *Slum and the Ghetto*, 131–33.

72. Spear, *Black Chicago*, 142, 146.

73. Baldwin, *Chicago's New Negroes*, 23.

74. Wilkerson, *Warmth of Other Suns*, 217–18.

10. "That Was Music": Chicago Jazz

1. Charles A. Sengstock Jr., *Jazz Music in Chicago's Early South Side Theaters* (Northbrook, IL: Canterbury Press of Northbrook, 2000), 9.

2. "Jazz Most Popular Music of the Day," *Chicago Defender*, May 31, 1924, 6.

3. From Sidney Bechet's *Treat It Gentle* (1960), quoted in Robert Gottlieb, *Reading Jazz* (New York: Vintage Books, 1996), 8.

4. John Chilton, *Sidney Bechet: The Wizard of Jazz* (Cambridge, MA: Da Capo Press, 1996), 27.

5. Howard Reich and William M. Gaines, *Jelly's Blues: The Life, Music, and Redemption of Jelly Roll Morton* (Cambridge, MA: Da Capo Press, 2004), 45.

6. Burton Peretti, *The Creation of Jazz: Music, Race, and Culture in Urban America* (Urbana: Univ. of Illinois Press, 1994), 45. Membership in the American Federation of Musicians jumped from 83,992 in 1917 to 146,421 in 1928. Ibid., 157.

7. Dave Peyton, "The Musical Bunch," *Chicago Defender*, Nov. 19, 1927, 6. Peyton later came to disparage jazz, feeling that black people should seek more musical training and a more elevated kind of music. Many jazz musicians agreed with him up to a point and sought to raise the music from its "low" southern origins and make it more "artistic."

8. Dave Peyton, "The Musical Bunch," *Chicago Defender*, Dec. 12, 1925, 7.

9. Tim Brooks, *Lost Sounds: Blacks and the Birth of the Recording Industry, 1890–1929* (Urbana: Univ. of Illinois Press, 2004), 337. See also Mark Berresford, *That's Got 'Em: The Life and Music of Wilbur C. Sweatman* (Jackson: University Press of Mississippi, 2010). Sweatman made some fascinating, but not very jazzy, recordings before World War I.

10. Peretti, *Creation of Jazz*, 21, 43, 45.

11. Sengstock, *Jazz Music*, 10–11, 27.

12. Thomas Bauman, *The Pekin: The Rise and Fall of Chicago's First Black-Owned Theater* (Urbana: Univ. of Illinois Press, 2014), 38.

13. In 2011 Chicago's Old Town School of Folk Music presented a revue entitled *Keep a Song in Your Soul*, which surveyed black vaudeville.

14. Brooks, *Lost Sounds*, 271.

15. "Europe's Band," *Chicago Defender*, May 3, 1919, 9.

16. Musicians who play brass or wind instruments or most string instruments can "bend" a note—that is, cause it to slide up or down in pitch. This is impossible on the piano, so players try to get a similar effect by playing flattened, or "blue," notes.

17. Many thanks to the late jazz historian James S. Patrick for sharing his insights into the relationship of ragtime to jazz and for reviewing the text of this chapter, which is dedicated to his memory.

18. Gottlieb, *Reading Jazz*, 5.

19. Lawrence Gushee, *Pioneers of Jazz: The Story of the Creole Band* (New York: Oxford Univ. Press, 2005), 100.

20. "Alberta Hunter Goes Over the Top at Dreamland," *Chicago Defender*, Jan. 28, 1922, 4.

21. Gordon Seagrove, "Blues Is Jazz and Jazz Is Blues," *Chicago Tribune*, July 11, 1915, E8. Seagrove later became a prominent advertising man best known for devising the slogan "Even your best friend won't tell you" for Listerine in 1922. His employment of the word *jazz* in the *Tribune* article has been called the first printed appearance of the term in reference to music.

22. Gary Giddins, *Visions of Jazz: The First Century* (New York: Oxford Univ. Press, 1998), 70.

23. Reich and Gaines, *Jelly's Blues*, 47.

24. "Jazz Music at Pekin Pavilion," *Chicago Defender*, Mar. 16, 1918, 12.

25. Gushee, *Pioneers of Jazz*, 302–7.

26. For a detailed analysis of this episode, much discussed in jazz history, see ibid., 169–73.

27. Chilton, *Sidney Bechet*, 30.

28. Ibid., 28.

29. Peretti, *Creation of Jazz*, 49.

30. Eddie Condon, *We Called It Music: A Generation of Jazz* (Cambridge, MA: Da Capo Press, 1992), 133.

31. "Jazz Music at Pekin Pavilion," *Chicago Defender*, March 16, 1918, 12.

32. Reed, *Knock at the Door of Opportunity*, 109.

33. Sandor Demlinger and John Steiner, *Destination Chicago Jazz* (Chicago: Arcadia Publishing, 2003), 34.

34. Kenney, *Chicago Jazz*, 18.

35. Peretti, *Creation of Jazz*, 50.

36. Kenney, *Chicago Jazz*, 10.

37. "At Royal Gardens," *Chicago Defender*, June 28, 1918, 8.

38. On the history of the Pekin in its various manifestations, see Bauman, *Pekin*.

39. Baldwin, *Chicago's New Negroes*, 26.

40. Peretti, *Creation of Jazz*, 40.

41. Chilton, *Sidney Bechet*, 27; Peretti, *Creation of Jazz*, 25.

42. Leonard Huber and Charles Dufour, *New Orleans: A Pictorial History* (Gretna, LA: Pelican Publishing, 1991), 12; Eric Arnesen, *Waterfront Workers of New Orleans: Race, Class, and Politics, 1863–1923* (Champaign: Univ. of Illinois Press, 1994), 217–22.

43. John H. Bernhard, *New Orleans: As the World's Greatest Port* (New Orleans: New Orleans Association of Commerce, 1921), 25–26.

44. Daniel Rosenberg, *New Orleans Dockworkers: Race, Labor, and Unionism, 1892–1923* (Albany: State Univ. of New York Press, 1988), 169.

45. Peretti, *Creation of Jazz*, 30, 49.

46. "Stale Bread's Sadness Gave 'Jazz' to the World," *Literary Digest*, Apr. 26, 1919, 132.

47. Charles A. Sengstock Jr., *That Toddlin' Town: Chicago's White Dance Bands and Orchestras, 1900–1950* (Urbana: Univ. of Illinois Press, 2004), 86.

48. Gushee, *Pioneers of Jazz*, 133.

49. On Frisco, see Paul M. Levitt, ed., *Joe Frisco: Comic, Jazz Dancer, and Railbird* (Carbondale: Southern Illinois Univ. Press, 1999).

50. Kenney, *Chicago Jazz*, 66–67. See also Samuel Barclay Charters, *A Trumpet around the Corner: The Story of New Orleans Jazz* (Jackson: University Press of Mississippi, 2008), 119.

51. Sengstock, *That Toddlin' Town*, 114.

52. Quoted in Sudhalter, *Lost Chords*, 11.

53. Sandor Demlinger and John Steiner, *Destination Chicago Jazz* (Charleston, SC: Arcadia, 2003), 20.

54. "Jazz.es Up' Radio," *Chicago Defender*, Sep. 2, 1922, 6.

55. Peretti, *Creation of Jazz*, 66.

56. Sudhalter, *Lost Chords*, 35.

57. Rick Kennedy, *Jelly Roll, Bix, and Hoagy: Gennett Studios and the Birth of Recorded Jazz* (Bloomington: Indiana Univ. Press, 1994), 57.

58. Gottlieb, *Reading Jazz*, 344.

59. "Lincoln Gardens," *Chicago Defender*, Sep. 1, 1923, 8; "King Oliver's Jazz Band," *Chicago Defender*, Aug. 11, 1923, 7. "King Oliver's Band," *Chicago Defender*, Oct. 6, 1923, 8.

60. Kenney, *Chicago Jazz*, 131.

61. Giddins, *Visions of Jazz*, 77.

62. Giddins feels that even if Armstrong had retired after his final recordings with the Hot Five and Hot Seven in 1928, "he would still be the most eminent figure in jazz history." Ibid., 94.

63. Ibid., 84.

11. "Sweet Home Chicago": The Chicago Blues

1. Elijah Wald, *Escaping the Delta: Robert Johnson and the Invention of the Blues* (New York: Amistad, 2005), 3, xiii.

2. Ibid., 13.

3. See Peter van der Merwe, "British Origins of the Blues," in *Origins of the Popular Style* (New York: Oxford Univ. Press, 1989), 171–83.

4. Francis Davis, *The History of the Blues* (Cambridge, MA: Da Capo Press, 1995), 90.

5. Ibid., 38.

6. Paul Oliver, *Songsters and Saints: Vocal Traditions on Race Records* (New York: Cambridge Univ. Press, 1984), 3. Oliver's book has excellent material on the wide repertoire of the songsters, and he points out that most were not full-time professional musicians, but part-timers who played mainly on weekends.

7. Ibid., 259.

8. Dave Oliphant, *Texan Jazz* (Austin: Univ. of Texas Press, 1996), 41.

9. Michael W. Harris, *The Rise of Gospel Blues: The Music of Thomas Andrew Dorsey in the Urban Church* (New York: Oxford Univ. Press, 1992), 60.

10. Elijah Wald, *The Blues: A Very Short Introduction* (New York: Oxford Univ. Press, 2010), 11.

11. Gerard Herzhaft, "Female Blues Singers," in *Encyclopedia of the Blues* (Fayetteville: Univ. of Arkansas Press, 1992), 110.

12. "Pace & Handy," *Chicago Defender*, July 31, 1920, 4; "New Records," *Chicago Defender*, Sept. 11, 1920, 5.

13. Will Friedwald, *A Biographical Guide to the Great Jazz and Pop Singers* (New York: Pantheon, 2010), 555.

14. William Howland Kenney, *Recorded Music in American Life: The Phonograph and Popular Memory, 1890–1945* (New York: Oxford Univ. Press, 2003), 114.

15. In 1923 a trade publication published a revealing interview with Heinemann: "Radio Aids Okeh Sales," *Wireless Age* 10, no. 9 (June 1923): 27–28.

16. "Pace & Handy," *Chicago Defender*, July 31, 1920, 4.

17. "'Mamie Smith Co.' Fills the Avenue," *Chicago Defender*, Mar. 5, 1921, 4.

18. "'In Bamville' in for a Run at Illinois," *Chicago Defender*, April 12, 1924, 6; "'Come along Mandy' at the Grand," *Chicago Defender*, May 10, 1924, 6.

19. Samuel B. Charters, *The Country Blues* (Cambridge, MA: Da Capo Press, 1975), 50.

20. Wald, *Escaping the Delta*, 30.

21. Davis, *History of the Blues*, 83.

22. The actual instrument Jackson played was an unusual six-string banjo; a photograph shows him holding a Gibson GB (guitar-banjo), which had a somewhat softer sound than the conventional five-string banjo.

23. Stephen Calt, "The Anatomy of a 'Race' Music Label: Mayo Williams and Paramount Records," in *R&B (Rhythm and Business): The Political Economy of Black Music*, ed. Norman Kelley (Brooklyn, NY: Akashic Books, 2005), 90–115.

24. Ibid., 109.

25. On the development of the blues tradition in Chicago, see Mike Rowe, *Chicago Blues: The City & the Music* (Cambridge, MA: Da Capo Press, 1975).

26. John Paulett and Rod Gordon, *Forgotten Chicago* (Mount Pleasant, SC: Arcadia Publishing, 2004), 98.

27. Lori Grove and Laura Kamedulski, *Chicago's Maxwell Street* (Mount Pleasant, SC: Arcadia Publishing, 2002), 15.

28. Irving Cutler, *The Jews of Chicago: From Shtetl to Suburb* (Champaign: Univ. of Illinois Press, 1996), 69.

29. David Whiteis, "The Blues Reality of Maxwell Street," in *BluesSpeak: Best of the Original Chicago Blues Annual*, ed. Lincoln T. Beauchamp Jr. (Champaign: Univ. of Illinois Press, 2010), 23.

30. Karen Hanson, *Today's Chicago Blues* (Chicago: Lake Claremont Press, 2007), 81–82.

31. Whiteis, "Blues Reality of Maxwell Street," 23.

32. Vladimir Bogdanov, Chris Woodstra, and Michael Erlewine, eds., *All Music Guide to the Blues* (Montclair, NJ: Backbeat Books, 2003), 139; Barry Hansen, *Rhino's Cruise through the Blues* (San Francisco: Miller Freeman Books, 2000), 19. However, black *musicians* born before Watson were recorded. In 1890, George Washington Johnson, who was born in 1846, recorded a cylinder for the Metropolitan Phonograph Company of New York, and Bert Williams, the Ziegfeld Follies star, made quite a few recordings before 1920. The folk song collector John A. Lomax recorded ballads sung in a Texas prison by Moses "Cedar Rock" Platt, who was born in 1862. Oliver, *Songsters and Saints*, 229. The earliest-born musician of any kind to have been recorded seems to have been the German composer-pianist Carl Reinecke (1824–1910). On Johnson, the first black performer to be recorded, see Tim Brooks, *Lost Sounds: Blacks and the Birth of the Recording Industry, 1890–1919* (Urbana: Univ. of Illinois Press, 2004), 17–71.

33. D. Thomas Moon, "Talkin' 'bout Maxwell Street," in the liner notes to the recording *And This Is Free: The Life and Times of Chicago's Legendary Maxwell Street*, Shanachie Entertainment, 2008. Some songsters played an instrument called the "stovepipe," an actual metal stovepipe that resonated like a jug in a jug band, but Watson's nickname came from his Lincolnesque tall hat. A Cincinnati musician named Sam Jones, who went by Stovepipe No. 1, did play the stovepipe and left a series of recordings.

34. Rowe, *Chicago Blues*, 49.

12. "Coming to Stay": The Beginning of Mexican Chicago

1. Ray Hutchinson, "Historiography of Chicago's Mexican Community," *La Voz de Aztlan*, accessed February 28, 2012, http://aztlan.net/chicagoh.htm. As Michael D. Innis-Jiménez wrote, "The study of the history of Mexicans in the industrial Midwest is a relatively new development and that of Mexicans in the Chicago area an even more recent one" Michael D. Innis-Jiménez, *Steel Barrio: The Great Mexican Migration to South Chicago, 1915–1940* (New York: New York Univ. Press, 2013), 6.

2. "Yellow peril" was a term used by nativist Europeans and Americans in the late nineteenth and early twentieth centuries to describe fears that the huge populations of Asia, especially China, represented a racial threat to Western culture. In the United States it was thought that this threat was most likely to be realized by large-scale immigration.

3. Innis-Jiménez, *Steel Barrio*, 26.

4. Lawrence A. Cardoso, *Mexican Emigration to the United States, 1897–1931* (Tucson: Univ. of Arizona Press, 1980), 2–3.

5. Paul Friedrich, *Agrarian Revolt in a Mexican Village* (Chicago: Univ. of Chicago Press, 1977), 3.

6. Cardoso, *Mexican Emigration*, 7.

7. Ibid., 6.

8. Ibid., 4.

9. Jean Edward Smith, *Grant* (New York: Simon & Schuster, 2001), 71.

10. Michael J. Gonzales, *The Mexican Revolution, 1910–1940* (Albuquerque: Univ. of New Mexico Press, 2002), 45.

11. Rita Arias Jirasek and Carlos Tortolero, *Mexican Chicago* (Chicago: Arcadia Publishing, 2001), 9.

12. Cardoso, *Mexican Emigration*, 38–39.

13. Louise Año Nuevo Kerr, "Chicano Settlements in Chicago: A Brief History," in *En Aquel Entonces: Readings in Mexican-American*

History, ed. Manuel G. Gonzales and Cynthia M. Gonzales (Bloomington: Indiana University Press, 2000), 9.

14. Quoted in Jirasek and Tortolero, *Mexican Chicago*, 8.

15. Perry R. Duis, *Challenging Chicago: Coping with Everyday Life, 1837–1920* (Urbana: Univ. of Illinois Press, 1998), 160.

16. "Hot Tamales Return with the Corn," *Chicago Tribune*, Aug. 31, 1896, 7.

17. "Chicken and Pigs' Feet for Soldiers," *New York Times*, April 6, 1901.

18. Warren Belasco and Roger Horwitz, *Food Chains: From Farmyard to Shopping Cart* (Philadelphia: Univ. of Pennsylvania Press, 2008), 163.

19. Wilfredo Cruz, *City of Dreams: Latino Immigration to Chicago* (Lanham, MD: University Press of America, 2007), 9.

20. Cutler, *Chicago*, 176.

21. Cruz, *City of Dreams*, 9.

22. Jirasek and Tortolero, *Mexican Chicago*, 10.

23. Ibid., 9.

24. "Importation of Colored Folks Causing Rumpus on the South Side," *(Chicago) Day Book*, Apr. 7, 1917, 10.

25. Cruz, *City of Dreams*, 28.

26. Sarah Kelly Oehler, *They Seek a City: Chicago and the Art of Migration* (Chicago: Art Institute of Chicago, 2013), 50.

27. Cruz, *City of Dreams*, 16.

28. Gabriela F. Arredondo, *Mexican Chicago: Race, Identity, and Nation, 1916–39* (Urbana: Univ. of Illinois Press, 2008), 23.

29. Cruz, *City of Dreams*, 10.

30. Innis-Jiménez, *Steel Barrio*, 31.

31. Michael D. Innis-Jiménez, *Persisting in the Shadow of Steel: Community Formation and Survival in Mexican South Chicago, 1919–1939* (Ann Arbor, MI: ProQuest, 2006), 44.

32. Innis-Jiménez, *Steel Barrio*, 28–30.

33. Ibid., 32, 35.

34. Arredondo, *Mexican Chicago*, 60.

35. Nicholas de Genova, *Working the Boundaries: Race, Space, and "Illegality" in Mexican Chicago* (Durham, NC: Duke University Press, 2005), 114.

36. Innis-Jiménez, *Steel Barrio*, 33.

37. Juan R. García, *Mexicans in the Midwest, 1900–1932* (Tucson: Univ. of Arizona Press, 2004), 38; Innis-Jiménez, *Steel Barrio*, 47. When a Mexican worker did become a foreman, he was given only Mexican workers to supervise.

38. David Brody, *Steelworkers in America: The Nonunion Era* (Urbana: Univ. of Illinois Press, 1998), 266.

39. Innis-Jiménez, *Steel Barrio*, 78.

40. Innis-Jiménez, *Persisting in the Shadow of Steel*, 319.

41. Arredondo, *Mexican Chicago*, 39.

42. Ibid., 51.

43. Ibid., 42.

44. Elizabeth Hughes of Chicago's Bureau of Social Surveys, quoted in Innis-Jiménez, *Steel Barrio*, 61.

45. "Human Exhibits Evidence Used against Pay Cut," *Chicago Tribune*, Apr. 3, 1922, 15.

46. Arredondo, *Mexican Chicago*, 61.

47. "Hit or Miss," *Chicago Daily Herald*, Feb. 14, 1919, 5.

48. Arredondo, *Mexican Chicago*, 106.

49. "Depicts Mexican Immigrants as Health Menace," *Chicago Tribune*, Oct. 19, 1928, 20.

50. "Immigration of Mexicans Looms as U.S. Problem," *Chicago Tribune*, Mar. 1, 1924, 25.

51. "Immigrant Tide from Mexico Still Vexes U.S.," *Chicago Tribune*, August 11, 1928, 8.

52. Innis-Jiménez, *Steel Barrio*, 144.

53. T. H. Watkins, *The Hungry Years: A Narrative History of the Great Depression in America* (New York: Henry Holt & Co., 1999), 399.

54. Cheryl R. Ganz and Margaret Strobel, eds., *Pots of Promise: Mexicans and Pottery at Hull-House, 1920–40* (Urbana: Univ. of Illinois Press, 2004), 41.

55. Innis-Jiménez, *Steel Barrio*, 119.

56. Oehler, *They Seek a City*, 50.

57. On the history and goals of the National Museum of Mexican Art, see Rosa M. Cabrera, *Beyond Dust, Memories and Preservation: Roles of Ethnic Museums in Shaping Community Ethnic Identities* (Ann Arbor, MI: ProQuest, 2008).

58. Arredondo, *Mexican Chicago*, 157.

59. Innis-Jiménez, *Steel Barrio*, 120.

60. Juan R. Garcia, *Mexicans in the Midwest, 1900–1932* (Tucson: Univ. of Arizona Press, 2004), 158.

61. Marcia Farr, *Rancheros in Chicagoacán: Language and Identity in a Transnational Community* (Austin: Univ. of Texas Press, 2006), 91. In more recent years, however, indications are that Hispanics are entering the melting pot in much the same way as Italians did before them. "Study after study shows current Hispanic immigrants are picking up English at an impressive clip, roughly as quickly as earlier immigrant groups. They are making steady gains in homeownership rates, job status and social identity. By the second generation, according to a Pew Research Center study released earlier this year, 61 percent of immigrants think of themselves as 'typical Americans.'" David Brooks, "Beyond the Fence," *New York Times*, May 6, 2013. Statistics have also showed that 26 percent of the second generation of Latinos marry outside their ethnic group. David Leonhardt, "Hispanics, the New Italians," *New York Times*, Apr. 20, 2013.

13. The End of Kultur: The Plight of Chicago's Germans

1. Robert Loerzel, "Native Numbers: How Many Chicagoans Were Born in the City?," *WBEZ*, accessed Feb. 13, 2014, http://www.wbez.org/series/curious-city/native-numbers-how-many-chicagoans-were-born-city-109680?utm_campaign=E-Update%202–13–14&utm_medium=email&utm_source=Eloqua. See also "The Book on Chicago," *Chicago Sun-Times*, May 16, 2010, 15A.

2. "Germany to Win, Annenberg Says," *Chicago Tribune*, Aug. 15, 1914, 1.

3. "Rain Fails to Dampen Ardor of Throng Which Honors Goethe," *Chicago Tribune*, June 14, 1914, 3.

4. Edward A. Steiner, *The Confession of a Hyphenated American* (New York: Fleming H. Revell, 1916), 6. Steiner, who emigrated from Vienna, was defending the patriotism of the immigrant.

5. David M. Kennedy and Thomas Bailey, *The American Spirit: U.S. History as Seen by Contemporaries* (Florence, KY: Wadsworth Publishing, 2009), 2:268.

6. Fleming, *Illusion of Victory*, 61.

7. In 1920 a novel by Lida C. Schem (who also wrote under the name Margaret Blake) titled *The Hyphen* was published. At over one thousand pages in two volumes, it must be the world's longest treatise devoted to a punctuation mark and is hefty testimony to the hullabaloo over the hyphen during the war years. A survey of World War I literature calls it "a careful, conscientious, and well-documented study of the trials of German-Americans during this period." Patrick J. Quinn, *The Conning of America: The Great War and American Popular Literature*, Amsterdam-Atlanta: Rodopi, 2001), 112.

8. "Dernberg Lays Blame for War on the English," *Chicago Tribune*, Dec. 11, 1914, 3.

9. Hugo Münsterberg, *The War and America* (New York: D. Appleton, 1914), 3.

10. Holli, "Great War Sinks Chicago's German *Kultur*," 478.

11. Hugo Münsterberg, *The Peace and America* (New York: D. Appleton, 1915), 146.

12. Holli, "Great War Sinks Chicago's German *Kultur*," 488.

13. "German Plots to Cripple U.S. Are Laid Bare," *Chicago Tribune*, Oct. 11, 1917, 2.

14. "Irish and German Join in Protest," *Chicago Tribune*, Dec. 2, 1914.

15. Holli, "Great War Sinks Chicago's German *Kultur*," 467–68.

16. Ibid., 491–92.

17. Ibid., 495.

18. Miles Franklin, *On Dearborn Street* (St. Lucia: University of Queensland Press, 1981), 119.

19. Quoted in Frederick C. Luebke, *Bonds of Loyalty: German-Americans and World War I* (De Kalb: Northern Illinois Univ. Press, 1974) 225.

20. Rudolf A. Hofmeister, *The Germans of Chicago* (Champaign, IL: Stipes Publishing Co., 1976), 69.

21. David Traxel, *Crusader Nation: The United States in Peace and the Great War, 1898–1920* (New York: Vintage, 2007), 316.

22. "Arrest Karl Muck as an Enemy Alien," *New York Times*, Mar. 26, 1918.

23. "Mr. Stock Will Put Native Music in All Orchestra Programs," *Chicago Tribune*, Sept. 26, 1917, 15.

24. Watkins, *Proof through the Night*, 22.

25. "Mr. Stock's Resignation," *Chicago Tribune*, Oct. 3, 1918, 6.

26. "Frederick Stock, Orchestra Head, Now U.S. Citizen," *Chicago Tribune*, May 23, 1919, 11.

27. "Weissensel Gets 10-Year Sentence for His Remarks," *Chicago Tribune*, Nov. 2, 1918, 8.

28. Historians' narratives of this mania have usually contained a hint of condescension, suggesting that Americans of today are above such folly, but when the French declined to support the Iraq War in 2003, the push to use "freedom fries" and "freedom toast" showed that the tendency survives.

29. After the armistice, the Bismarck Hotel's German-born owners quickly restored the original name. The hotel was rebuilt in the 1920s and renamed the Hotel Allegro in 1998.

30. Holli, "Great War Sinks Chicago's German *Kultur*," 508.

31. "Argue Blotting German Names from City Map," *Chicago Tribune*, Jan. 3, 1919, p. 13.

32. "'Bismarck Dead, Respect Him'—Big Bill's Board," *Chicago Tribune*, July 19, 1917, 5.

33. "Poles Denounce Plan to Change School Names," *Chicago Tribune*, Apr. 26, 1918, 12.

34. "Bismarck Loses to Funston in 10 Month Fight," *Chicago Tribune*, May 2, 1918, 3.

35. "Go Easy on Poor Kaiser, Verdict of School Board," *Chicago Tribune*, Aug. 8, 1917, 5.

36. "They're Tearing Kaiser out of Their Spellers," *Chicago Tribune*, Aug. 9, 1917, 3.

37. "Shoop Storms Kaiser's Last Spelling Trench," *Chicago Tribune*, Sept. 4, 1917, 9.

38. Holli, "Great War Sinks Chicago's German *Kultur*," 502. "By summer of 1918, approximately half of all the states had curtailed or abolished instruction in the German language, and several, along with dozens of counties, cities, and villages, had restricted the freedom of citizens to speak German in public." Luebke, *Bonds of Loyalty*, 252.

39. Hofmeister, *Germans of Chicago*, 74.

40. "Hun Doctrines Spread by Book in City Library," *Chicago Tribune*, June 18, 1918, 17.

41. The operetta, with music taken from the compositions of Franz Schubert, was adapted into English under several titles. It was filmed in English in 1934 with the title *Blossom Time*, starring the great tenor Richard Tauber.

42. "Tears Down Hun Theater Sign; Lands in Cell," *Chicago Tribune*, Jan. 2, 1918, 3.

43. "Only German Theater in U.S. Survives Here," *Chicago Tribune*, Dec. 18, 1918, 5. The Bush Temple building, however, still stands.

44. "Use Nothing German,'" *Chicago Tribune*, July 9, 1918, 7.

45. Holli, "Great War Sinks Chicago's German *Kultur*," 511.

46. Ibid.

47. Luebke, *Bonds of Loyalty*, 331.

48. Daniel Okrent, *Last Call: The Rise and Fall of Prohibition* (New York: Simon & Schuster, 1910), 54.

49. Thomas R. Pegram, *Battling Demon Rum: The Struggle for a Dry America, 1800–1933* (Chicago: Ivan R. Dee, 1998), 139.

50. Richard F. Hamm, *Shaping the 18th Amendment: Temperance Reform, Legal Culture, and the Polity, 1880–1920* (Chapel Hill: Univ. of North Carolina Press, 1995), 240.

51. "'Pro-German,' Charge against Brewers' League," *Chicago Tribune*, Oct. 9, 1918, 9.

52. Capozzola, *Uncle Sam Wants You*, 95.

53. Pegram, *Battling Demon Rum*, 146.

54. Ibid., 144.

55. G. K. Chesterton, *What I Saw in America* (London: Hodder and Stoughton, 1922), 96–97.

One Chicagoan's War
Thomas A. Dorsey:
The Father of Gospel Music

1. Robert L. Taylor, *Thomas A. Dorsey, Father of Black Gospel Music: An Interview* (Bloomington, IN: Trafford Publishing, 2014), 15.

2. Robert M. Marovich, *A City Called Heaven: Chicago and the Birth of Gospel Music* (Urbana: Univ. of Illinois Press, 2015), 72.

3. Harris, *Rise of Gospel Blues*, 46.

4. Marovich, *A City Called Heaven*, 72.

5. Harris, *Rise of Gospel Blues*, 96.

6. Joe C. Clark, "Thomas Andrew Dorsey," in *Encyclopedia of American Gospel Music*, ed. William K. McNeil (New York: Routledge, 2005), 105–7.

7. Harris, *Rise of Gospel Blues*, 241.

8. Marovich, *A City Called Heaven*, 312.

9. Taylor, *Thomas A. Dorsey*, 16.

Emil G. Hirsch: The Mistrusted Rabbi

1. David Einhorn Hirsch, *Rabbi Emil G. Hirsch: The Reform Advocate* (Chicago: Whitehall Co., 1968), 3–6.

2. Cutler, *Jews of Chicago*, 34.

3. Hirsch, *Rabbi Emil G. Hirsch*, 26.

4. Holli, "Great War Sinks Chicago's German *Kultur*," 479.

5. "Dernberg Lays Blame for War on the English," *Chicago Tribune*, Dec. 11, 1914, 3.

6. Holli, "Great War Sinks Chicago's German *Kultur*," 505.

7. "Germans in U.S. to Rebuild Town Russians Ruined," *Chicago Tribune*, Feb. 20, 1916, A2.

8. Susan Roth Breitzer, *Jewish Labor's Second City: The Formation of a Jewish Working Class in Chicago, 1886–1928* (Ph.D. diss., University of Iowa, 2007), 268.

9. "Dr. Hirsch Seeks 100 Stars for Service Flag," *Chicago Tribune*, Nov. 10, 1917, 6.

10. "Dr. Hirsch Voices Loyalty before Crowd of 3,000," *Chicago Tribune*, April 25, 1918, 5. Like many, Hirsch distinguished between Germany and Prussia, saying, "I was educated in Germany and naturally learned to love the German people but I am unalterably opposed to Prussianism." *Decatur (IN) Daily Democrat*, April 12, 1918, 1.

11. "Hirsch Defends Loyalty from Temple Pulpit," *Chicago Tribune*, April 28, 1919, 17.

Part Six. After the War

14. "Taking New Heart": Organized Labor and the Postwar Strikes

1. Zieger, *America's Great War*, 117.

2. Hutchins Hapgood, *The Spirit of Labor* (New York: Duffield & Co., 1907), 12.

3. Elizabeth McKillen, *Chicago Labor and the Quest for a Democratic Diplomacy, 1914–1924* (Ithaca, NY: Cornell Univ. Press, 1995), 14.

4. Harold Underwood Faulkner, *The Decline of Laissez-Faire, 1897–1917* (Armonk, NY: M. E. Sharpe, 1977), 108.

5. Wilson J. Warren, *Tied to the Great Packing Machine: The Midwest and Meatpacking* (Iowa City: Univ. of Iowa Press, 2006), 34.

6. Barrett, *Work and Community in the Jungle*, 191.

7. McKillen, *Chicago Labor and the Quest*, 85.

8. "Packing House Workers Press for U.S. Seizure," *Chicago Tribune*, Jan. 22, 1918, 12.

9. Venzon, *United States in the First World War*, 792, s.v. "Wilson, William Bauchop."

10. "Arbitrator," *Chicago Tribune*, Feb. 8, 1918, 9.

11. "Alschuler Sees All Phases of Packers' Work," *Chicago Tribune*, Feb. 16, 1918, 5.

12. "Long Hours Forced by War, Packers' Defense at Inquiry," *Chicago Tribune*, Feb. 26, 1918, 11.

13. "Gompers Styles Packers' Pleas 'State of Mind,'" *Chicago Tribune*, Mar. 1, 1918, 4.

14. Barrett, *Work and Community in the Jungle*, 198–99.

15. "600,000 Profit by Wage Raise at Stockyards," *Chicago Tribune*, Mar. 31, 1918, 9.

16. Zieger, *America's Great War*, 258.

17. McKillen, *Chicago Labor and the Quest*, 217.

18. Barrett, *Work and Community in the Jungle*, 200.

19. Reed, *Not Alms but Opportunity*, 87.

20. Reed, *Knock at the Door of Opportunity*, 260.

21. "Angry at Guards, 10,000 Workers at Yards Strike," *Chicago Tribune*, July 19, 1919, 2.

22. Barrett, *Work and Community in the Jungle*, 242.

23. On the conflict between the SLC and the AMC (which operated as part of the AFL), see David Brody, *The Butcher Workmen: A Study of Unionization* (Cambridge, MA: Harvard Univ. Press, 1964).

24. Ibid., 246.

25. Brody, *Steelworkers in America*, 214.

26. Kennedy, *Over Here*, 135.

27. Brody, *Steelworkers in America*, 190, 184, 198.

28. William Z. Foster, *The Great Steel Strike and Its Lessons* (New York: B. W. Huebsch, 1920), 17.

29. Ibid., 25.

30. Ibid., 77.

31. Kennedy, *Over Here*, 270.

32. Zieger, *America's Great War*, 211.

33. Brody, *Steelworkers in America*, 218–19.

34. Pacyga, *Polish Immigrants and Industrial Chicago*, 196.

35. Foster, *Great Steel Strike*, 100–101.

36. Lizabeth Cohen, *Making a New Deal: Industrial Workers in Chicago, 1919–1939* (New York: Cambridge Univ. Press, 1990), 41.

37. Brody, *Steelworkers in America*, 228.

38. Ibid., 247, 244.

39. Zieger, *America's Great War*, 213.

40. Brody, *Steelworkers in America*, 250.

41. Ibid., 254.

42. Cohen, *Making a New Deal*, 12.

43. Elizabeth McKillen, "Chicago Federation of Labor," in Eric Arnesen, ed., *Encyclopedia of U.S. Labor and Working-Class History* (New York: Routledge, 2007), 1:227.

44. Andrew E. Kersten, "Dominance and Influence of Organized Labor: 1940s," in ibid., 1:375.

15. "Eyes to the Future": Chicago in 1919

1. "Chicago's New Year Is Gay, but Fun Is Kept Indoors," *Chicago Tribune*, Jan. 1, 1919, 1.

2. "Governors of Valley States Vision New Year," *Chicago Tribune*, Jan. 1, 1919, A1.

3. "Mayor Calls for After War Effort in 1919," *Chicago Tribune*, Jan. 1, 1919, 6.

4. "City Plan Stirs Chicago Spirit to Realization," *Chicago Tribune*, Jan. 1, 1919, A1.

5. Gary Krist, *City of Scoundrels: The Twelve Days of Disaster That Gave Birth to Modern Chicago* (New York: Crown, 2012), 113.

6. Reed, *Knock at the Door of Opportunity*, 16.

7. Pacyga, *Chicago*, 208.

8. Krist's *City of Scoundrels* is an entire book about the events that transpired in Chicago in 1919. The same topics are described in Richard Lindberg, "A Summer of Lost Innocence, May to August 1919," in *Chicago Ragtime: Another Look at Chicago, 1880–1920* (South Bend, IN: Icarus Press, 1985), 214–55.

9. At least thirty race riots took place in the United States in 1919. Part of the reason seems to have been that many whites feared that returning black soldiers would become more aggressive in asserting their civil rights. See Keene, *Doughboys*, 164.

10. Krist, *City of Scoundrels*, 18.

11. Robert M. Lombardo, *Organized Crime in Chicago: Beyond the Mafia* (Urbana: Univ. of Illinois Press, 2013), 71–77.

12. Ibid., 73.

13. Reed, *Knock at the Door of Opportunity*, 91.

14. Baldwin, *Chicago's New Negroes*, 50–51.

15. John Kobler, *Capone: The Life and World of Al Capone* (Boston: Da Capo Press, 2003), 66.

16. Gus Russo, *The Outfit* (New York: Bloomsbury USA, 2003), 32.

Index

Page numbers followed by *f* refer to figures.

Joseph Gustaitis is a freelance writer and editor living in Chicago. His first book, *Chicago's Greatest Year, 1893: The White City and the Birth of a Modern Metropolis*, received a Superior Achievement Award from the Illinois State Historical Society. He is also the author of many articles in the popular history field. After working as an editor at *Collier's Year Book*, he became the humanities editor for *Collier's Encyclopedia*. He has also worked in television and won an Emmy Award for writing for ABC-TV's *FYI* program.